BTEC
Level 2

edexcel
advancing learning, changing lives

PERFORMING ARTS LEVEL 2

BTEC First

Sally Jewers | Carolyn Carnaghan

Rob East | Julie Read

Published by Pearson Education Limited, a company incorporated in England and Wales, having its registered office at Edinburgh Gate, Harlow, Essex, CM20 2JE. Registered company number: 872828

www.pearsonschoolsandfecolleges.co.uk

Edexcel is a registered trademark of Edexcel Limited

Text © Pearson Education Limited 2010

First published 2010

13 11 10
10 9 8 7 6 5 4 3 2 1

British Library Cataloguing in Publication Data
A catalogue record for this book is available from the British Library.

ISBN 9780435026516

Edited by Julia Bruce
Designed by Wooden Ark
Produced by Pearson
Original illustrations © ODI
Cover design by Visual Philosophy, created by EMC Design
Picture research by Thelma Gilbert
Index by Indexing Specialists (UK) Ltd
Cover photo/illustration © Arenapal: Elliott Franks
Back cover photos © Arenapal: Elliott Franks
Printed and bound in Great Britain at Scotprint, Haddington

Hotlinks
There are links to relevant websites in this book. In order to ensure that the links are up to date, that the links work, and that the sites are not inadvertently linked to sites that could be considered offensive, we have made the links available on the following website: www.pearsonschoolsandfecolleges.co.uk/hotlinks. When you access the site, search for either the express code 6516V, title BTEC First Performing Arts Student Book or ISBN 9780435026516.

Disclaimer
This material has been published on behalf of Edexcel and offers high-quality support for the delivery of Edexcel qualifications. This does not mean that the material is essential to achieve any Edexcel qualification, nor does it mean that it is the only suitable material available to support any Edexcel qualification. Edexcel material will not be used verbatim in setting any Edexcel examination or assessment. Any resource lists produced by Edexcel shall include this and other appropriate resources.

Copies of official specifications for all Edexcel qualifications may be found on the Edexcel website: www.edexcel.com

Every effort has been made to contact copyright holders of material reproduced in this book. Any omissions will be rectified in subsequent printings if notice is given to the publishers.

Contents

About your **BTEC Level 2 BTEC in First Performing Arts**

Credits

The publisher would like to thank the following individuals for their help and advice on this project:
Paul Webster
Ashley Hunt

The publisher would like to thank the following for their kind permission to reproduce their photographs:

Alamy Images: Don Hammond 310, Pawel Libera Images 254, David Lyons 83, Moodboard 18, 305, Moodboard 18, 305, Keith Morris 37, 48, Alex Segre 261, Adrian Sherratt 42, Travelshots.com 86, Rob Walls 239, WorldFoto 99; **Arenapal**: Hanal Chahal 23, Rowena Chowdey 79, Rowena Chowdrey 111, Fritz Curzon 77, 90, 91, 208, 210, 225, Fritz Curzon 77, 90, 91, 208, 210, 225, Fritz Curzon 77, 90, 91, 208, 210, 225, Fritz Curzon 77, 90, 91, 208, 210, 225, Fritz Curzon 77, 90, 91, 208, 210, 225, Elliott Franks 127, 213, 224, 241, Elliott Franks 127, 213, 224, 241, Elliott Franks 127, 213, 224, 241, Elliott Franks 127, 213, 224, 241, Image Works / Topfoto 252, 312, Image Works / Topfoto 252, 312, Pete Jones 57, Marilyn Kingwill 30, 35, 201, 269, Marilyn Kingwill 30, 35, 201, 269, Marilyn Kingwill 30, 35, 201, 269, Marilyn Kingwill 30, 35, 201, 269, Eleni Leoussi 66, Nigel Norrington 125, Eric Richmond 64, 106, Eric Richmond 64, 106, Topfoto / John Powell 27, UPP / Topfoto 233, Colin Wiloughby 84; **Candoco Dance Company**: 237; **Corbis**: 179, 183, Jim Craigmyle 59, Randy Faris 181, Roy McMahon 157, Gideon Mendel 52, Sigrid Olsson 133, Michael Pole 131, Thomas Rodriguez 20, Charles E. Rotkin 102; **Jenny Court**: 61, 61/2, 62, 265; **Education Photos**: 118, 220; **Mary Evans Picture Library**: 87; **Getty Images**: 196, 203, 204, Altrendo Images 302, Mark Andersen 39, Bridgeman Art Library 116, Pando Hall 272, Tony Hutchings 67, Sandy Jones 74, Lawrence Lucier 129, Milk & Honey Creative 167, George Shelley Productions 97, Inti St. Clair 108, Thinkstock 115, WireImage 194, WireImages 70, 175, WireImages 70, 175; **iStockphoto**: bibi57 177, Fitzer 285, Jasminam 11, jlmatt 227, Charles Knox 81, Peepo 309, TriggerPhoto 13, wrangel 258; **Kobal Collection Ltd**: Universal 288; **Lebrecht Music and Arts Photo Library**: 25, Dee Conway 113, 216, Dee Conway 113, 216, Tristram Kenton 103, 255, Laurie Lewis 95, Rob Moore 153, Odile Noel 199, Graham Salter 186; **Pearson Education Ltd**: 235, 287, 307; **Photolibrary.com**: Peter Cook 47, North Wind Picture Archives 85, Ingram Publishing RF 49; **Photostage Ltd**: 93, 243; **Rex Features**: 155, 163; **Roger Scruton**: 140, 278; **Shutterstock**: 101; **TopFoto**: 159

Cover images: Front: **Arenapal**: Elliott Franks Back: **Arenapal**: Elliott Franks, Elliott Franks

All other images © Pearson Education

About the Authors

Carolyn Carnaghan is an External Verifier and a Principal Moderator for the Performing Arts and Drama sectors. Carolyn has written several books about the arts and the teaching of dance and drama. She has also worked on the development of a number of arts qualifications and has many years of teaching experience. Carolyn has performed as a professional dancer and in 1988 she founded and ran her own dance consortium, The Dance Workshop. She also created a dance ensemble called Splitz. She has worked as a performer/choreographer on stage, in schools and colleges.

Rob East is a Senior Verifier. He has been working with Edexcel for over 8 years: as an External Verifier, supporting centres through training events and writing support materials. Prior to his work with Edexcel, Rob taught BTEC Performing Arts at First, National and Higher levels. Rob also has many years professional experience working as an actor and director.

Sally Jewers has over 20 years experience of the delivery and assessment of BTEC performing arts programmes and is currently a Senior Verifier and Senior Examiner for the Performing Arts, Music and Creative and Media areas. Sally leads national and centre based training events for Edexcel as well as offering guidance as part of the 'Ask the Expert' service. She is an experienced author and has written for Edexcel to support both BTEC and Diploma. Sally has also produced a range of interactive whiteboard resources including a KS4 Music Resource and is a regular contributor to Teaching Drama Magazine.

Julie Read has worked for the past 10 years as an External Verifier. She has also spent time working as a Performing Arts lecturer in FE for 18 years. Julie trained at the Wimbledon School of Art and worked as a freelance set and costume designer nationally and internationally. She has worked as the Theatre Design Leader for Cheshire combining designing for large scale county productions with running a drama centre that offered drama, dance and design courses for Cheshire schools.

About your BTEC Level 2 First in Performing Arts

Choosing to study for a BTEC Level 2 First Performing Arts qualification is a great decision to make for lots of reasons. This qualification will allow you to look into different areas of the Performing Arts, leading you into a whole range of professions and sectors and allowing you to explore your creativity in many different ways.

Your BTEC Level 2 First in Performing Arts is a **vocational** or **work-related** qualification. This doesn't mean that it will give you all the skills you need to do a job, but it does mean that you'll have the opportunity to gain specific knowledge, understanding and skills that are relevant to your future career.

What will you be doing?

The qualification is structured into mandatory units (ones you must do) and optional units (ones you can choose to do). This book covers 10 units in full and an overview of a further 13 units in the Projects section – giving you a broad choice no matter what size your qualification.

- BTEC Level 2 First **Certificate** in Perfoming Arts: 1 mandatory unit and 1 optional unit that provide a combined total of 15 credits
- BTEC Level 2 First **Extended Certificate** in Performing Arts: 1 mandatory unit and 2 or more optional units that provide a combined total of 30 credits
- BTEC Level 2 First **Diploma** in Performing Arts: For Dance, Acting and Production pathways: 4 mandatory units, 2 specialist optional units and 1 or more optional units. For Performance pathway: 3 mandatory units, 1 specialist optional and 3 or more optional units that provide a combined total of 60 credits

The following table shows the units covered or partially covered in this book and whether they are Mandatory (M), Specialist Optional (S) or Optional (O) units for the Certificate (C), Extended Certificate (E) and Diploma (D).

Unit Number	Credit value	Unit Name	Mandatory or Optional											
			Dance			Acting			Performance			Production		
			C	E	D	C	E	D	C	E	D	C	E	D
A1	5	Working in the Performing Arts Industry	O	O	M	O	O	M	O	O	M	O	O	M
A2	5	Professional Development in the Performing Arts Industry	O	O	M	O	O	M	O	O	M	O	O	M
A3	10	Performing Arts Production Process		O	M		O	M		O	M		O	M
B4	10	Acting Skills and Techniques			O	M	M	M		O	O			O
B5	10	The Development of Drama					O	S	S	S	S			O
B6	10	Devising Plays					O	S		O	O			O
B7	10	Performing Scripted Plays					O	S		O	O			O
B8	10	Musical Theatre Performance		O	O		O	S		O	O			O
B9	10	Developing Physical Theatre Performance		O	S		O	S		O	O			O

Unit Number	Credit value	Unit Name	Mandatory or Optional											
			Dance			Acting			Performance			Production		
			C	E	D	C	E	D	C	E	D	C	E	D
C10	10	Contemporary Dance		O	S			O		O	O			O
C11	10	Exploring Urban Dance Styles		O	S			O		O	O			O
C12	10	Jazz Dance		O	S			O		O	O			O
C13	10	Performing Dance	M	M	M			O		O	O			O
C14	10	The Development of Dance		O	S			O	S	S	S			O
D16	10	Crewing for Stage Performance			O			O		O	O	M	M	M
D17	10	Design for Performance			O			O		O	O		O	S
D20	10	Mask Making			O			O		O	O		O	S
D21	10	Set Construction			O			O		O	O		O	S
E26	10	Exploring Musical Composition			O			O		O	O			O
E28	10	Developing Musical Theory			O			O		O	O			O
E30	10	Solo Musical Performance			O			O		O	O			O
E31	10	The Development of Music			O			O	S	S	S			O
E32	10	Working as a Musical Ensemble			O			O		O	O			O

How to use this book

This book is designed to help you through your BTEC Level 2 First Performing Arts course. It has two sections:

- **A knowledge and skills** section with chapters covering each of the mandatory units in depth giving detailed information about each of the learning outcomes and including helpful advice for your assessments.

- **A projects** section with chapters covering a number of units. Each chapter guides you through the relevant learning outcomes to complete the project and includes activities to polish your skills and advice on evidence and assessment.

This book contains many features that will help you use your skills and knowledge in work-related situations and assist you in getting the most from your course.

Introduction

These introductions give you a snapshot of what to expect from each unit – and what you should be aiming for by the time you finish it!

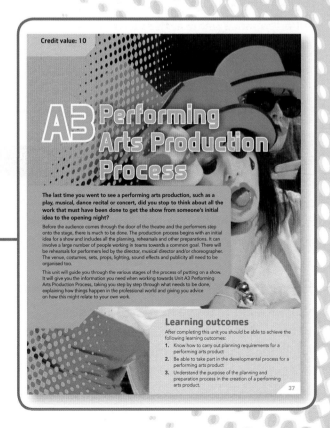

Credit value: 10

A3 Performing Arts Production Process

The last time you went to see a performing arts production, such as a play, musical, dance recital or concert, did you stop to think about all the work that must have been done to get the show from someone's initial idea to the opening night?

Before the audience comes through the door of the theatre and the performers step onto the stage, there is much to be done. The production process begins with an initial idea for a show and includes all the planning, rehearsals and other preparations. It can involve a large number of people working in teams towards a common goal. There will be rehearsals for performers led by the director, musical director and/or choreographer. The venue, costumes, sets, props, lighting, sound effects and publicity all need to be organised too.

This unit will guide you through the various stages of the process of putting on a show. It will give you the information you need when working towards Unit A3 Performing Arts Production Process, taking you step by step through what needs to be done, explaining how things happen in the professional world and giving you advice on how this might relate to your own work.

Learning outcomes

After completing this unit you should be able to achieve the following learning outcomes:

1. Know how to carry out planning requirements for a performing arts product.
2. Be able to take part in the developmental process for a performing arts product.
3. Understand the purpose of the planning and preparation process in the creation of a performing arts product.

37

Assessment and grading criteria

This table explains what you must do in order to achieve the assessment criteria for each unit. For each assessment criterion in the table, shown by the grade button **P1**, there is an assessment activity

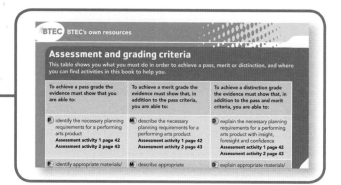

Assessment

Your tutor will set **assignments** throughout your course for you to complete. These may take a variety of forms, from research, presentations, performances and evaluations to reports and posters. The important thing is that you collect evidence of your skills and knowledge to date.

Stuck for ideas? Daunted by your first assignment? These students have all been through it before…

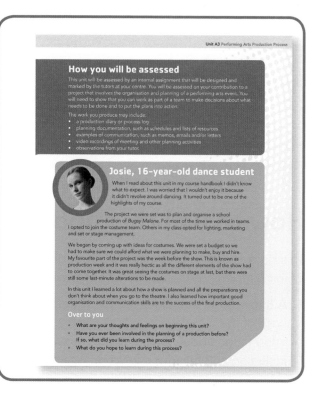

Personal, learning and thinking skills

Throughout your BTEC Level 2 First Performing Arts course, there are lots of opportunities to develop your personal, learning and thinking skills. Look out for these as you progress.

PLTS

Setting deadlines for your tasks and keeping to them will use your skills as a **self manager**.

Functional skills

It's important that you have good English, maths and ICT skills – you never know when you'll need them, and employers will be looking for evidence that you've got these skills too.

Functional skills

The production of your action plan will require you to use **writing skills**.

Activities

Assessment activities are suggestions for tasks that you might do as part of your assignment and will help you demonstrate your knowledge, skills and understanding. Each of these has **grading tips** that clearly explain what you need to do in order to achieve a merit or distinction grade.

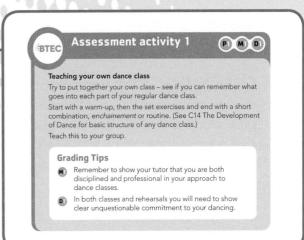

BTEC **Assessment activity 1** P M D

Teaching your own dance class

Try to put together your own class – see if you can remember what goes into each part of your regular dance class.

Start with a warm-up, then the set exercises and end with a short combination, *enchainement* or routine. (See C14 The Development of Dance for basic structure of any dance class.)

Teach this to your group.

Grading Tips

M Remember to show your tutor that you are both disciplined and professional in your approach to dance classes.

D In both classes and rehearsals you will need to show clear unquestionable commitment to your dancing.

There are also suggestions for activities that will give you a broader grasp of the industry, stretch your imagination and deepen your skills

Activity: Marking out the performance space

Produce a scale drawing of the stage/performance space of the venue you will be using showing the stage and the entrances and exits.

Use this drawing to mark out your rehearsal space.

Key terms

Technical words and phrases are easy to spot, and definitions are included. The terms and definitions are also in the glossary at the back of the book.

Key term

Budget – the amount of money allocated to a production.

WorkSpace

Case studies provide snapshots of real workplace issues, and show how the skills and knowledge you develop during your course can help you in your career.

WorkSpace **Big Hat Theatre Company**
production schedule

Big Hat Theatre Company is a small touring theatre company that specialises in Theatre in Education as well as traditional family productions. It is planning a production of the family pantomime Aladdin. The show will be performed at the Newtown Arts Centre for three weeks from 14th Dec.

The company begins its planning activities by drawing up a production schedule. The schedule identifies the planning requirements for the production by setting out what needs to be done and the dates by which the various milestones must be reached.

The schedule includes:
- An initial production meeting to discuss design requirements for sets, costumes, lighting and marketing strategy
- A production meeting to finalise designs and marketing
- A read-through
- Props meeting
- Marking out rehearsal space and beginning rehearsals
- When marketing material is distributed and tickets go on sale
- Building the set
- A production meeting to review props, set, costumes and lighting
- A production meeting to make final arrangements for production week
- The final run in rehearsal space
- The get in, fit up, focus and plotting
- The tech rehearsal, dress rehearsals and photo call
- The run.

Think about it!

1. Why do you think there are so many meetings included in the production schedule?

2. What do you think the following terms mean?
   - read through
   - costume call
   - props
   - photo call
   - final run in rehearsal space
   - marketing materials

55

Just checking

When you see this sort of activity, take stock! These quick activities and questions are there to check your knowledge. You can use them to see how much progress you've made or as a revision tool.

Edexcel's assignment tips

At the end of each chapter, you'll find hints and tips to help you get the best mark you can, such as the best websites to go to, checklists to help you remember processes and really useful facts and figures.

Don't miss out on these resources to help you!

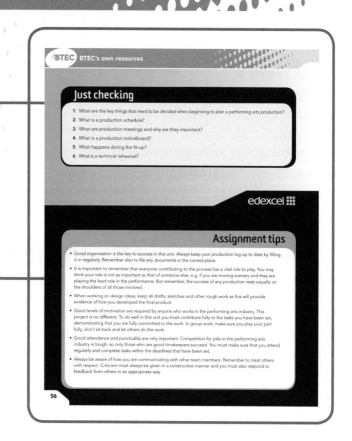

:BTEC BTEC's own resources

Just checking

1. What are the key things that need to be decided when beginning to plan a performing arts production?
2. What is a production schedule?
3. What are production meetings and why are they important?
4. What is a production noticeboard?
5. What happens during the fit-up?
6. What is a technical rehearsal?

edexcel :::

Assignment tips

- Good organisation is the key to success in this unit. Always keep your production log up to date by filling it in regularly. Remember also to file any documents in the correct place.
- It is important to remember that everyone contributing to the process has a vital role to play. You may think your role is not as important as that of someone else, e.g. if you are moving scenery and they are playing the lead role in the performance. But remember, the success of any production rests equally on the shoulders of all those involved.
- When working on design ideas, keep all drafts, sketches and other rough work as this will provide evidence of how you developed the final product.
- Good levels of motivation are required by anyone who works in the performing arts industry. This project is no different. To do well in this unit you must contribute fully to the tasks you have been set, demonstrating that you are fully committed to the work. In group work, make sure you play your part fully; don't sit back and let others do the work.
- Good attendance and punctuality are very important. Competition for jobs in the performing arts industry is tough, so only those who are good timekeepers succeed. You must make sure that you attend regularly and complete tasks within the deadlines that have been set.
- Always be aware of how you are communicating with other team members. Remember to treat others with respect. Criticism must always be given in a constructive manner and you must also respond to feedback from others in an appropriate way.

56

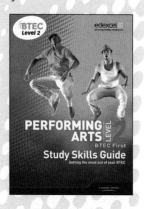

Have you read your BTEC Level 2 First Study Skills Guide? It's full of advice on study skills, putting your assignments together and making the most of being a BTEC Performing Arts learner.

Your book is just part of the exciting resources from Edexcel to help you succeed in your BTEC course. Visit www.edexcel.com/BTEC or www.pearsonfe. co.uk/BTEC 2010 for more details.

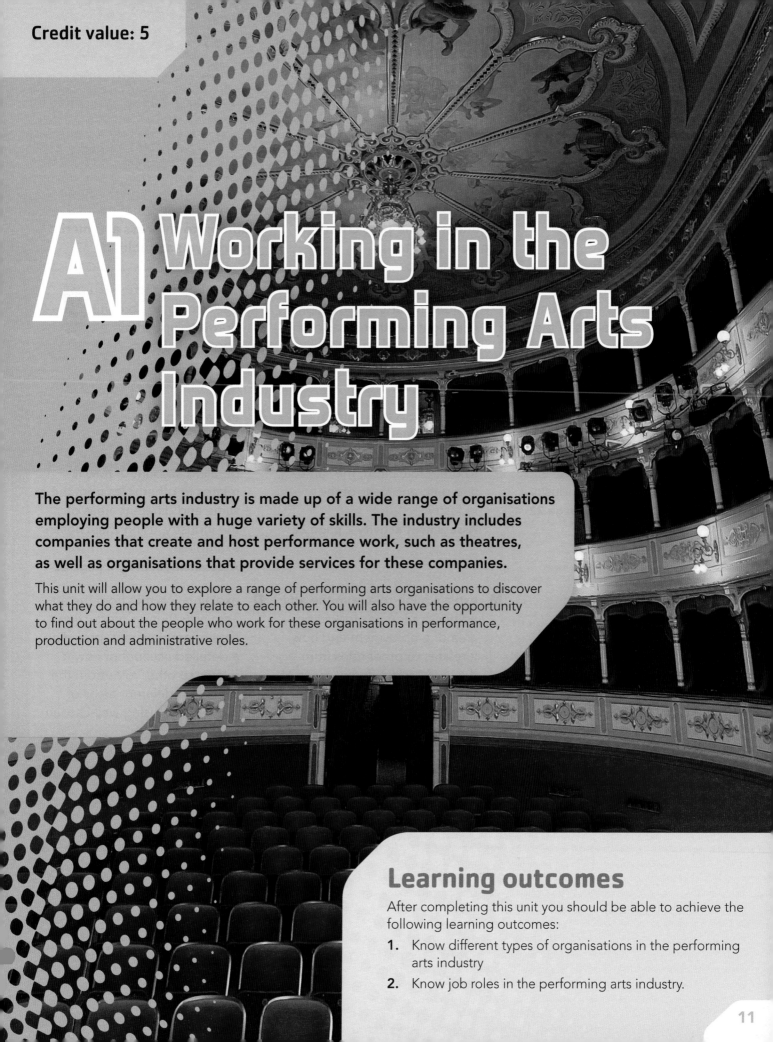

A1 Working in the Performing Arts Industry

The performing arts industry is made up of a wide range of organisations employing people with a huge variety of skills. The industry includes companies that create and host performance work, such as theatres, as well as organisations that provide services for these companies.

This unit will allow you to explore a range of performing arts organisations to discover what they do and how they relate to each other. You will also have the opportunity to find out about the people who work for these organisations in performance, production and administrative roles.

Learning outcomes

After completing this unit you should be able to achieve the following learning outcomes:

1. Know different types of organisations in the performing arts industry
2. Know job roles in the performing arts industry.

Assessment and grading criteria

This table shows you what you must to in order to achieve a pass, merit or distinction and where you can find activities in this book to help you.

To achieve a pass grade the evidence must show that you are able to:	To achieve a merit grade the evidence must show that, in addition to the pass criteria, you are able to:	To achieve a distinction grade the evidence must show that, in addition to the pass and merit criteria, you are able to:
P1 describe a performing arts organisation, its function and relation to other areas of the industry **Assessment activity 1 page 18**	**M1** explain the function of a performing arts organisation, relating it to other areas of the industry **Assessment activity 1 page 18**	**D1** explain the function of a performing arts organisation, drawing supported conclusions about its relation to other areas of the industry **Assessment activity 1 page 18**
P2 describe a job role from the performance area of employment and how it relates to other roles in the same and different areas of the industry **Assessment activity 2 page 22**	**M2** explain a job role from the performance area of employment and how it relates to other roles from the same and different areas of the industry **Assessment activity 2 page 22**	**D2** explain a job role from the performance area of employment, providing a detailed account of how it relates to other roles from the same and different areas of the industry, using well-chosen examples **Assessment activity 2 page 22**
P3 describe a job role from the arts administration or production area of employment and how it relates to other roles from the same and different areas of the industry **Assessment activity 2 page 22**	**M3** explain a job role from the arts administration or production area of employment and how it relates to other roles from the same and different areas of the industry. **Assessment activity 2 page 22**	**D3** explain a job role from the arts administration or production area of employment, providing a detailed account of how it relates to other roles from the same and different areas of the industry, using well-chosen examples. **Assessment activity 2 page 22**

How you will be assessed

This unit will be assessed by an internal assignment that will be designed and marked by the tutors at your centre. You will be assessed on your ability to demonstrate your understanding of different organisations and job roles in the performing arts industry.

The work you produce may include:
- a research plan and notes
- a written report
- a verbal presentation.

Sara, trainee marketing assistant and ex-performing arts student

I'm a trainee marketing assistant at Hendon Arts Centre. I first got interested in working in marketing when I studied Unit A1 Working in the Performing Arts Industry during my BTEC First in Performing Arts. Back then I wanted to be an actress, but the unit got me interested in all the other jobs that are vital to the performing arts industry. As part of the unit, we visited a local theatre and spoke to their marketing manager. As I was doing an art GCSE alongside my BTEC, I was already interested in graphic design so the work of the marketing department really interested me. I was fascinated by how the various productions were promoted and by the design work that went into the posters and leaflets that were produced. Now I'm involved in publicity work myself, and although I'm at the bottom of the ladder, my ambition is to manage a marketing department one day.

Over to you

- What career would you like to follow in the performing arts industry?
- Are there any other careers in the industry that you are really interested in learning about?

13

1.1 Different types of organisations in the performing arts industry

Warm up

Performing arts organisations...

When people think of companies and organisations in the performing arts industry, it's usually performance companies and venues that come to mind. However, the industry is made up of many different types of organisation. In small groups, come up with a list of as many types as you can.

Here are a couple to get you started:

* costume hire companies
* ticket agencies.

Share and discuss your ideas with the rest of your class.

1.1.1 Production companies and venues

Producing theatres

A producing theatre (sometimes known as a repertory theatre) has an artistic director and a company of performers who produce a number of shows each year. Producing theatres are often subsidised. This means they receive funding from the Arts Council and/or their local council. The Stephen Joseph Theatre in Scarborough and the Lyric Theatre in Belfast are examples of producing theatres.

Receiving theatres

Receiving theatres, also known as non-producing theatres, buy in productions from touring companies rather than producing shows themselves. Unlike producing theatres, some receiving theatres are run on a commercial basis. This means they do not receive any subsidies or government funding and have to rely entirely on money made from ticket sales, bar and restaurant takings, and merchandising. Most West End theatres in London are receiving theatres, along with many regional theatres.

Arts centres

Arts centres are subsidised venues that buy in a large variety of productions. The programme of performances at an arts centre may include music, dance and drama. Arts centres may also screen films and have galleries for visual art exhibitions.

Key term

Arts Council – An organisation that distributes government funding (money) for the arts.

PLTS

These activities will allow you to show off your skills as a **team worker** when you carry out the research in pairs, and also use your skills as an **independent enquirer**.

Activity: Producing and receiving theatres

Working in pairs, use the Internet to investigate one producing and one receiving theatre. Create a fact file for each theatre that includes the following information:

- the type of theatre it is (producing or receiving)
- a brief history of the theatre
- how the theatre is funded (if it is subsidised or run on a commercial basis)
- recent productions staged at the theatre
- any education work the theatre does
- facilities (including access for people with mobility, sight or hearing difficulties).

The following theatres may be useful.

Producing theatres:

- Stephen Joseph Theatre, Scarborough
- Lyric Theatre, Belfast.

Receiving theatres:

- Theatre Royal, Newcastle-upon-Tyne
- Theatre Royal, Norwich

To access their websites, go to the hotlinks section on p.2.

Touring production companies

Touring companies are theatre and dance companies that do not belong to a particular theatre. They produce the shows that are bought in by receiving theatres and arts centres. Many companies also perform in other venues, such as schools and community centres. Some touring companies are subsidised while others are run on a commercial basis.

Functional skills

During your research you will need to use your **IT** skills.

Activity: Touring theatre companies

Working in pairs, use the Internet to investigate the work of a touring production company. Aim to answer the following questions:

- Where is the company based?
- What kind of work does the company produce?
- How is the company funded?
- What kinds of venue does the company perform in?

You should also give details of a recent production by the company.

PLTS

Setting deadlines for your tasks and keeping to them will use your skills as a **self-manager**.

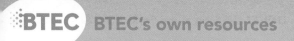

1.1.2 Arts administration

Funding bodies

Subsidised venues and companies rely on the grants they receive from their local branch of the Arts Council. For example, the Arts Council of Wales has given a grant of £280,000 to the Dylan Thomas Theatre in Swansea and the Arts Council England has awarded almost £190,000 to Perfect Pitch Musicals, aimed at showcasing new musicals. Local councils also sponsor venues and companies.

Unions

The three main unions for people working in the performing arts industry are Equity, the Musicians' Union (MU) and the Broadcasting Entertainment Cinematograph and Theatre Union (BECTU). They provide their members with advice and support, and agree minimum rates of pay with theatres and other employers. Many people who work in the performing arts industry do so on a freelance or casual basis rather than being permanent employees. This means the backing of a union is a vital form of support for them; protecting their rights and making sure they have reasonable working conditions.

PLTS

Researching Equity, BECTU and the Musician's Union will develop your personal learning and thinking skills as an **independent enquirer**.

Activity: Unions

Take a look at the websites of Equity, BECTU and the Musicians' Union to find out more about their history and what they do for their members.

To access their websites, go to the hotlinks section on p.2.

Agencies

An agency is a company that represents an individual or organisation. Many performers have theatrical agents who help them find work. Theatres and other venues may also use employment agencies to help them recruit front-of-house staff, such as cleaners, bar staff and security personnel. Some venues also use ticket agencies to help them sell tickets for their shows on the Internet, by phone and at outlets in city centres.

1.1.3 Services

This area of the performing arts industry provides support and other services for theatres and production companies.

Hire and supply companies

Hire companies service theatres and touring companies by supplying a wide range of materials and equipment. Many companies hire specialist materials and equipment, such as costumes, props and items of set. Specialist sound and lighting equipment is also often hired for specific productions. Companies that supply products such as make-up, wigs, textiles and timber and paint for sets, are also vital to the industry.

Transport companies

Touring theatre and dance companies often rely on specialist transport companies to move their sets, costumes and other equipment, as well as personnel, from one venue to another during a tour.

1.1.4 How it all fits together

The types of organisations and companies we have looked at in this chapter often have close links with each other. A typical touring theatre company, for example, is likely to have connections with a variety of different organisations.

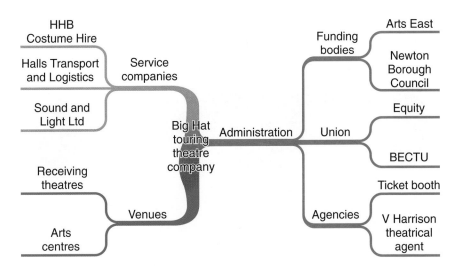

Figure 1: The network of connections made by the Big Hat Touring Theatre Company with various other organisations and companies.

BTEC **Assessment activity 1** P1 M1 D1

Planning meeting

You should take part in a meeting where you will discuss the planning requirements for your production. Start by listing all the things that need to be done before the opening night of your show. Place them in the order in which they need to be done and produce a production schedule that includes deadlines for each stage of the process.

During the meeting you should make notes and afterwards write up in your process file the plans you have discussed and agreed, describing the planning requirements you have identified.

Grading Tips

M1 Remember to provide detailed explanations of the organisation and how it operates and its connections with other areas of the industry.

D1 As well as explaining what the performing arts organisation does and how it relates to other organisations from other areas of the industry, you should also mention specific examples to support your explanations.

Functional skills

You will use your **English** skills when speaking and writing during the meeting when you discuss the planning requirements and make notes on it.

Make sure you make notes through the meeting and listen to the views of other people.

1.2 Job roles in the performing arts industry

Job roles in the performing arts...

Warm up

The performing arts industry relies on people with a wide variety of different skills.

In small groups, come up with as many job titles found in the industry as you can think of.

Here are a few to get you started:

- choreographer
- stage manager
- programme seller

When you have compiled your list, share it with the rest of your group to create a master list of all the job roles identified.

1.2.1 Performers

Performance jobs are central to the performing arts industry. As well as actors, dancers and musicians, this area of the industry also employs directors, musical directors and choreographers, who create and direct performances.

1.2.2 Arts administration

Like any other area of business, the performing arts industry needs people who work on such things as finance, publicity and the day-to-day running of an organisation.

A typical producing theatre will employ staff in:

- **marketing** – including a marketing manager and graphic designer who produce promotional materials and publicity campaigns
- **front-of-house (FOH)** – including a front-of-house manager, bar staff, ushers, cleaners and security personnel
- **finance** – including a head who manages the budget for the organisation
- **box office** – those who sell tickets for the performances.

The Performing Arts industry has many more job roles than just the creative ones.

1.2.3 Production

The production team for a performance is composed of people who undertake a wide range of jobs in construction, design, backstage and technical areas. A typical producing theatre may have a production team made up of the following job roles.

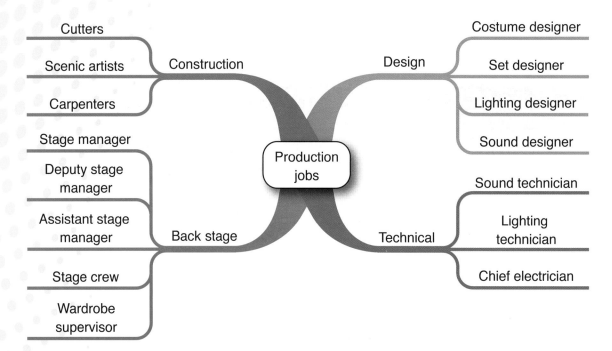

Cutters
Scenic artists — Construction
Carpenters

Stage manager
Deputy stage manager
Assistant stage manager — Back stage
Stage crew
Wardrobe supervisor

Production jobs

Costume designer
Set designer — Design
Lighting designer
Sound designer

Sound technician
Lighting technician — Technical
Chief electrician

Figure 2: Typical production roles in a producing theatre.

Who does what?

Costume/set designer	Works with the director to design the costumes and scenery for the production. In some companies, the role may be taken by one designer. In larger companies, there may be separate set and costume designers.
Lighting designer	Designs the lighting and other visual effects for a performance.
Sound designer	Creates any sound effects and/or music required by the director.
Lighting technician	Responsible for rigging and focusing the lights for the production. The lighting technician may also operate the lights during the show.
Sound technician	Responsible for rigging and focusing the sound equipment for the production. The sound technician may also operate the sound equipment during the show.
Chief electrician	Also known as the chief LX, the chief electrician is in overall charge of all lighting, sound, special effects and other electrical equipment.
Cutter	Responsible for cutting out and making costumes. Larger companies may also employ a range of specialists, such as dyers, milliners (hat makers), wig makers, etc.
Carpenter	Constructs scenery and furniture for the production.
Scenic artist	Applies paint and other effects to scenery.
Stage manager (SM)	Is in overall control of the backstage areas during a performance.
Deputy stage manager (DSM)	Works with the director and cast during rehearsals to create the prompt copy. During the show they supervise all cues. (See WorkSpace case study for more details.)
Assistant stage manager (ASM)	Assists the SM and DSM during preparations for the show. During the show itself they will work with the stage crew to change scenery.
Stage crew	Assists with the get-in and fit-up of a show. During the show they will be responsible for scene changes.
Wardrobe supervisor	Responsible for all costume and wardrobe matters during the run of a show making sure costumes remain in good condition, organising repairs, alterations and cleaning.

PLTS

The research aspect of this task will show your skills as an **independent enquirer**.

Functional skills

When producing the job advert you will need to use your **English** writing skills.

 BTEC Assessment activity 2

Job roles

Choose two job roles, one from the performing area of employment and another from the arts administration or production area of employment.

Find out what each job entails and how it relates to other job roles from the same and different areas of employment.

Gather your research findings together and use them to create a detailed job advert for each role. The advert must explain:

- the day-to-day responsibilities of the role
- how the role relates to other roles from the same area of the industry (e.g. members of staff in the same team/department)
- how the role relates to job roles in different areas of employment (e.g. staff from other departments).

Grading Tips

M2
M3 You should aim to provide as much detail as possible, remembering to include responsibilities. You must explain how the roles link to other roles from the same areas of the industry and other areas of the industry.

D2
D3 You should aim to provide detailed explanations of the characteristics of the job roles you investigate. Consider the responsibilities of the role:

- How do they contribute to the work of the company?
- Why are they important to the success of the work?

Consider how the job role fits into the 'bigger picture' within a company or organisation:

- Who do they work with?
- How does their work relate to the work undertaken by others?

Jane Newsome
Deputy stage manager

Interview with Jane Newsome, DSM at a large producing theatre.

My job involves attending all rehearsals where I am 'on book'. This means taking note of what the director wants and making notes in a special script known as the prompt copy of all lighting and sound cues as well as details of blocking and calls for the actors.

The prompt copy is vital to the smooth running of the show. During performances I sit at the prompt desk. In some theatres this is at the side of the stage but here we have a soundproof box at the back of the auditorium.

It is the nerve centre of the production from where I use the prompt copy to ensure the show runs as it should from a backstage point of view. I can communicate with backstage and front-of-house staff via my headset or 'cans'.

I love the buzz of working backstage. I started my career working for a touring theatre company where we had a very small production team and I pretty much needed to be a 'jack of all trades'. My work in this job is different. The production/technical team includes a large number of full-time staff. When we are working on a big production, the Christmas show or a musical, for example, we also use an agency to find casual staff to increase the team.

Think about it!

1. What do the following terms mean?
   - blocking
   - auditorium
   - casual staff.
2. What role would you like to do backstage in a show? Why?

Just checking

1. What is the difference between a producing theatre and a receiving theatre?

2. How might an arts centre differ from a theatre?

3. What is a touring production company?

4. What are costume hire and transport companies examples of?

5. What kind of organisation is Equity?

6. Actors, dancers and musicians are all examples of jobs from which area of the performing arts industry.

7. What does FOH stand for?

edexcel

Assignment tips

- Try to use a wide range of sources when undertaking your research work. Websites and books will be useful. However, primary research, undertaken by visiting venues and companies and talking to people who work in the industry, will give you first-hand information.

- When undertaking research activities, always keep a log of the websites, books and other materials/resources you use.

- Always record your research findings in your own words.

- Remember to record your thoughts about what you find out, for example, what did you find interesting? Did you find out anything unexpected?

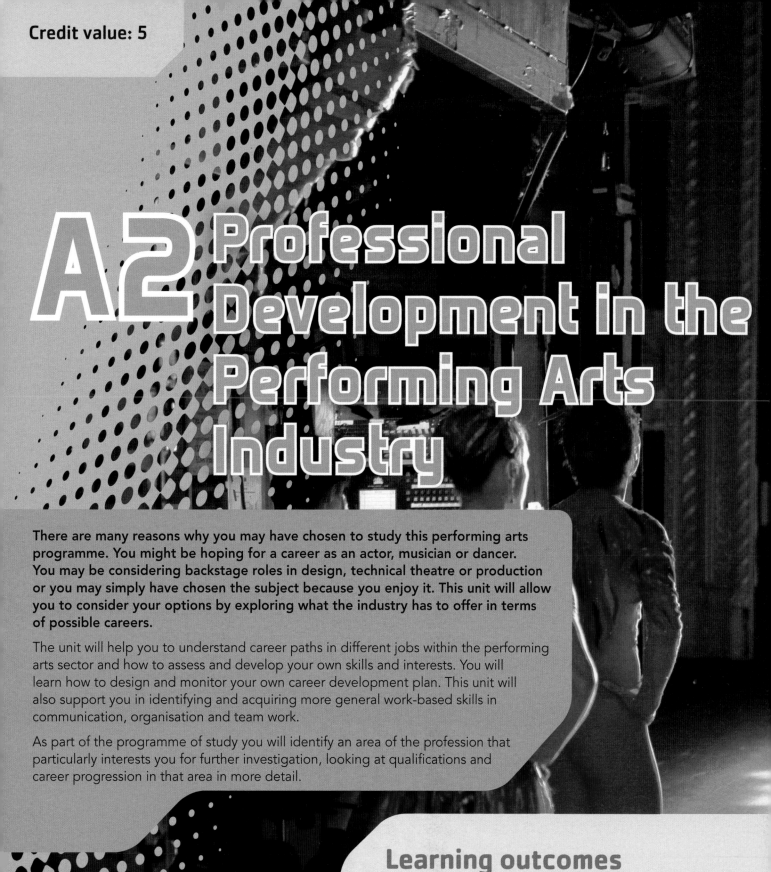

A2 Professional Development in the Performing Arts Industry

There are many reasons why you may have chosen to study this performing arts programme. You might be hoping for a career as an actor, musician or dancer. You may be considering backstage roles in design, technical theatre or production or you may simply have chosen the subject because you enjoy it. This unit will allow you to consider your options by exploring what the industry has to offer in terms of possible careers.

The unit will help you to understand career paths in different jobs within the performing arts sector and how to assess and develop your own skills and interests. You will learn how to design and monitor your own career development plan. This unit will also support you in identifying and acquiring more general work-based skills in communication, organisation and team work.

As part of the programme of study you will identify an area of the profession that particularly interests you for further investigation, looking at qualifications and career progression in that area in more detail.

Learning outcomes

After completing this unit you should be able to achieve the following learning outcomes:

1. Know career and progression opportunities within the performing arts industry
2. Be able to design and monitor a professional development plan.

Assessment and grading criteria

This table shows you what you must to in order to achieve a pass, merit or distinction and where you can find activities in this book to help you.

To achieve a pass grade the evidence must show that you are able to:	To achieve a merit grade the evidence must show that, in addition to the pass criteria, you are able to:	To achieve a distinction grade the evidence must show that, in addition to the pass and merit criteria, you are able to:
P1 identify the training requirements and experience required for a career path in the performing arts **Assessment activity 1 page 31**	**M1** describe the training requirements and experience required for a career path in the performing arts with reference to examples **Assessment activity 1 page 31**	**D1** explain the training requirements and experience required for a career path in the performing arts with reference to well-cited examples **Assessment activity 1 page 31**
P2 design a professional development plan that identifies current skill levels and sets targets **Assessment activity 2 page 33** **Assessment activity 3 page 34**	**M2** design a professional development plan that describes current skill levels and sets considered targets **Assessment activity 2 page 33** **Assessment activity 3 page 34**	**D2** design a professional development plan that provides an explanation of current skill levels and sets well-defined and measurable targets **Assessment activity 2 page 33** **Assessment activity 3 page 34**
P3 monitor a professional development plan, identifying progress towards targets. **Assessment activity 4 page 34**	**M3** monitor a professional development plan describing progress towards targets. **Assessment activity 4 page 34**	**D3** monitor a professional development plan giving detailed explanations of progress towards targets. **Assessment activity 4 page 34**

How you will be assessed

This unit will be assessed by an internal assignment that will be designed and marked by the tutors at your centre. You will be assessed on your ability to demonstrate your understanding of a career path in the performing arts industry. You will also be required to produce an action plan for your own development.

The work you produce may include:
- a research plan and notes
- a written report
- a skills audit
- a professional development plan.

Kem, an acting student

I have always been into drama. I really started to see it as a possible career when I studied a BTEC First in Performing Arts at school. It really provided me with a focus in terms of what I wanted to do and how to achieve it. In Unit A2 on professional development we investigated career paths and I found out about different drama schools and how to apply for them. I also found out how much competition for places there is. In the unit I also produced an action plan that really helped me to focus on the skills I needed to develop and improve.

Three years later I won the place I'd hoped for and, although I'm facing years of hard work, I am much closer to my dream.

Over to you

- Do you want to go to drama school?
- What would you put in your action plan to achieve your goals?

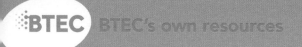

2.1 Career and progression opportunities within the industry

2.1.1 Careers

The performing arts industry offers a range of employment opportunities in performing, production and administration. Details of different types of job role can be found in Unit A1: Working in the Performing Arts Industry.

Different types of employment

People working in the performing arts industry are employed in a number of different ways.

- **Full-time employment**. Having a full-time job means working on a permanent basis for at least 35 hours a week.

- **Part-time employment**. Working part time means undertaking fewer hours than employees who work on a full-time basis.

- **Freelance, contract or casual employment**. This type of work is very common in the performing arts industry where performers, designers and production staff might be employed for a single project.

You can also do unpaid work to gain experience, for instance, as a volunteer or on a work experience placement.

Activity: Types of employment

In small groups, discuss the advantages and disadvantages of working full time, part time and freelance. Share your findings with the rest of the class.

2.1.2 Training

Most performers working professionally in the performing arts industry will have undertaken some kind of professional training at a drama, dance or music school or at a university or college. Although it is always possible to find successful performers who have had no training, most working actors, singers and dancers have undertaken some sort of professional training.

There are many schools, colleges and other institutions offering training for people wanting a career in performing arts. These will vary from evening classes to A Levels and BTECs, right through to degrees in Professional Acting, Musical Theatre or Stage Management. There may be some courses in your own region or you may have to go further afield to find something. They will vary in size and the types of course they offer.

Performing arts training in schools, colleges and universities do tend to vary slightly from the training you would have in specialist drama, music or dance schools. As a very general rule, schools, colleges and universities tend to teach learners about the industry, whereas specialist schools will train learners to work in the industry. There may therefore be more practical work in the specialist schools.

Activity: Training courses

1. Divide into pairs or small groups and choose one of the following schools:

- Arts Educational Schools London
- Bristol Old Vic Theatre School
- East 15 Acting School
- Central School of Ballet
- Mountview Academy of Theatre Arts
- Royal Welsh College of Music & Drama
- Birmingham School of Acting
- Central School of Speech and Drama
- Guildhall School of Music and Drama
- London Academy of Music and Dramatic Art
- Royal Academy of Dramatic Art

Find out about the types of course they run.

2. Now search for a university or college in your region offering courses in performing or production arts. Choose a course that interests you and find out about what the course entails.

3. Share your findings from these two activities with the rest of your class.

2.1.3 Application procedures

When considering applying for any educational or training course you should find out about:

- the entry requirements, e.g. do they require certain types or levels of qualification such as GCSEs, BTECs or A Levels?
- application procedures, e.g. do you need to apply directly to the institution by writing a letter or through UCAS?
- do need to supply a personal statement outlining your skills and showing your enthusiasm for the course?

Auditions

Most courses will shortlist applicants and invite those who seem appropriate to an interview or audition. Depending on the type of course you are applying for you might be asked to:

- prepare a monologue or a song
- take part in a dance audition
- present a portfolio of designs.

As the performing arts industry is very difficult to get into, due to its popularity, you should always be prepared to show your enthusiasm by talking about your experiences or your knowledge of the industry. Auditions for jobs are likely to have the same structure as those to enter your chosen course. When choosing your monologue, song or specific designs in your portfolio, it is a good idea to think about what skills, knowledge or experience are needed for that job (e.g. comedy experience or knowledge of 1970s styling) and ensure it will help demonstrate you are aware of these requirements and either already possess them or can acquire them.

CVs and portfolios

The performing arts business is very competitive. A vital tool for anyone looking for work is an up-to-date CV. The CV of an actor or someone working backstage in the performing arts is very different from someone applying for an office job, such as a marketing assistant. CVs for all aspects of the performing arts industry can be seen on the websites of theatrical agencies, for example, United Agents. To obtain a link to their website, please see the hotlinks section on p.2. These CVs generally list all of the productions that have been worked on, plus any relevant skills and education.

If you are looking for work in the design area of the industry it is important to show examples of what you can do, so you should put together a portfolio of designs from recent projects undertaken.

Actors will always work closely with the director.

Key term

CV/curriculum vitae – A brief account of your qualifications, experience and education

Those who have successful careers in the performing arts industry never really stop learning and improving their skills. Whether you have recently perfected a new accent or learned to use a new piece of technological equipment, it is important that your CV and portfolio are kept up to date.

Casting

Casting happens in a number of stages. First, a production company will employ a casting director to find actors for a particular show. The casting is then advertised and agencies will put their clients forward for an audition, or actors can send their CVs directly to the casting director. The casting director will then audition all actors who sound suitable for the part and cast the play. There will often be more than one round of auditions as it is always important to get the best people for the parts. If an agency gets their client paid work, they will usually take a cut of their pay – this is how the theatrical agencies generate their income, as they don't usually charge clients for simply being on their books.

Assessment activity 1 P1 M1 D1

Creating a careers booklet

Choose a career path to investigate. You should find out about:

- the training requirements for entry into the career
- the career ladder.

Present your findings as a chapter for inclusion in a careers booklet that focuses on careers in the performing arts industry.

You may use diagrams and other images to illustrate your chapter.

Grading Tips

D1 You should provide detailed explanations of the type of training a person needs to enter a chosen career. This might include:

- examining the content of specific HE courses that are relevant to the role
- considering how well each course prepares someone for entry into the profession
- considering what other experience and attributes are needed for the role.

PLTS

Your investigation into a career path will use your skills as an **independent enquirer**.

Functional skills

Producing a chapter for a careers booklet will require that you use your **English** writing skills.

2.2 Designing and monitoring a professional development plan

Warm up

What are you good at now?

What skills need improvement?

A professional development plan should begin with an honest appraisal of the skills and attributes you already have and those you need to acquire, develop or improve.

On a piece of paper, write down three things you think you are good at and three things you struggle with. Consider personal and work skills as well as skills within the area of performing arts.

2.2.1 Skills audit

A skills audit is a good way of identifying the skills needed for a particular career path and assessing your own abilities against these skills. For example, someone aspiring to have a career as an actor would need to develop the following skills:

- **vocal** – breath control, projection, articulation, pitch, tone quality, vocal colour

- **physical** – balance, spatial awareness, weight placement, use of gesture, facial expression

- **interpretive** – ability to analyse the physical characteristics of a role, applying research findings to a role, using improvisation

- **performance** – communication with audience, interaction with other performers

- **personal** – ability to get on with others, ability to meet deadlines, punctuality, reliability.

Once the relevant skills have been identified, an audit or assessment of those skills will help you to understand where improvements need to be made.

Unit A2 Professional Development in the Performing Arts industry

 Assessment activity 2

Skills audit

1. Choose a career path that appeals to you.
2. Make a list of the skills needed for your chosen career path. Remember to include personal skills and attributes as well as professional skills.
3. Rate yourself against the skills you have identified, providing a brief comment about your current ability and any improvements that need to be made.

Grading Tips

M2 You should describe your strengths and weaknesses with regard to your skills and indicate how the improvement of these skills might help you achieve your goals. Remember to make long- and short-term targets specific and detailed.

D2 You must provide full details of your current skill levels in the area you have chosen. You need to show a detailed understanding of your strengths and weaknesses. When you set your targets, remember to prioritise your goals as well as making them realistic and time-bound.

2.2.2 Setting targets

A vital key to success is often said to be the setting of clearly defined goals or targets. Setting a target means making a commitment to working towards that target. It helps bridge the gap between where you are at present and where you want to be. Some targets might be things you wish to achieve in the long term e.g. the completion of a higher education course. Some targets might be achievable in the short term e.g. improvement of vocal or movement skills.

SMART targets

Having identified the skills you need to develop and improve you should the set yourself a series of targets.

Your targets should be SMART. This means they should be:

S – Specific: designed to address specific skills that need to be developed and improved.

M – Measurable: designed in a way that will allow you to measure your progress towards them.

A – Achievable: designed to be feasible. Small steps are best.

R – Relevant: designed to be appropriate to the career path you have identified.

T – Time bound: that is you should set appropriate timescales for their achievement.

 PLTS

Rating yourself against the skills you would need for your chosen career path will show you to be a **reflective learner**.

 Functional skills

Making a list of skills you will need will use your **English** writing skills.

2.2.3 Tracking progress

Once a development plan has been created it must be monitored at regular intervals to:

- check progress towards targets through self evaluation and feedback – have milestones been hit?

- make adjustments to targets – have skills improved faster or slower than you expected or have your aspirations changed?

- add new targets as necessary.

PLTS

Setting targets and monitoring your progress towards them is an excellent opportunity to develop your personal learning and thinking skills by working as a **reflective learner**.

 Assessment activity 3

Professional development plan

Design a professional development plan for yourself that includes:

- an overview of what you are hoping to achieve over a specified period of time (e.g. by the end of your BTEC course)
- a set of SMART targets for the development and improvement of skills
- review dates to allow you to monitor your progress.

Grading Tips

M2 Remember to make long- and short-term targets specific and detailed.

D2 Your plan should include a detailed explanation of the skills you want to improve. When you set your targets, remember to prioritise your goals as well as making them realistic and time bound.

 Assessment activity 4

Monitoring your plan

You should revisit your professional development activity on at least two occasions during your BTEC course.

When you do so you should identify and discuss the progress made towards your targets and make adjustments to your plan as appropriate.

Grading Tips

M3 You will need to describe the progress you have made towards your targets.

D3 When reviewing your plan you should provide detailed explanations of your progress towards the targets that were set.

Performer biogs

Look in the programme of any professional theatrical production and you will find the 'biogs' (brief biographies) of those involved. These biogs often give details of the training and experience of the performers.

Alison Harris (Dancer)

Born in Nottingham, Alison began singing and dancing at an early age and after completing a BTEC National Diploma in Performing Arts at Franklinborough FE College attended the Rambert School. She has worked in the West End in the ensemble of *My Fair Lady* and *Carmen Jones* and recently completed a national tour of *Starlight Express*.

Jennifer Gattis (Actor)

Jennifer was born and went to school in the West Midlands where she was a keen member of her school theatre group. After studying 'A' levels in Theatre Studies, English Literature and German she went on to train at Central School of Speech and Drama. Since completing her training she has worked in repertory theatre throughout the UK. Recent roles include Adelaide In *Guys and Dolls* and Prince Charming in *Cinderella* for the Northern Repertory Theatre. Her TV credits include *The Bill*, *Holby City* and *Doctors*.

Stephen Greene (Actor)

Stephen became interested in drama in his 20s through a friend who took him along to an amateur drama group. Three years later he quit his job in IT to take up a place at Mountview Theatre School. This is Stephen's first professional role.

Think about it!

1. What do the following terms mean?
   - amateur drama group
   - ensemble
   - national tour
   - repertory theatre
   - TV credits
2. Write your own biography, of no more than 100 words. Include all productions you have either been in or worked behind the scenes on. If you have not yet taken part in any shows, you could make up a few to complete the biography.

Just checking

1. What is the difference between full-time and freelance employment?
2. What does the term 'entry requirements' mean in relation to higher education institutions?
3. What is a CV?
4. Why is goal or target setting important to professional development?
5. What does SMART stand for in target setting?

Assignment tips

- When researching job opportunities, begin by looking at a wide range of job roles before choosing a particular career path.
- Always consult a range of sources when researching your chosen career path.
- When undertaking your skills audit, gather information from your tutors to help you assess your current skill levels.
- Set a series of manageable targets when designing your plan. You can always add new targets when they are achieved.

A3 Performing Arts Production Process

The last time you went to see a performing arts production, such as a play, musical, dance recital or concert, did you stop to think about all the work that must have been done to get the show from someone's initial idea to the opening night?

Before the audience comes through the door of the theatre and the performers step onto the stage, there is much to be done. The production process begins with an initial idea for a show and includes all the planning, rehearsals and other preparations. It can involve a large number of people working in teams towards a common goal. There will be rehearsals for performers led by the director, musical director and/or choreographer. The venue, costumes, sets, props, lighting, sound effects and publicity all need to be organised too.

This unit will guide you through the various stages of the process of putting on a show. It will give you the information you need when working towards Unit A3 Performing Arts Production Process, taking you step by step through what needs to be done, explaining how things happen in the professional world and giving you advice on how this might relate to your own work.

Learning outcomes

After completing this unit you should be able to achieve the following learning outcomes:

1. Know how to carry out planning requirements for a performing arts product
2. Be able to take part in the developmental process for a performing arts product
3. Understand the purpose of the planning and preparation process in the creation of a performing arts product.

Assessment and grading criteria

This table shows you what you must do in order to achieve a pass, merit or distinction, and where you can find activities in this book to help you.

To achieve a pass grade the evidence must show that you are able to:	To achieve a merit grade the evidence must show that, in addition to the pass criteria, you are able to:	To achieve a distinction grade the evidence must show that, in addition to the pass and merit criteria, you are able to:
P1 identify the necessary planning requirements for a performing arts product **Assessment activity 1 page 42** **Assessment activity 2 page 43**	**M1** describe the necessary planning requirements for a performing arts product **Assessment activity 1 page 42** **Assessment activity 2 page 43**	**D1** explain the necessary planning requirements for a performing arts product with insight, foresight and confidence **Assessment activity 1 page 42** **Assessment activity 2 page 43**
P2 identify appropriate materials/equipment suitable for a performing arts product **Assessment activity 3 page 46**	**M2** describe appropriate materials/equipment suitable for a performing arts product with an attempt at shaping the nature of the work in development **Assessment activity 3 page 46**	**D2** explain appropriate materials/equipment suitable for a performing arts product in a way that shows a positive and artistic contribution to the work in development **Assessment activity 3 page 46**
P3 communicate with other team members and/or event personnel as appropriate **Assessment activity 4 page 50**	**M3** communicate with other team members and/or event personnel using appropriate channels and methods to ensure communication achieves its objective **Assessment activity 4 page 50**	**D3** communicate effectively with other team members and/or event personnel **Assessment activity 4 page 50**
P4 carry out a role in the development process showing a grasp of the task requirements and with some commitment **Assessment activity 5 page 52**	**M4** carry out a role in the development process showing that the task requirements are handled with some thought and attention to detail and with some commitment **Assessment activity 5 page 52**	**D4** carry out a role in the development process showing that the task requirements are handled with efficiency, commitment and independence **Assessment activity 5 page 52**
P5 evaluate the main strengths and weaknesses of the product with reference to the planning and preparation process. **Assessment activity 6 page 54**	**M5** evaluate strengths and weaknesses of the product with reference to the planning and preparation process and with some reasoning. **Assessment activity 6 page 54**	**D5** evaluate in detail the effectiveness of the product with reference to the planning and preparation process and with considered conclusions. **Assessment activity 6 page 54**

How you will be assessed

This unit will be assessed by an internal assignment that will be designed and marked by the tutors at your centre. You will be assessed on your contribution to a project that involves the organisation and planning of a performing arts event. You will need to show that you can work as part of a team to make decisions about what needs to be done and to put the plans into action.

The work you produce may include:
- a production diary or process log
- planning documentation, such as schedules and lists of resources
- examples of communication, such as memos, emails and/or letters
- video recordings of meeting and other planning activities
- observations from your tutor.

Josie, 16-year-old dance student

When I read about this unit in my course handbook I didn't know what to expect. I was worried that I wouldn't enjoy it because it didn't revolve around dancing. It turned out to be one of the highlights of my course.

The project we were set was to plan and organise a school production of *Bugsy Malone*. For most of the time we worked in teams. I opted to join the costume team. Others in my class opted for lighting, marketing and set or stage management.

We began by coming up with ideas for costumes. We were set a budget so we had to make sure we could afford what we were planning to make, buy and hire. My favourite part of the project was the week before the show. This is known as production week and it was really hectic as all the different elements of the show had to come together. It was great seeing the costumes on stage at last, but there were still some last-minute alterations to be made.

In this unit I learned a lot about how a show is planned and all the preparations you don't think about when you go to the theatre. I also learned how important good organisation and communication skills are to the success of the final production.

Over to you

- What are your thoughts and feelings on beginning this unit?
- Have you ever been involved in the planning of a production before? If so, what did you learn during the process?
- What do you hope to learn during this process?

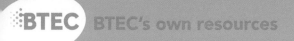

3.1 Carry out planning requirements for a performing arts product

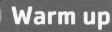

How many people does it take...

Imagine you are a member of a theatre company that is about to produce a family pantomime. Other than the performers, what other people are likely to be involved in the process of producing the show?

Make a list of who might be needed and what they would do.

Key term

Budget – the amount of money allocated to a production.

3.1.1 Planning and decisions

All performing arts productions begin with a series of decisions. A professional company may begin by selecting an idea for a performance. Any company planning a production must take into account a number of practical issues which will affect the decisions they make. These are likely to include:

- the time available
- the nature of the venue(s) where the performance will be staged
- the resources available to the company
- the budget available for the production.

The performance

Your work for this unit may begin with a decision about the type of performance you will produce. If your tutor allows you to choose the piece you will need to weigh up the pros and cons of several ideas to decide which is most suitable. However, your tutor may have chosen a specific play, musical or dance piece based on the size of your group, your skills and the resources available.

The venue

You must also consider where the performance will be staged. Theatrical spaces come in a variety of shapes and sizes and some productions will have certain requirements or may be more suited to one theatre than another. For your production you'll need to think about:

- the size and shape of the stage
- where the audience will be in relation to the performers
- what technical equipment (e.g. light and sound) is available.

The design concept

In the professional world, the planning process begins with a series of meetings. The director of the production will discuss their ideas for what the production will look like with other members of the creative team. These ideas are sometimes known as the design concept. The director will discuss the design of the set, costumes, lighting and sound. In your production you may be working under the direction of your tutor. You should, however, go through a similar process to a professional team as the design concept for the production is discussed and agreed.

Budget

Budgeting is central to any performing arts production. In the professional world, an administrator or finance officer will allocate a budget to cover production and marketing costs. The budget may then be divided into separate allocations for costumes, set, hire of technical equipment, etc. It is vital that costs are kept within the allocated budget. In your production you may also be allocated a small budget. It is important that you discuss how this money will be used.

The production schedule

At the beginning of the planning process the company must decide when the major deadlines for the production will be, most importantly the 'opening night' of the production. The organisation of any production then begins with the drawing up of a production schedule working back from that date. This is essentially a timeline that sets out the important dates and deadlines for the project. It should begin with an initial production meeting and end with the opening of the show. Depending on the type of production being organised it will include the dates of the get-in and fit-up as well as the technical and dress rehearsals. It should also include deadlines for the distribution of publicity materials and the completion of sets and costumes.

Production meetings

The production process will begin with a series of meetings in which design requirements are discussed and rehearsal and production schedules are drawn up. As the production of a performing arts event involves a lot of different activities carried out by many different people these meetings are vital to ensure that everyone understands what they need to do and that progress towards deadlines is monitored.

Remember

During your work on this unit you should keep a record of your activities and the decisions you make in a production file.
Get started by producing an outline of the performance event you will be planning and organising. Remember to include details about:

- the production being planned
- the venue
- the design concept or 'look' of the production
- the budget
- the main deadlines.

Key terms

Get-in – the process of moving scenery, lighting and other equipment into the venue.

Fit-up – the process of setting up scenery, lighting and other equipment for a show.

Technical rehearsal – a run-through of the show to allow the technical members of the production team to practise their cues and identify any problems.

Dress rehearsal – the final rehearsal before the opening night where the show is run in full costume.

PLTS

Working as a member of the production team during meetings and other activities is an excellent opportunity to develop your **team worker** skills by working confidently with others.

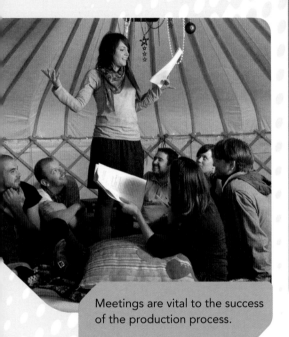

Meetings are vital to the success of the production process.

BTEC **Assessment activity 1** (P1) (M1) (D1)

Take part in a meeting to discuss the planning requirements for your production. Start by listing everything that needs to be done before the opening night. Place them in the order in which they need to be done and produce a production schedule that includes deadlines for each stage of the process.

During the meeting you should make notes and afterwards write up in your process file the plans you have discussed and agreed, describing the planning requirements you have identified.

Grading Tips

(M1) You could consider the following questions:
- How long will each task take?
- How will each role fit into the process?

(D1) Explain the importance of the planning requirements you have listed. You could do this by considering the following:
- Why is each task you have identified necessary?
- Why did you place them in the order you did on the production schedule?
- Can you foresee any potential problems with the tasks identified and deadlines agreed?
- How might these problems be avoided?

Your job

Once you have drawn up your plans and agreed your production schedule you will then need to decide who does what. Depending on the type of production you are planning, there will be a need for designers, technicians, backstage and front-of-house staff, and marketing people.

If you are working as part of a large group you may wish to divide up into teams with each team being allocated a role, e.g. marketing team, stage-management team, costume team. Alternatively, you may be allocated a specific role by your tutor. You may have to have an interview for the job you would like. Either way it is important that you understand precisely what you are personally required to do at each stage of the production process.

Assessment activity 2

P1 M1 D1

To show that you know your role and the responsibilities you have been given you will need to draw up an action plan for your work on this unit. It should include:

- a job description of the role you are carrying out
- deadlines for the individual tasks you are required to undertake
- details of others you will be working with (your team)
- an explanation of how your role will contribute to the production.

Grading Tips

D1 Your action plan should show that you know how your role fits into the production process by explaining:

- the importance of the tasks you will be undertaking
- why you need to meet the set deadlines.

PLTS

Setting deadlines for your tasks and keeping to them will use your skills as a self manager.

Functional skills

The production of your action plan will require you to use writing skills.

3.1.2 Marketing

A performing arts company bases its choice of production on what it knows will sell. Like other businesses, theatre and dance companies need to understand their customers – the audience. The type of audience a production might appeal to will need to be taken into account when the show is marketed. Different groups of people enjoy different types of show. For example, families with young children will be the main audience for a pantomime while productions such as *High School Musical* will be mainly watched by pre-teens and a show like *Phantom of the Opera* will attract older teenagers and adults. Each type of audience will need a different sort of marketing.

For your production, make sure you identify your target audience and use appropriate forms of marketing to attract them to your show.

Activity: Marketing

What is the target audience for your production?

In groups, produce marketing materials for your production. You should use at least one form of marketing. Choose from a poster, press release or flyer.

Key terms

Artistic policy – the type of work a company produces and the reasons why they produce it.

Season – a period in the company's calendar e.g. September–January. Many production companies produce two 'seasons' of work per year.

3.1.3 Product

Large production companies often produce a range of different types of show each season. For example, each season they might produce:

- a family show for the Christmas market

- a work by a new playwright

- a play that is a set text for English or drama examinations

- a play based on a local or regional theme.

Smaller touring companies sometimes specialise in a particular style of work. Walk the Plank, for example, specialise in large outdoor events that include fireworks and other specials effects, while Trestle Theatre is known for its mask-based work.

Some companies are commissioned to produce work, for example, a Theatre in Education company might be asked to create a piece to respond to a particular issue, such as road safety or healthy eating. The APE Theatre Company, for instance, toured with *Too Much Punch for Judy* about drink-driving, *Vicious Circle* about carbon emissions and *Pills Thrills @ Automobiles* about drugs. Other Theatre in Education companies tour schools with classic plays. For example, The Young Shakespeare Company visits primary and secondary schools, performing Shakespeare plays.

Activity: What's on in your region?

In groups, look at the programme of shows produced during a season by a theatre or dance company based in your region. You could do this by looking at a copy of their brochure or by visiting their website.

Consider the following questions:

1. Does the company have an artistic policy that influences their choices of performance?

2. What does the range of work they produce tell you about the company?

3. Is any of the work seasonal, e.g. do they produce a family show at Christmas?

4. What does the type of work they produce tell you about the kind of audience the company is targeting? Do they appear to be trying to attract a wide and diverse group, or a narrower audience, such as a certain age-group, an ethnic audience or audience interested in a certain type of theatre?

3.2 The developmental process for a performing arts product

Warm up

Lists, lists and more lists!

The development process of a performing arts production usually begins with a series of lists being drawn up to identify all the different materials and equipment that will be needed for the show.

What kind of list will you have to draw up for your role?

3.2.1 Development

Once your plans have been agreed and you have been allocated a role, the real work can begin. If you are performing you will begin to explore the material – rehearsing, working on choreography and so on. Further meetings will be scheduled to discuss and agree the design requirements for costumes, set and props. The marketing of the production will be considered and ideas for publicity materials agreed. You will then need to draw up a list of appropriate materials and equipment required for the production area you are responsible for.

Case study: Aladdin – props list

Mick, the assistant stage manager for Big Hat Theatre Company, is drawing up a list of props needed for the show. He goes through the script, identifying what is needed and describing each prop. He then notes whether the item is in the company's stock of props or if it needs to be made, bought or hired.

The ASM makes use of the final column to track items that have been found or made.

Props List: Act One – Scene One			
Item	**Description**	**Source**	**Done**
Basket	Shallow wicker washing basket with handles.	From stock.	
Washing	Various general items e.g. shirts, vests.	Some from stock.	
	3 pairs of large 'comedy bloomers' similar to those worn by Widow Twankey. Must be colourful e.g. spots/stripes.	'Comedy bloomers' to be made in house.	
Paper money	20 bank notes, larger than standard size.	Make.	
Lamp	Genie style.	Buy.	

1. Why is it important to include a description of each item?

2. Who will Mick need to contact with regards to the 'bloomers'?

Did you know?

The word prop is short for property and refers to any object that is held or used on stage. Smaller props that are used by one particular performer, e.g. a handkerchief, are known as personal props and become the responsibility of the performer during the run of the performance.

Functional skills

Presenting your ideas to the group will require you to use your **English** skills in speaking and listening.

BTEC **Assessment activity 3**   P2 M2 D2

1. Identify the equipment and/or resources required for the area of the production you are working on. For example, if you are working as part of the costume team you will need to draw up a list of the costume requirements for each performer. You should include detailed descriptions of each item you have identified.

2. Present your ideas to the whole group at a production meeting. You will need to:

   - list the materials and/or equipment you have chosen and explain the reasons for your choices

   - use sketches, drawings or diagrams where necessary to illustrate your ideas.

Grading Tips

M2 You should describe the materials and equipment you think you will need as well as how they will be used.

D2 You should explain why your choices are suitable for the production and why you think they will make a positive contribution to the show. For example, if you are involved in marketing and publicity you might explain why your design for a poster suits the theme and content of your production and will attract your target audience.

Preparing for rehearsals

Few performance companies rehearse in the space in which they will actually perform, so before rehearsals can begin, the space they are going to use needs to be prepared. The shape and size of the performance space will need to be marked out with coloured tape to match the dimensions of the actual performance space. If a drama piece is being rehearsed, the position of any large items of set will also need to be marked out. This job is normally carried out by the stage management team.

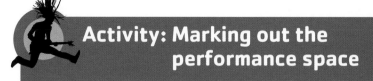

Activity: Marking out the performance space

Produce a scale drawing of the stage/performance space of the venue you will be using showing the stage and the entrances and exits.

Use this drawing to mark out your rehearsal space.

The rehearsal period

The first rehearsal of a production marks an important phase in the production process and marks the start of a busy time for all involved.

- Performers will work with the director, musical director and/or choreographer.

- Members of the production teams will be busy building sets and/or making props and costumes.

- Technical members of staff will ensure that any lighting/sound equipment needed is available, perhaps by hiring specialist equipment.

- Those involved in marketing and administration will ensure publicity materials are produced and distributed.

- The stage management team will play a vital role recording what goes on in rehearsals and communicating requirements to the technical and production teams. The deputy stage manager (DSM) will attend all rehearsals and prepare the 'book' or prompt script.

Key terms

Prompt Script – an annotated script showing information about all aspects of the show, including lighting, sound, cues, blocking and where props and scenery will be used.

Cue – a signal for something to happen, for example a lighting or sound effect.

Blocking – the physical arrangement of the actors on stage.

Performers will work with directors right through the rehearsal period, in the rehearsal room and the theatre itself.

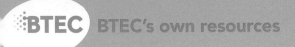
3.2.2 Technical

Production week

The final stage of the production process is known as production week. It involves the following processes.

The process	What needs to be done	Who is involved
The get-in	The set and other equipment are moved into the performance venue.	Stage management team Lighting and sound technicians
The fit-up	The lights are rigged (attached to the lighting grid and front-of-house lighting bars) and focused. Sound equipment is installed. The set is moved into place.	Stage management team Lighting and sound technicians
Plotting	Sound levels are set. All lighting cues are rehearsed and adjusted where necessary. Set changes are rehearsed.	Stage management team Lighting and sound technicians
Technical rehearsal	The show is run through to allow the technical team and stage crew to practise their cues. Often known as the 'tech', this is also an opportunity for the performers to get used to working with the lighting and sound cues.	Stage management team Lighting and sound technicians Director, choreographer, performers
Dress rehearsals	Before the opening night the show is normally run twice in full costume. The dress rehearsal is treated like a performance and some companies will run an 'open dress' with an invited audience. This is the first time the designers will see their work in action. They will attend and make any necessary last minute adjustments.	Stage management team Lighting and sound technicians Director, choreographer, performers Wardrobe team Set and costume designers

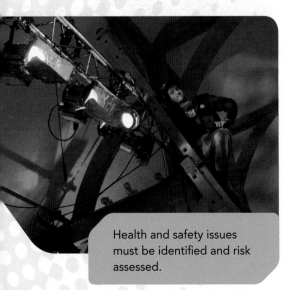

Health and safety issues must be identified and risk assessed.

Working safely

The theatre can be a dangerous place, particularly during production week. Many jobs may involve the lifting and moving of heavy or bulky equipment. Some jobs involve working at height or with electrical equipment. Where health and safety is an issue a risk assessment must be carried out. A risk assessment:

- identifies potential hazards in the workplace
- identifies who might be at risk
- puts in place actions to minimise the risk.

Organisation during production week

Whether you are working for a large theatre company or on a student production, good organisation is vital to the success of a production week. The get-in and fit-up must be planned meticulously. Having a written plan like the one below will ensure everything runs smoothly.

Plan for Fit-up Tues 7th – Thurs 9th May.		
Date/Time	**Activity**	**Personnel**
Tues 8.30–3.30	Rig on-stage lights	Kevin, James, Jim
Tues 3.30–4.30	Hang backdrop up stage	Laurie, Mick
Tues 4.30–6.30	Install rostra	Laurie, Mick, Harry, Ben
Wed 8.30–12.30	Rig front-of-house lights and sound	Kevin, James, Jim, Raj
Wed 1.30–6.30	Focus lights	Kevin, James, Jim, Raj
Thurs 8.30–10.30	Install large items of set	Laurie, Mick, Harry, Ben
Thurs 10.30–2.30	Plotting (Tidy backstage area and set up props table)	Kevin, James, Gina, (Harry & Ben)
Thurs 2.30–3.30	Sound check	Raj, Mary
Thurs 3.30–4.30	Scene change rehearsal	Laurie, Mick, Harry, Ben
Thurs 5.00–6.00	Health and safety session with cast (walk the set)	Full company and crew

3.2.3 Production team

With lots of different activities going on it is vital that safeguards are in place to make sure deadlines are met. It is also important that any decisions made by one person or team that might have an impact on the work of others are clearly communicated.

Meetings

Regular meetings are essential for communication during the production process. They provide opportunities for members of the various teams to meet, provide updates on progress and identify and deal with problems. An agenda should be drawn up before each meeting stating what needs to be discussed. The decisions made at meetings should also be recorded in the form of minutes or a report and distributed to all affected personnel.

Production week is when the technical team swings into action.

Functional skills

Producing memos and notices and recording your contribution to meetings will call for you to use your **English** writing skills.

:BTEC **Assessment activity 4** (P3) (M3) (D3)

Keep a log of the method you use to communicate with other team members in your production file and keep copies of any memos or notices you produce.

Record your contribution to meetings by producing a report of what was discussed and the decisions that were made.

Your tutor may also produce an observation record of how well you use communication skills when working with members of your team during practical activities.

Grading Tips

(M3) Think carefully how you communicate with other members of the production team. Be as supportive as you can to other team members and show that you are happy to share tasks.

(D3) Make sure that your written and verbal communication is clear so that others understand. You should also show that you are supportive of others by being patient and appreciative of their efforts.

Case study: Production meeting agenda

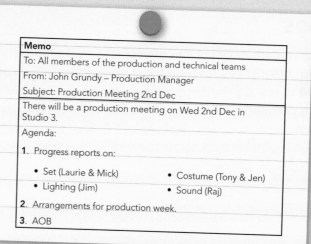

Memo
To: All members of the production and technical teams
From: John Grundy – Production Manager
Subject: Production Meeting 2nd Dec
There will be a production meeting on Wed 2nd Dec in Studio 3.
Agenda:

1. Progress reports on:

- Set (Laurie & Mick)
- Lighting (Jim)
- Costume (Tony & Jen)
- Sound (Raj)

2. Arrangements for production week.

3. AOB

1. What information might Laurie and Mick provide in their progress report?

2. What does AOB mean?

Using a production noticeboard

Professional theatre companies usually make use of a production noticeboard to exchange information between meetings. The DSM will post a call sheet on the notice board to inform performers of when they are required to attend rehearsals. Other team members may post reminders about meetings and other business.

Case study: Big Hat – production noticeboard

Big Hat Theatre Company is now in its second week of the production process. Take a look at their production noticeboard.

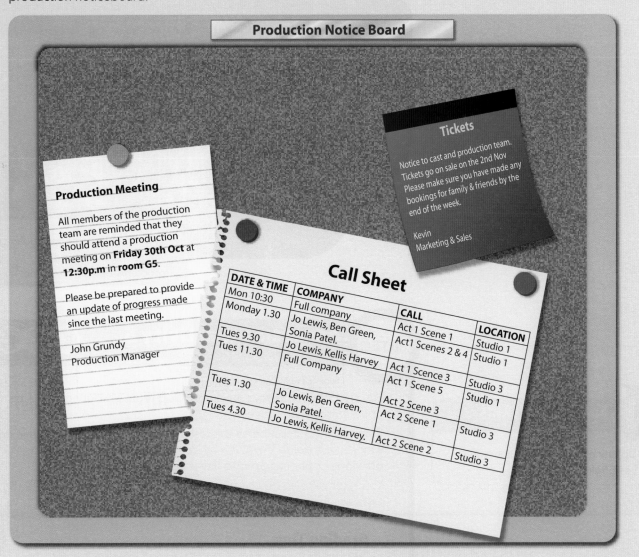

Production Notice Board

Production Meeting

All members of the production team are reminded that they should attend a production meeting on **Friday 30th Oct** at **12:30p.m** in **room G5**.

Please be prepared to provide an update of progress made since the last meeting.

John Grundy
Production Manager

Tickets

Notice to cast and production team. Tickets go on sale on the 2nd Nov Please make sure you have made any bookings for family & friends by the end of the week.

Kevin
Marketing & Sales

Call Sheet

DATE & TIME	COMPANY	CALL	LOCATION
Mon 10:30	Full company	Act 1 Scene 1	Studio 1
Monday 1.30	Jo Lewis, Ben Green, Sonia Patel.	Act1 Scenes 2 & 4	Studio 1
Tues 9.30	Jo Lewis, Kellis Harvey	Act 1 Scence 3	Studio 3
Tues 11.30	Full Company	Act 1 Scene 5	Studio 1
Tues 1.30	Jo Lewis, Ben Green, Sonia Patel.	Act 2 Scene 3	Studio 3
Tues 4.30	Jo Lewis, Kellis Harvey.	Act 2 Scene 1	Studio 3
		Act 2 Scene 2	Studio 3

You should now set up your own production noticeboard in your workspace to communicate important messages. Remember to check it every day.

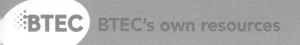

Front-of-house

During the run of the show, the front-of-house team will swing into action making sure the audience is looked after. This will include ensuring that the audience are seated for the performance, dealing with any problems and keeping disruption in the auditorium to a minimum. Backstage, the production will be overseen by the stage management team. In the professional theatre, the stage manager will produce a report after each show recording anything that did not go to plan.

If everything has been well planned the show should run smoothly. However, the unexpected can happen even in the professional world. If a problem arises it is important to deal with it calmly. The audience is often unaware of minor glitches provided no one panics.

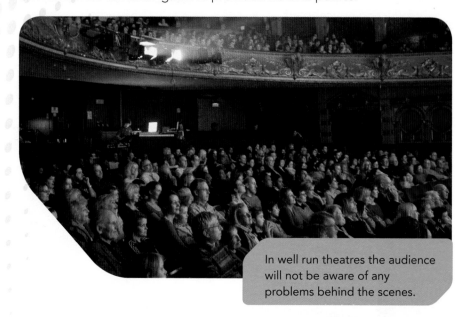

In well run theatres the audience will not be aware of any problems behind the scenes.

Functional skills

Updating your log will allow you to use **English** writing skills.

 Assessment activity 5 P4 M4 D4

You should update your production log regularly during all stages of the production process.

Remember to describe all the tasks you are undertaking, explaining why you are doing them. It may be helpful to include diagrams, drawings or photographs to illustrate your activities.

You tutor will also be observing your progress as you complete the tasks associated with your role.

Grading Tips

D4 You must show that you are working efficiently by meeting your deadlines. You should also show that you can remain committed to the project by staying on task and working without constant supervision.

3.3 The purpose of the planning and preparation process in the creation of a performing arts product

3.3.1 Evaluation

When the final curtain falls on your production you will need to consider how successful your planning and development activities were. You will do this by evaluating the work carried out during each phase of the production process. In doing this you should show that you have understood the purpose of the various activities you have undertaken.

You should begin by looking at the way in which you made your initial plans for the production. How were early decisions made? Did you correctly identify all the necessary planning requirements for the show? Was anything overlooked?

Use of materials and equipment

Each company member will have been responsible for using the materials and/or equipment as well as they could. For example, if you were a member of the marketing team you may have created posters using a camera to produce photos of the cast and a computer software program. Consider whether you used the equipment well and safely to design effective and eye catching materials. Did you damage any equipment?

Effectiveness of processes and techniques

During each phase of the production process you will have taken part in activities using a range of processes and techniques. During production week you may have used technical skills to rig and focus lights as well as team working skills to ensure tasks were completed within deadlines. How effectively did you undertake these activities?

Professional relationships and team working

A professional relationship is one that is built on trust and shared responsibility. If you work as part of a team, each person in that team will contribute to the success of the final production. In your evaluation you will need to consider:

- whether the team worked effectively

- how well you communicated with each other.

Functional skills

Taking part in the group meeting will allow you to use your **English** skills in speaking and listening.

PLTS

Evaluating your skills over the course of the production will allow you to show that you are a **reflective learner**.

3.3.2 Evaluating the final product and audience response

Did the audience respond to the work as you had planned and anticipated? If your aim was to provide the audience with a near-professional piece of theatre you will need to work out if this happened. This could be done by gathering verbal responses from people as they leave the show or by asking people to complete an audience questionnaire.

BTEC **Assessment activity 6**

Take part in a group meeting after the performance where you discuss how successful your planning and development activities were. You should consider how well:

- you made initial plans
- you used materials and equipment
- individual roles and responsibilities were decided
- you operated as a team
- you completed the tasks and processes you undertook
- the audience response to the production.

You should the make notes to record your own opinion about the strengths and weaknesses of the work of the group and your own individual contribution.

Grading Tips

M5 Show that you have understood why the planning process was so important to the final production. What might have happened if you didn't plan? You must also describe how you met the requirements of your role, and whether you would change how you do things in future performances.

D5 Always illustrate the points you make about strengths and weaknesses by referring to specific examples from the work you did.

Big Hat Theatre Company

production schedule

BIG HAT THEATRE

Big Hat Theatre Company is a small touring theatre company that specialises in Theatre in Education as well as traditional family productions. It is planning a production of the family pantomime Aladdin. The show will be performed at the Newtown Arts Centre for three weeks from 14th Dec.

The company begins its planning activities by drawing up a production schedule. The schedule identifies the planning requirements for the production by setting out what needs to be done and the dates by which the various milestones must be reached.

The schedule includes:

- An initial production meeting to discuss design requirements for sets, costumes, lighting and marketing strategy
- A production meeting to finalise designs and marketing
- A read-through
- Props meeting
- Marking out rehearsal space and beginning rehearsals
- When marketing material is distributed and tickets go on sale
- Building the set
- A production meeting to review props, set, costumes and lighting
- A production meeting to make final arrangements for production week
- The final run in rehearsal space
- The get in, fit up, focus and plotting
- The tech rehearsal, dress rehearsals and photo call
- The run.

Think about it!

1. Why do you think there are so many meetings included in the production schedule?

2. What do you think the following terms mean?

- read through
- props
- final run in rehearsal space
- costume call
- photo call
- marketing materials

Just checking

1. What are the key things that need to be decided when beginning to plan a performing arts production?
2. What is a production schedule?
3. What are production meetings and why are they important?
4. What is a production noticeboard?
5. What happens during the fit-up?
6. What is a technical rehearsal?

edexcel

Assignment tips

- Good organisation is the key to success in this unit. Always keep your production log up to date by filling it in regularly. Remember also to file any documents in the correct place.

- It is important to remember that everyone contributing to the process has a vital role to play. You may think your role is not as important as that of someone else, e.g. if you are moving scenery and they are playing the lead role in the performance. But remember, the success of any production rests equally on the shoulders of all those involved.

- When working on design ideas, keep all drafts, sketches and other rough work as this will provide evidence of how you developed the final product.

- Good levels of motivation are required by anyone who works in the performing arts industry. This project is no different. To do well in this unit you must contribute fully to the tasks you have been set, demonstrating that you are fully committed to the work. In group work, make sure you play your part fully; don't sit back and let others do the work.

- Good attendance and punctuality are very important. Competition for jobs in the performing arts industry is tough, so only those who are good timekeepers succeed. You must make sure that you attend regularly and complete tasks within the deadlines that have been set.

- Always be aware of how you are communicating with other team members. Remember to treat others with respect. Criticism must always be given in a constructive manner and you must also respond to feedback from others in an appropriate way.

B4 Acting Skills and Techniques

This unit is designed to develop your skills in using the essential tools of the actor's trade: your voice, body and imagination. Like any musician mastering an instrument, or athlete training to the peak of their abilities, the actor needs to practise, exercise and fine-tune their own 'instrument' (body, voice and creativity) in order to meet the demands of creating and performing characters on the stage.

This unit will teach you many techniques to develop vocal, movement and characterisation skills through exercises and workshops, leading to opportunities to put these skills into practice in performances to an audience. You will learn how to interpret and develop characters through workshops, explorations and research, including improvisations and work on published plays, allowing you to apply your acting skills to contrasting characters and types of play.

Assessment opportunities will include the improvement in your vocal and movement skills; approaches to the creation, interpretation and development of characters from rehearsal through to performance; and then the 'icing on the cake' – assessment of your performance to an audience in at least two separate shows.

Learning outcomes

After completing this unit you should be able to achieve the following learning outcomes:

1. Be able to use vocal skills
2. Be able to use movement skills
3. Be able to interpret and develop characters
4. Be able to perform in an acting role.

Assessment and grading criteria

This table shows you what you must to in order to achieve a pass, merit or distinction and where you can find activities in this book to help you.

To achieve a pass grade the evidence must show that you are able to:	To achieve a merit grade the evidence must show that, in addition to the pass criteria, you are able to:	To achieve a distinction grade the evidence must show that, in addition to the pass and merit criteria, you are able to:
P1 take part in vocal exercises and show improvement in the use of vocal techniques **Assessment activity 1 page 65**	**M1** take part in vocal exercises and show marked improvement of vocal techniques **Assessment activity 1 page 65**	**D1** take part in vocal exercises and demonstrate significant improvements to vocal techniques **Assessment activity 1 page 65**
P2 use vocal skills in a way that is appropriate to the acting role with technical control **Project 7 page 284**	**M2** use vocal skills in ways that demonstrate a good degree of technical control in an acting role **Project 7 page 284**	**D2** demonstrate a strong technical command of vocal skills within an acting role **Project 7 page 284**
P3 take part in movement exercises and show improvement in body control **Assessment activity 2 page 75**	**M3** take part in movement exercises and show marked improvement in body control **Assessment activity 2 page 75**	**D3** take part in movement exercises and show complete body control **Assessment activity 2 page 75**
P4 use movement skills in a way that is appropriate to the acting role with technical control **Project 7 page 284**	**M4** use movement skills in ways that demonstrate a good degree of technical control in an acting role **Project 7 page 284**	**D4** demonstrate a strong technical command of movement skills within an acting role **Project 7 page 284**
P5 demonstrate ways of exploring, researching and creating a character/role **Project 7 page 274, 279**	**M5** demonstrate responsive ways of exploring, researching and creating a character/role **Project 7 page 274, 279**	**D5** demonstrate highly flexible and creative ways of exploring, researching and creating a character/role **Project 7 page 274, 279**
P6 develop a character and make decisions about interpretation **Project 7 page 274, 279**	**M6** develop a character and make considered decisions about interpretation **Project 7 page 274, 279**	**D6** develop a character which shows use of imagination and/or insight in the choices and decisions made about interpretation **Project 7 page 274, 279**

To achieve a pass grade the evidence must show that you are able to:	To achieve a merit grade the evidence must show that, in addition to the pass criteria, you are able to:	To achieve a distinction grade the evidence must show that, in addition to the pass and merit criteria, you are able to:
P7 Perform a role showing a basic handling of the role with commitment **Project 7 page 284**	**M7** Perform a role that is handled with commitment and some attention to detail **Project 7 page 284**	**D7** Perform a role with focus, commitment, imagination and some sense of ease **Project 7 page 284**
P8 Communicate with an audience with occasional lapses in consistency **Project 7 page 284**	**M8** Communicate with an audience and remain focused and engaged in the drama **Project 7 page 284**	**D8** Communicate effectively with an audience and remain focused and engaged in the drama throughout **Project 7 page 284**

How you will be assessed

This unit will be assessed by internal assignments that will be designed and marked by the tutors at your centre. Each assignment will allow you to demonstrate understanding and apply skills and techniques you have learned in order to meet the grading criteria.

The work you produce may include:
- DVD/video recording of workshops, skills development and performances
- an Actor's Log that could include written entries, audio/video diaries and blogs
- tutor observations and statements
- skills progress audits charting improvement in vocal technique and movement.

Parmjeet, 17–year–old student

I'm on a performing arts course at college and am a member of a local youth theatre. I have a soft voice and find it difficult to do any accents or put on the right voice for parts I have played. In acting classes, we do voice warm-ups every lesson, and our tutor teaches us exercises to help us support our voices on stage with breathing and voice control. I often do these exercises myself at home. What I have learned is that actors need to make the best use of the voice they have, and that you don't have to always put on a 'special voice'. You should use your own voice well.

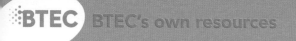
4.1 Using vocal skills

Warm up

What makes a good actor?

Choose an actor who, in your opinion, is a master of their profession. Consider the following questions, then share and discuss your views with the rest of your class.

1. What kind of character or style of drama is the actor associated with?

2. Do they work in theatre, film or TV, or all three?

3. What skills, qualities or 'hallmarks' make the actor special?

4. What is good and interesting about their voice?

5. What qualities do you see in their movement, expression and gesture?

PLTS

Completing the Warm up activity is evidence of your abilities as an **independent enquirer**.

4.1.1 Technique

Throughout the unit you will be taught and guided by your tutor to use exercises and techniques to develop your voice and your body for performance. Professional actors need to train and exercise to improve and maintain their voice and body in order to meet the demands that acting makes. You can do the following activities in classes and workshops with the rest of your group or on your own at home and before rehearsals as part of your preparation before going on stage.

Activity: Facial limber

Before you begin vocal exercises you need to warm up your face with a facial limber. This gets the face and mouth (lips, teeth and tongue) ready for speech work.

1. Start by massaging your face with your fingertips – gently work your fingers over your whole face and jawline.
2. Imagine you are a cow chewing hay – move your jaw, lips, tongue and teeth around in exaggerated eating motions.
3. Stick out your tongue and try to touch the tip of your nose and the end of your chin.
4. Pucker your lips and blow kisses to someone in the class or an imaginary person at home.
5. Blow raspberries at the same person.
6. With mouth and eyes wide open, make your face as big as possible.
7. Then scrunch your face up as small as it will go.
8. Give a huge silent yawn to open up your throat.

Vocal technique

Being able to control breathing on stage is vital to an effective vocal technique. It supports your voice and enhances projection. It will also help you to avoid running out of breath during long sentences. Breathing exercises are an important part of an actor's preparation for work, and will help you develop a good vocal technique.

Activity: Breathing exercises

Exercise 1

1. Stand centred and relaxed (shake your body out or undertake the centring exercise described later in this unit if necessary).
2. Give a silent yawn to open your throat, then inhale quickly trying to get as much air into your body as you can. When your lungs are full, hold your breath for a count of five.
3. Then exhale very quickly, pushing all the breath out of your body as fast as you can. It will help if you collapse to a crouch as you do this.
4. Repeat, but this time, after the count of five, release your breath as slowly as possible, while collapsing slowly into a crouch as the breath leaves your body.

Exercise 2

You can try this exercise while lying on the floor following a relaxation exercise (see page 67) or while standing. Place your hands on your ribs to allow you to feel your breathing at work.

1. Stand with your mouth and jaw relaxed and your hands placed on your ribcage, tips of your middle fingers touching in the middle.
2. Breathe in slowly through your nose, to a count of three.
3. Gently hold your breath for a count of three.
4. Exhale slowly through your mouth for a count of three.
5. Repeat, increasing the number of counts each time, but don't make these so long that tension creeps into your chest and shoulders.
6. On the outward breath, add a comfortable sung note on an 'ahh' sound, or count out each number as you exhale.

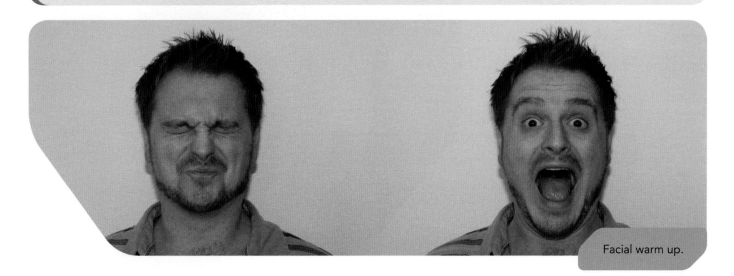

Facial warm up.

Voice projection

Voice projection is important because, if you don't project your voice effectively on stage, the audience won't hear or understand you. How much you need to project will vary according to the size and nature of the place where you are performing.

Good voice projection isn't simply about raising the voice and being loud. An actor needs to consider the vocal quality and tone required to accurately express the thoughts, feelings and situation of the character. Good voice projection should fill the performance space without placing strain on the actor's vocal apparatus or assaulting the eardrums of the audience.

Activity: Fill space with sound

You should test and practise your voice projection skills in several ways. This exercise will increase your skill and confidence.

1. Centre and relax your body (see exercises below for details of how to do this). Pick a phrase, a sentence (perhaps saying one important thing about yourself) or a line from a play or poem.
2. Place your hand 15 centimetres in front of your face. You should be able to feel your breath on your hand as you speak if you are projecting with enough breath and volume.
3. Put your hand down and now focus on a point some distance across the room. Direct your voice to that point, using deeper breathing and control to support your voice to allow it to reach the point.

Try this exercise in different spaces, listening to your ability to fill each space with sound. How does a small room compare with a theatre or a corridor? What happens out of doors?

Find yourself different opportunities to speak, calling for gradual increases in volume, such as speaking while the TV is on, then above a noisy crowd.

When you test your projection in different spaces, ask a friend or your tutor to comment on the quality and clarity of your voice in each location.

Feeling your breath.

Articulation

Articulation makes what you say clear, allowing you to express the meaning of what you are saying precisely. Some words and combinations of words are often difficult to speak clearly or fluently. The mouth and face need exercises to help overcome these obstacles. The following tongue twisters are effective warm-ups and exercises for speaking clearly.

- A proper cup of coffee in a proper coffee pot.

- A glowing gleam glowed grey and green.

- The feathered thrush flew through the fiery flue.

- Red lorry yellow lorry/red leather yellow leather.

- A big, black bug bit a big black bear and made the big black bear bleed blood.

- The sixth sheikh's sixth sheep's sick.

- The Leith police dismisseth us, the Leith police are thorough. The Leith police admitteth us, into their lawful borough.

Tongue twisters can be very frustrating, but with practice, are very useful and effective exercises. However, you need to have done some of the facial limbering and warm-up exercises in order to be fully prepared to attemp tongue twisters.

Vocal exercises

The following vocal exercises help the actor develop vocal skills and techniques to allow them to express character, mood and feeling through varying use of the voice, allowing flexibility and variation in pitch, tone, intonation and inflection.

Key terms

Pitch – the correct level and sound of the voice as required for the character and role at any particular moment of a vocal performance.

Intonation – the rise and fall of the voice when speaking.

Inflection – changes in how high and how low the voice is when speaking.

Activity: Resonance

Experimenting with resonators helps you make many adjustments to the quality of your voice.

To warm up and exercise your resonators:

1. Try humming through closed lips, at first gently and then with increasing force. Feel the tingling in your lips.
2. Place the hum further up in your head, as if humming from the top of your nose. You will notice the sound of the hum is different (a higher pitch) and the tingling higher up behind your face. Then experiment by imagining you are moving the hum into different parts of your face, throat and chest.
3. With an open mouth and throat, pant like a dog, making a 'huh, huh' sound.
4. Now give the pant a 'voice', and say the following 'Ha-Ha-Ha; Hee-Hee-Hee, Ho-Ho-Ho, Hey-Hey-Hey; Hi-Hi-Hi; Haw-Haw-Haw, Hoo-Hoo-Hoo'. Work your mouth and face to emphasise each different sound.

Resonance

This is what allows you to make different sounds – your chest, throat, mouth, nose and head have hollows, shapes and features that add different qualities to the noises you make when you turn breath into sound.

Learning your lines

Strong technical control and correct use of the voice are important, but you must also know the lines you are speaking. While practising the interpretation and delivery of any scripted dialogue, don't forget to learn your lines thoroughly. Some actors learn each line by saying it out loud repeatedly until they have memorised it before moving onto the next line. Others record their lines on a Dictaphone or MP3 and listen back. A good method is to use the script, covering your next line with a piece of paper, reading the other character's lines (your cue to speak) then saying your line in response before lifting the paper and checking you've got it right. It's also often helpful to be tested on your lines – ask a friend or family member to read you the cue lines and prompt when necessary.

4.1.2 Expression and modulation

Modulation is what we do to express feeling through altering the voice to signal what that emotion is. These are very fine adjustments that we make to volume, speed, sound, tone and emphasis. It adds colour and depth to speech, and is very important to actors, who need to modulate their speech to allow the audience to fully understand what the character is thinking and feeling.

Did you know?

Your face, breathing and voice respond to different emotions. Think about how they change when you:
- find something funny
- are angry
- love someone
- are scared
- have been disappointed
- feel proud
- find something pleasurable or disgusting.

PLTS

Applying appropriate modulation and articulation to express mood, feeling and meanings shows you are a **creative thinker**.

Participating in all the activities in voice classes will show you can be an **effective participator**.

Working in groups in vocal warm-ups requires co-ordination and working sensitively with others, and will allow you to demonstrate you are a **team worker** especially if leading voice warm-ups or being led by others.

What is the feeling?

Activity: Practising what you have learned

1. Take some simple phrases: 'Hey – how are you?', 'What are you doing?', 'You, over there!', 'I can't do that!', 'Cuthbert!'

   Use your imagination to find different reasons for saying each one, then use the modulation of your voice to express what that reason is (e.g. you are amused, scared, angry, etc.).

   Speak the phrases to a partner. With their eyes closed, can they guess the feeling behind what you are saying? Get them to tell you what it was in your voice that conveyed the feeling.

2. Now look at the following descriptive phrases. Each one suggests a mood and paints a picture. Use your voice to paint that picture with sound.
   - Rain drops spitting, dripping.
   - Light feet skipping, flitting.
   - Tongues of fire flaming, scorching.
   - Wild winds whistling, thrashing.
   - Sad voices crying, wailing.
   - Faint echoes whispering, dying.
   - Soft snow drifting, floating.
   - Bright stars sparkling, exploding.

3. Take the tongue twisters you tried earlier and this time exaggerate every syllable, using your whole face to emphasise each word.

 ## Assessment activity 1

Vocal improvement

Throughout your BTEC First in Performing Arts you will take part in regular voice-training workshops. These will include relaxation and breathing, warm-ups and techniques to develop your vocal acting skills.

Keep notes on your progress in worksheets and self-assessments provided.

Following a 'skills check' at the start of the course, improvement of your vocal skills will be assessed in a series of 'milestone' activities. These may include: leading the rest of the group in voice exercises, prepared readings, short scenes for stage and radio acting, acting in different spaces, improvisation, and theatre games.

Your performances to audiences in the Acting Skills and Techniques and Performing Scripted Plays units may provide evidence of vocal improvement. Your vocal skills in an acting role will also be assessed for Unit B4 Acting Skills and Techniques P2, M2 and D2.

Grading Tips

M1 You will demonstrate obvious progress with improvements in areas such as clarity of speech, use of breath, effective modulation, phrasing and projection.

D1 You will show significant improvements, with growing confidence and mastery of vocal skills and techniques.

4.2 Using movement skills

Plays make particular movement demands on the actor. Classical plays, for example, may require actors to adopt stances and gestures typical to a historical period or society. Professional theatres often employ specialist movement coaches, such as fight co-ordinators and choreographers, to help actors with specialised movement. An actor's work on character movement requires research and observation, such as analysing body language, ageing or physical illnesses to help perform them accurately. Actors must make sure they have physical co-ordination, flexibility and stamina to perform a range of roles and actions. This is where good movement training and regular exercise pay dividends.

4.2.1 Technique

To work effectively in performance and rehearsals, the actor's body must first be warmed-up and relaxed to meet and respond to the challenges and demands of acting and to prevent danger of injury. The relaxation and centring exercises described below are good ways of preparing for movement work. They will help with your general relaxation and balance and with developing the control, flexibility and co-ordination of your body to prepare you for work on stage.

Specialist movement skills are required of performers in the DV8 Physical Theatre company.

Activity: Relaxation exercise

This is a good exercise as it includes relaxation, co-ordination and body control.

1. Lie on your back (supine) on the floor, with your arms either side, palms facing down. Bring your knees up with your feet flat on the floor. Knees and feet should be slightly apart, but not so far that you tense your legs.

2. In this position, make sure your whole body, from head to toe, is relaxed – you do this by identifying any areas that feel stiff or tense, and willing them to relax (imagine warmth spreading through your body, like hot treacle, as stiffness and tension seep away). The picture should give you an idea, but your tutor will guide you to make sure you are positioned correctly and check for any tension in your body.

3. Clench and tighten every part of your body from your toes to the top of your head. Your whole body should be squeezed as tightly as possible.

4. Clench and squeeze even more.

5. Then relax: let everything release and loosen. Spend a while checking no tension has crept back in.

6. Now, imagine your body is split down the middle from your head to your toes (visualise a downward line splitting your body into two equal halves).

7. Repeat the clenching and squeezing, but this time tensing one half of your body, while keeping the other half completely free and relaxed

8. Relax the whole body, then repeat, tensing the opposite side of your body before relaxing.

Hints

- Place a paperback book or cushion underneath your head to make sure your head isn't tilting forward or back, which could create neck discomfort.
- Keep checking regularly to make sure no tension has crept back in.
- Don't fall asleep – keep your eyes open to avoid this happening.

Relaxation exercise: semi-supine position.

Did you know?

Relaxing your body helps you to avoid tension, something that can creep into the actor's body (a symptom of stage fright) and prevent accurate movement and characterisation.

The centring exercise that follows is based on Alexander Technique, which is a method of improving the use of the body and its muscles. The technique's originator, F.M. Alexander identified that every day when we walk, stand, speak and sit, we place unnecessary strain on our bodies through incorrect use and posture, leading to strain, injury and even speaking difficulties. His methods are particularly useful to actors, dancers and musicians, whose professional work can place strain on both the voice and the body.

PLTS

Some team games, along with exercises in spatial awareness, allow you to show evidence of your ability as a **team worker**.

Taking part in movement work, physical training and development exercises shows you are an **effective participator**.

Exercises requiring you to express concepts and emotions physically show you can be a **creative thinker**.

Activity: Centring exercise

1. Stand up and check to make sure you are relaxed. Vigorously shake out your arms, then legs, then your whole body to get rid of any tension.
2. Centre yourself by imagining a piece of string is attached to the top of your head, and someone is slowly pulling you up.
3. As you pull up onto your tiptoes, keep your balance. If you start to tip forward or back, your posture is incorrect and you should relax and start again.
4. When you are comfortably balanced, imagine the string is gradually being released, and slowly let your feet come to rest flat on the floor while concentrating on trying to keep your head at the height you were pulled up to.

The result is a satisfying stretch in your back, improved posture and you will feel a lot taller. Now walk around, keeping that sense of height and posture, but do not allow any tension to creep back in.

Games

Playing games is a good way of loosening up and releasing tensions and inhibitions in a fun way, leaving you free to work. They will also provide you with a burst of fresh energy, which can be useful during rehearsals if things are flagging.

There are hundreds of games that will fit the bill. Your tutor will usually suggest the best ones, but you may be called upon to come up with ideas yourself. Some excellent examples are:

- Grandmother's footsteps
- Wizards, dwarves, giants
- Stuck in the mud
- Prisoner
- ball games.

Group warm-up game for a quick energy boost

Team games are also useful. They provide valuable training to help develop essential movement skills such as trust, co-ordination, movement memory and working with others.

Spatial awareness and relationships

On stage, actors need to be highly aware of where they are in relation to other characters, the set and furniture, the audience and the theatre space as a whole. This helps avoid masking, upstaging and bumping into scenery or other actors.

Activity: Fill space with movement

1. The whole class walks around the studio, avoiding collisions.
2. Experiment with speed and pace, going from very slow walking to fast running.
3. Avoid 'following the leader' or patterns – everyone should change direction regularly and quickly, observing others carefully to avoid collisions.
4. Leave no spaces in the studio – everyone must think quickly and be ready to fill any gaps or empty areas of the room.

Variation:
On the command of the tutor everyone in the class stops and closes their eyes.
The tutor then names one person in the room. With eyes still shut, everyone has to point to where they think that person is standing. Start moving again, and repeat.

Weight placement

How we place our weight tells us a lot about character. When developing a character, a useful way to approach the physical portrayal of the role is to experiment with how they stand and walk. When developing a character in a play or through improvisation, experiment with weight placement along with the pace and tempo of their movement to reflect their personality, mood and motivations (what is driving them). You will need to adjust these, especially if you are to act naturally in the role, but experimentation in rehearsal can really help you tune in to a character.

The walking exercises on the next page will help you see how using weight in different ways generates different characteristics.

Remember

Whenever you take part in a game or exercise, you should keep a note in your Actor's Log, describing the game, its purpose and its benefit to you as an actor and/or to your group as a working team.

Did you know?

Sometimes a director will intentionally ask an actor to mask or upstage another actor, or speak with their back to the audience, in order to achieve a particular effect.

Key terms

Masking – standing in front of other actors, blocking the audience's view.

Upstaging – standing towards the rear of the stage from the actor who is speaking to you, making it difficult for them to deliver the line as they have to face away from the audience.

Activity: Walking exercises

1. Walk neutrally. This means walk just for the sake of walking, without consciously showing intention, character or mood. It is best to carry out a relaxation exercise before attempting this. Get others to watch you and point out what they observe. You need to cancel out anything that does not appear neutral (such as deliberately swinging an arm, clenching a fist or having your head at an angle).

2. Then imagine you are being led by different parts of your body, for example, your chin, as if someone has attached a string and is pulling you. Try this with your stomach, chest, forehead, hips, knees and so on.

What does this do to your balance and what is the effect on the rest of your body?

How does each different walk make you feel? Does leading with the chin, for instance, make you feel haughty and proud, or leading with the knees tired and depressed?

Pace and tempo

We all move differently and have our own rhythms. How an actor moves on stage in terms of speed, rhythm and how they place their weight will tell the audience a great deal about the character.

What does the way your friends walk and use gestures tell you about them?

Activity: The rhythms of life

Think about people you know (relatives, friends, people in your acting class, your tutors). What kind of rhythms do you associate with them? (Think of how people walk, talk, eat and use gestures such as slowly rubbing the chin or rapidly scratching behind the ear.) What do these rhythms tell you about the person or the situation?

Movement memory

Control of your movements is very important because everything you do on stage, even the tiniest gesture, is seen by the audience, and they will interpret it as part of the play. The gestures, movements and mannerisms of your character need to be carefully considered to make sure they are sending the right signals to the audience. These exercises will help you develop control and detail in your physical acting.

Activity: Pass the remote

1. List some familiar actions you perform every day. Examples could include doing your make-up, cleaning your teeth, tying shoelaces, pouring a drink.
2. Recreate one or more of these actions without the actual objects (as a mime). Be very careful to keep the exact detail of the action – to do this, it helps to really imagine the feel, weight and texture of any objects involved.
3. When you are confident the action feels real, imagine you are being controlled by a television remote control.
4. First do the action in slow motion. Remember that although the speed has changed, the accuracy and detail must stay the same.
5. Now set the remote to rewind, so you perform the action in reverse.
6. Add in the occasional pause command.
7. Now fast-forward the action.
8. Improvise – experiment with pause, rewind, fast-forward, slow-motion, to create a bizarre piece of choreography.

Remember

Movements can be interpreted in more than one way. We often, for instance, associate quick jerky movements with nervous insecure characters, and slower controlled gestures with the more confident. But other factors need to be considered when looking at what our bodies project: quick movements could be due to being late or being cold, and slowness due to feeling bored or hot.

4.2.2 Expression

Gesture

Gestures are movements we make with our bodies, heads, faces and hands to express a particular meaning. When developing a character it is important to consider carefully all the gestures you perform, as every single gesture is interpreted by the audience as saying something about the character, their attitude, feeling and state of mind at that moment.

Professional actors spend a great deal of time observing or people watching to gain useful information on how and what people communicate through gestures. Get used to watching people around you – your family, people in the street, friends at your centre. What do their gestures, movements, expressions convey? Observation of this kind is an invaluable resource for the actor.

Physicalising internal feelings

Try these activities to practise making internal feelings visible in outward movements and gestures.

PLTS

Observation work when developing characterisation skills and preparing for an acting role is evidence of your skills as an **independent enquirer**, a **self manager** and a **reflective learner**.

Activity: Physicalising feelings

In the mood

Perform a series of familiar actions, perhaps the same ones as in the activity Pass the remote. This time perform each action as if you are affected by a particular emotion or mood. For example, you could be doing your hair after splitting with your girl/boyfriend (you could either be sad or relieved about this); or making a cup of tea for a guest you really wish would leave.

It's just a chair

1. Place a chair in the middle of the studio.
2. Each actor has to approach the chair in such a way as to show they feel a certain way, on which the chair has an effect. For example, they could be simply feeling tired and wanting to sit down, or could be a prisoner stepping up to the electric chair.
3. Others in the group have to guess what is going on. The more controlled and expressive the movement, the more able they will be to guess correctly.

Facial expression

The face's many muscles and features can be arranged to express feeling and emotion ranging from the tiniest expression of embarrassment (a slight flush of the cheek and downward glance) to extreme passions (floods of tears, flaring nostrils, trembling snarls).

Facial expression is an important tool for the actor, but you must be careful that expressions are not painted on or adopted like masks. The reason our faces change is because we feel something (you don't put on an angry face – something has to first make you angry; then the feeling of anger results in a scowl, flared nostrils and hard stare).

Look at Unit B5: The Development of Drama. This will give you some clues about when and why different acting styles are called for.

Activity: Big versus subtle

Sit opposite a partner and start with simple and broad expressions to include the following: fear, happiness, sadness, disgust, shock, anger, pain, love, etc.

Don't tell your partner what the expression is – let them decide.

Then try a range of subtle, less obvious, expressions: embarrassment, pride, shame, pity, boredom, uncertainty.

Now try to show the larger expressions you started with in a more subtle way.

Think about these questions:

1. What kind of acting situations or roles would call for the larger broad expressions?
2. When would actors need to tone down their performance to make it more subtle and natural?

PLTS

Participating in the weight placement and facial expression exercises shows skills as an **effective participator**, a **team worker** and a **creative thinker**.

Handling props

The ability to handle props convincingly on stage is surprisingly difficult to master. Inexperienced actors often suffer from on-stage nervousness, resulting in them fumbling with items so that the audience becomes less than convinced in the reality of what they are seeing. How a character handles a prop tells the audience a lot about what they are feeling and their relationship to the scene and other characters. It also helps to create the illusion of reality if handled naturally and realistically. Assessment activity 2 deals with prop handling as an assessment exercise. Here is a practice activity you could undertake.

Activity: Handling props

Rehearse an action that involves using one or more objects and which is fairly complex. You need to use real objects as props. Examples include:

- making a cup of tea
- sending a text message
- putting on make-up
- making a sandwich.

When you have rehearsed this so that it looks natural and convincing, act a short scene with dialogue involving another character while performing the same activity. The scene could be a script you have learned in advance, or could be improvised.

The objective is to convey the dialogue and communicate the scene effectively while handling the props convincingly. Get your tutor to video the scene, so you can see on playback how well you have managed.

Spatial awareness

Spatial awareness includes understanding the relationship between the characters, as the distance between characters on stage often depends on this relationship.

What do you think these girls might be doing? What does the space between the two girls and the one at the back tell you?

Activity: Spatial relationship

In groups, make tableaux showing spatial relationships (decide on the characters, location and situation) then see how effectively the tableaux tell the story by asking others in the class to say what they think is going on. You could start with the following examples:

- Four girls huddled closely together whispering; a fifth girl stands apart from them reading a book.
- Three pairs on a train: one pair sits with hips touching and sharing iPod earphones; another pair sit opposite each other talking; the third pair sit on the same seat, one looking out of the window, the other close but not touching, arms folded.

4.3 Interpreting and developing character

When developing a character in a scripted play or when devising, the actor needs to spend a lot of time researching, discussing, observing and experimenting in order to come up with an interpretation. How the actor interprets the text will result in decisions about the character's voice, gestures, mannerisms, rhythms, habits, appearance, etc, which the actor will need to show in performance. Try not to make your characterisations too complicated. Too much to remember and too many quirks can just detract.

Project 7 page 269 provides detailed guidance on how to analyse a play in order to make decisions about interpretation of character.

The C.R.O.W. concept below is a quick and easy way to get you started and thinking about the interpretation of character.

Key Concept – C.R.O.W.

When working on an exercise or improvisation, it is important for each actor in the scene to know the following information, otherwise the scene will be disjointed and will have difficulty moving on:

C Character – who is my character?

R Relationship – what is their relationship with the other characters?

O Objective – what does my character want to do, what is their goal?

W Where – where does the scene take place, and when?

PLTS

Working in groups in physical warm-ups, games and exercises requires co-ordination and working sensitively with others, and will allow you to demonstrate you are a **team worker**. Your participation will also demonstrate you are an **effective participator**.

Remember

All notes on the exercises, as well as any worksheets and self-assessment forms should be kept in your logbook.

BTEC **Assessment activity 2** (P3) (M3) (D3)

Moving on

1. You will have regular movement training through warm-ups, games, exercises to improve control, spatial awareness, expression and interpretation of character through movement and gesture.

2. Keep notes on the exercises, their purpose, what you have learned and a review of the development of your physical acting skills. You will be given worksheets and self-assessments to help you.

   Your participation in acting classes and workshops will occasionally be recorded on video and by tutor observation.

3. On at least three milestone occasions, your improvement of movement skills will be assessed through activities such as character and animal movement workshops, performing emotion, handling props accurately while performing dialogue, and so on.

Your performances to audiences in this unit as well as others may provide evidence of improvement of movement skills. Your movement skills in acting roles will also provide assessment evidence for P4, M4 and D4.

Grading Tips

(M3) Show notable improvement in warm-ups, classes and workshops, general control, balance, relaxation, expression, use of space, etc. resulting in clear, accurate and effective physical performances.

(D3) You will improve continually, with growing skill and mastery of these techniques performed with confidence and assurance.

Further guidance

Further guidance and activities will be needed to work through Learning Outcome 3: Be able to interpret and develop characters and Learning Outcome 4: Be able to perform in an acting role, and are covered in Project 7 page 269. The project looks at the actor creating and developing a character and the preparation needed for successful performance.

Maggie Pryce
Artistic Director

Maggie Pryce is Artistic Director at the Lestat theatre in North London.

Question: What do you look for when you are auditioning and interviewing?

Maggie: Everything I look for in an actor is equally important. There are a number of things I am looking for:

1. Actors need 100 per cent commitment to detail in every aspect of rehearsal and performance. This extends to every single eye movement, use of the hands, handling an object, how they exit, even down to their boots.

2. Stage presence. Even a character who has nothing to say and isn't involved in the main action of the scene needs to be totally immersed in doing something and having a reason for being there. The audience must see every actor on stage as having a purpose, not just as background.

3. Energy and focus. Both plays we are rehearsing are fast paced, with each scene blending into the next like a kaleidoscope. The actors need to be fast, decisive and totally disciplined to maintain the pace.

4. A sense of humour. Laughter is a great release and a necessary part of the creative process.

5. Knowledge and understanding. Every actor needs to know the story and the world of the play. Obviously this means total understanding of the character they are playing and their part in the story, but they must also understand the part that every other character plays.

6. Patience. In rehearsals, every actor is vulnerable, as is the director. Sensitivity is needed as well as the ability to adjust to the demands of the play and to what other actors are doing. There is no room for preciousness in the company.

7. The willingness to take risks. An actor must take risks.

8. Actors who give – I like actors who input ideas, asking questions as well as providing some of the answers.

9. Team workers. This is essential. Rehearsal is a long, sometimes hard journey, and we are all working together, creating the story and the world of the play.

Think about it!

1. How do you think actors can find and maintain the energy levels necessary for rehearsals and performance?
2. Why does Maggie suggest laughter is both a release and a necessary part of the creative process?
3. Maggie says 'preciousness' should have no place in her company. What does she mean?
4. Why is it important for an actor to be able to take risks?

Just checking

1. What parts of your body should you warm up before rehearsals or performances?

2. What do the following words mean?
   - pitch
   - intonation
   - inflection

3. What does C.R.O.W. stand for?

edexcel

Assignment tips

- For rehearsals, practical workshops and particularly for performances, always arrive in good time to prepare. If your group or company are there before the tutor/director, use the time to warm-up and prepare yourselves ready to work.

- Take it in turns to lead vocal and physical warm-ups and exercises. This is good for team working.

- Dress comfortably. Be prepared for anything you might be asked to do, including working on the floor, lifting other people, etc. Don't wear any jewellery and remove watches. Also remember to have soft footwear, or be prepared to work in bare feet.

- No matter how much or how little your character is doing, always know the following:

  - Who am I?   - Where have I just come from?

  - Where am I?   - What do I want?

  - Why am I here?   - What am I going to do (next)?

- On stage: Good theatre depends on detail. Attend to every element of your performance – your facial expressions, what you do with your hands, your feet, how and where you are standing, how you handle objects and props, etc, etc.

- On stage: Be sensitive to other actors. Whatever you do on stage, while it must be accurate and convincing, it mustn't steal the focus from other performers at the wrong time.

- By openly experiencing, observing and asking questions about your own life and the world around you, you will develop the understanding and experience good acting demands. Have a good time.

Credit value: 10

B5 The Development of Drama

Anyone involved in making theatre needs a good general knowledge of the work they are producing; not just the process of developing and putting on a show, but also the importance and relevance drama has for us today, just as it has for societies and cultures across many centuries of theatre history.

Theatre is a vast and varied area, and every actor, director, technician and designer learns and applies a range of specialist creative techniques – a 'language of theatre' –essential to making successful, entertaining and meaningful drama.

This unit will allow you to explore how drama is made – how it develops from an original idea to the finished article. It will help you gain a better understanding of dramatic forms, genres and the history of drama when you are creating and performing your own play, whether as a performer, a technician or an aspiring director. You will discover what makes a play and the features that give certain forms of drama their unique style and characteristics. You will find out how and why theatre and acting techniques have developed through history. You will explore some key processes in making theatre; learning and practising different acting and staging techniques in producing two pieces of drama.

Learning outcomes

After completing this unit you should be able to achieve the following learning outcomes:

1. Know about the social and historical context in the development of drama
2. Know the structures and characteristics of drama
3. Be able to apply the processes of creating dramatic work.

Assessment and grading criteria

This table shows you what you must to in order to achieve a pass, merit or distinction and where you can find activities in this book to help you.

To achieve a pass grade the evidence must show that you are able to:	To achieve a merit grade the evidence must show that, in addition to the pass criteria, you are able to:	To achieve a distinction grade the evidence must show that, in addition to the pass and merit criteria, you are able to:
P1 identify social and historical factors that have influenced the development of drama **Assessment activity 1 page 90**	**M1** describe social and historical factors that have influenced the development of drama **Assessment activity 1 page 90**	**D1** explain in detail social and historical factors that have influenced the development of drama **Assessment activity 1 page 90**
P2 identify two dramatic genres and their major characteristics **Assessment activity 1 page 90**	**M2** describe two dramatic genres and their major characteristics **Assessment activity 1 page 90**	**D2** explain in detail two dramatic genres and their major characteristics **Assessment activity 1 page 90**
P3 demonstrate the processes of creating dramatic work. **Assessment activity 2 page 92**	**M3** demonstrate the processes of creating dramatic work with purpose and commitment. **Assessment activity 2 page 92**	**D3** demonstrate the processes of creating dramatic work with confidence and attention to detail. **Assessment activity 2 page 92**

How you will be assessed

You will be assessed by internal assignments that will be designed and marked by the tutors at your centre. Each assignment will allow you to demonstrate understanding and apply knowledge, skills and techniques you have learned in order to meet the grading criteria.

The work you produce may include:
- presentations
- a portfolio
- a log book
- DVD of performances
- tutor observations and statements.

Ben, 16-year-old trainee actor

I found this unit really interesting, especially learning how and why theatres and acting styles have changed through history, and how the styles of my favourite actors, like Johnny Depp, Jude Law and Ben Whishaw, compare to actors of 100 years ago. Our 'Acting Through the Ages' project was a challenge, as I had to act in three versions of the same play, one naturalistic, one as Victorian melodrama and the third performing in masks in ancient Greek style. This was fun, and made me aware of the demands different styles place on the actor.

I also had the opportunity of performing Shakespeare in a showcase of scenes from Elizabethan theatre, playing Mark Antony in Julius Caesar. Once we'd talked through the scene, what was going on and how Antony felt about Caesar's assassination, the speeches made sense and really came to life for me. I applied page to stage rehearsal techniques to help develop the character and found speaking the verse was easy once I understood I was playing a real man with clear emotions and goals.

I hope to go to drama school, and finding out about the background and structure of different plays and styles of theatre will help me become more versatile, as well as giving me a good understanding of the roles I am performing.

Over to you

- How do you think this unit might help you develop your creativity and technique as an actor?
- Why do you think it is important for an actor to research and understand the background of the play and the world it presents?

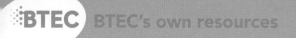

5.1 Social and historical context in the development of drama

PLTS

Experimenting with different staging types, and investigating strong acting positions for each is evidence of your abilities as a **creative thinker** and **effective participator**.

Did you know?

The word theatre comes from the Greek word theatron, meaning place of seeing.

Stage types

This unit tells you about key developments in the history of drama and refers to many different stage types. You should understand what the following stage types look like.

- **Arena** – where the stage is surrounded on three or four sides by the auditorium, which is raised and tiered higher than the stage.

- **Thrust** – a stage that projects out into the auditorium with the audience surrounding it on three sides.

- **In-the-round** – the acting space is in the centre of the audience.

- **Proscenium arch** – the stage is framed by a wall, typically with an arch or rectangular opening separating the front of the stage from the auditorium.

- **Traverse** – where the audience sit either side of the stage.

- **Rostra** – plural of rostrum, meaning a raised area.

5.1.1 Social and historical context

The following case studies provide a brief overview of some key developments in the history of drama, but you will need to carry out some investigation and research of your own.

When investigating social and historical factors, you should consider the following:

1. Think about the audiences, why they went to the theatre and what their tastes in entertainment were.

2. What was the dominant religion of the time? Did this have any effect on the content of the drama? Did religion have any influence on the job of the actors and how they were regarded by their society? Were there any connections between religious ceremonies, rituals and drama? (Hint: this is very important in understanding ancient Greek and medieval theatre).

3. How did the theatres exist financially? How were they funded and the actors paid? Did the audiences pay to see the plays? If so, how?

4. Were there any political factors that had an impact on the theme and content of the drama as well as on how the theatres operated? There may have been major historical events at the time, such as wars and revolutions – did these have any effect on drama?

5. You will need to research the actual theatres and the types of staging used. Also you should look at how theatre technology has changed and the impact this has had on the development of drama.

Did you know?

Medieval cycle plays were very long, often enacting both testaments of the Bible and lasting more than 20 hours!

Remains of a theatre from ancient Greece.

Case study: Actors in ancient Greece

Origins of theatre can be traced back over 2500 years to ancient Greece where the first tragedies and comedies were performed at religious festivals. There were never more than three main actors in Greek dramas, and as they each played more than one role, they wore masks and costumes to show different characters.

The dramas also featured a chorus of up to 50 performers, all male, who often played crowds, armies and smaller roles; singing, chanting verse and adding rhythmic movement to the plays.

Theatres were huge semicircular arenas built into hillsides, affording audiences, often as large as 10,000, a perfect view of the play which was performed on and behind a circular stage. Masks and costumes were colourful and padded and actors wore platform shoes to give them presence in large open-air theatres. The masks also amplified their voices, and they performed with large stylised gestures and movements.

Famous playwrights included Euripides and Sophocles, whose plays are still performed today. Greek dramas were advanced for their time, and many plot development features seen in plays nowadays, including crisis, conflict, reversals of fortune and resolution, were pioneered by the ancient Greeks.

1. What are stylised gestures?
2. Why was it important for the chorus to add movement and spectacle?
3. Imagine you were producing an ancient-Greek-style play nowadays. What are the kind of roles you could give the chorus?

PLTS

Answering the case study questions, reading play extracts and exploring staging of Ancient Greek plays will provide evidence of your abilities as an **independent enquirer**, **creative thinker**, **effective participator** and a **team worker**.

Key terms

Tragedy – serious drama, usually with a sad ending, where one or more main characters die.

Chorus – in ancient Greek drama, a group of actors who sang and danced, often commenting on the content of the play. Nowadays the term describes performers who sing and dance as an ensemble in musical theatre.

Plot – the events of the play and sequence in which they occur.

A performance of *Oedipus the King*.

Greek comedies and tragedies are still performed today, including:

- *Oedipus the King* by Sophocles
- *The Trojan Women* by Euripides
- *Lysistrata* by Aristophanes.

The best way to really understand what ancient Greek theatre was like is by reading one of the plays from that time and perhaps staging the play. If you stage the play, make sure you use stylised movement and chanting for the chorus, exaggerated gesture and use of masks. You could also stage it in the round.

Activity: A modern morality play

As a group, use either the Seven Deadly Sins or The Ten Commandments as a starting point to devise a short play. The play should provide moral instruction or a warning to the audience about not living a good and pure life. The characters/roles in your play should be personifications of the concept you are putting across to your audience.

Case study: Actors in medieval Britain

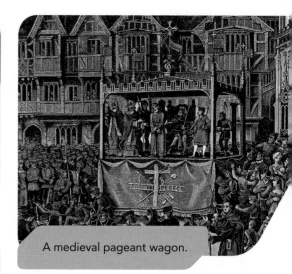

A medieval pageant wagon.

During the Middle Ages in Europe, drama was used purely as religious instruction. Plays were either performed in churches, or took place in public places on public holidays.

There were three types of play: passion plays, which depicted Christ's last days; morality and miracle plays, written to show the importance of living sin-free lives; and cycle plays, which enacted events from the Bible.

The plays were devised and acted by working tradesmen, not professional actors. Different scenes from the plays were performed in different parts of the town, using a mobile stage called a pageant wagon.

We know little about the style of acting, but it took on the form of popular street entertainment. Characters were either taken from the Bible or, in the morality plays, actors portrayed types of character representing concepts rather than real people. A famous example of this personification is the play *Everyman*, where characters include Knowledge, Death, Strength and Good Deeds. In morality plays actors might portray the Seven Deadly Sins, or the Ten Commandments.

1. What does personification mean, and how is it different from characterisation?

2. What are the Seven Deadly Sins?

3. When you have found out what they are, decide, for a modern version of a morality play, the kind of characters that might be used to represent each sin (for example: Greed could be a bank executive).

Functional skills

Writing – noting characters for a modern interpretation of a Medieval morality play and creating a short play as part of the activity.

Reading – participating in reading extracts from Greek plays in order to discuss staging and features of the plays.

PLTS

Devising a short instructional play in the style of a medieval morality play will allow you to demonstrate your skills as a **creative thinker**, **team worker** and **effective participator**.

85

Case study: The Elizabethan stage

During the Renaissance, religion-inspired drama gave way to the tragedies, romances, historical dramas, comedies and fantasies written by playwrights such as William Shakespeare and Christopher Marlowe.

The first proper indoor theatres were built in London from around 1570, and acting became a respectable full-time profession for men with companies of actors receiving financial support in the form of patronage from the nobility.

Theatres such as The Globe on London's South Bank were still open air, meaning plays had to be performed during the day, but audiences who could afford seats sat in enclosed galleries sheltered from the weather. The stage was known as thrust as it projected out, surrounded on three sides by the poorer audience who stood at ground level.

Elizabethan actors worked as companies, often performing a number of different plays in one week while rehearsing other plays at the same time. The plays demanded strong vocal skills of the actors to deliver the language with passion and feeling in large theatres, often competing with noisy audiences. Movement, expression and gesture were deliberate, clear and simple; and staging was often a question of actors finding the strongest position to deliver a speech or place a principal character or action.

1. Patronage was more than a financial arrangement. What other advantages do you think the support of a nobleman might give a theatre company?

2. Elizabethan actors spoke and used gestures and expression clearly and deliberately. List as many reasons you can think of why this was necessary.

PLTS

Answering the case study questions will show you are an **independent enquirer**.

Did you know?

Women weren't allowed to act in the theatre until the Restoration Period (in England from around 1660). Until then, all female parts were played by men.
In ancient Greece, a female character was usually indicated by the mask worn by the actor and yellow sleeves on their costume.
In Elizabethan theatre, female roles were played by boys or young men dressed as women and wearing wigs. This is one reason why so many of Shakespeare's comedies feature mistaken identities and women disguising themselves as men – as the actors were male, this wasn't a difficult deception.

Did you know?

An exact replica of the Globe Theatre (the theatre in which Shakespeare's plays were performed) was built approximately 200 yards away from the site of the original. The new theatre took 10 years to build, opening in 1997. Visit the Globe website for information, activities, interviews with actors, etc. See the hotlinks section on p.2 for how to access the website.
The 1943 colour film version of Shakespeare's Henry V (available on DVD) recreates an original performance of the play at The Globe, and is an interesting record of how the play would have been performed in the 1500s.

Shakespeare's Globe Theatre, Southwark, London, rebuilt in 1997.

Case study: The Victorian Melodrama

During the Industrial Revolution in Britain (late 18th and early 19th centuries), theatre-going became a popular entertainment for the masses who lived in the expanding and overcrowded cities. Theatre buildings had developed into large indoor spaces with proscenium staging, and for the first time used gas lighting, stage make-up, elaborate sets and staging.

Theatre companies knew the tired and oppressed audiences needed escapism through a good night out, with plenty of action, fun and spectacle – they had little time for the complicated plots and carefully written language of classical plays. The popular theatre of this period became known as melodrama (meaning drama with music). The plots were simple, centred on good triumphing over evil, and often based on topical news stories, popular novels, folk stories and fairy tales. One key feature was the use of music to underscore the action, create mood and announce characters' entrances with their own theme.

We nowadays associate melodrama with its stock characters; the villain dressed in black cape, laughing wickedly as he twiddles his moustache; the innocent heroine, wearing a simple white dress to show her purity and working-class origins, pleading to be spared an awful fate; or her lover, the faithful yet gullible hero, arriving at the very last minute to save the day, to much cheering from the audience.

1. What is a proscenium arch stage?
2. How did the audience and their needs influence the content, style and staging of Victorian melodrama?
3. Looking at the description of melodrama above, discuss why the acting style we associate with it had to be so over the top compared to today's standards.

Activity: Sweeney Todd

Sweeney Todd, the Demon Barber of Fleet Street was originally a melodrama based on a story serialised in a popular 19th-century magazine. More recently it has been turned into a musical by Stephen Sondheim and a movie starring Johnny Depp, directed by Tim Burton. Watch the movie and list all the features that make Sweeney Todd a classic melodrama.

PLTS

Answering the case study questions allows you to show you are an **independent enquirer**.

Did you know?

Victorian theatres were in competition for audiences. To win customers, they tried to outdo each other with the use of staging and special effects, which were spectacular for the time. One theatre managed to stage a convincing train crash, only to find a local rival went one better by not only staging a crash, but then having a second train crash into the first.

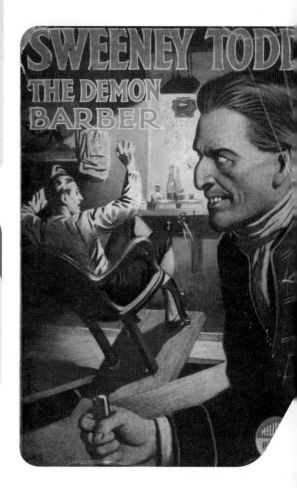

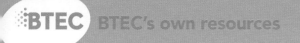
5.2 The structure and characteristics of drama

Find the genre

1. Make a list of ten different plays or shows by researching online or looking at the entertainment section of newspapers and magazines. You could also visit your school/college library and look for plays in the drama section.

2. Find out about the content and style of each play (the play may be described in a review, or a synopsis given as part of the script).

3. Create a chart or table either in your own notebook and/or on the wall of your drama room, placing each play under the appropriate heading from the list below in terms of the style or genre you think the play falls into:

- tragedy
- comedy
- musical theatre
- farce
- melodrama
- epic
- revue
- multimedia
- experimental/surrealistic.

If any of your choices don't fall into one of these categories, can you say what category it does fall into? Do any of your choices fall into more than one category? Discuss your findings in class.

5.2.1 Style

Style is the category of a play depending on the particular techniques it uses, including its language, action, movement and staging (technical elements) as well as costume, make-up, etc. Styles include:

Naturalistic – a 'realistic' drama aiming to depict life as it really is, or selecting aspects of reality on which the play draws.

Epic – theatre using techniques that aim to disrupt the illusion of reality by reminding the audience they are watching a play in a theatre. This technique is known as a 'distancing effect'. Epic dramas also aim to educate audiences and emphasise social and political issues.

Expressionistic – a style of drama focusing on expressing intense emotional states though stylised use of voice, movement, staging, design and technology.

Surrealistic/experimental – performances that challenge accepted conventions and norms in theatre. Surrealistic drama tends to make use of dream-like images and events to question what we term 'reality'.

PLTS

By completing the Warm up activity, researching different plays and genres you will show you are an **independent enquirer**; by contributing to group discussions and adding to a master chart, you will be an **effective participator**.

5.2.2 Constituent features

Constituent features are all the various elements that come together in the staging of a play. They include:

Action – the events that take place during the play. Action is a series of conflicts and their outcomes that form the story of the play and relates to what the characters do and say throughout the story.

Space – the staging in terms of the type of theatre (arena, thrust, proscenium, etc), and how the space is used in representing the world of the play in which the action takes place.

Emotion – the feelings of the characters as well as the intended effect and impact the play has on the audience.

Dynamics – the way the characters behave and react to one another and to the events and situations in the play; also how this in turn impacts on the audience.

Plot and narrative development – the plot is the main sequence of events in the play and how this develops. It includes the following:

- **a crisis** – the event at the beginning of the play that triggers the plot, usually presenting a conflict for the main character(s). The plot then follows a series of further crises and conflicts, each presenting an exciting and important dramatic climax, until the main climax towards the end of the play.

- **character development** – as a result of the crisis, conflict and resolution of the drama, the characters will have changed in some way. This change is known as character development. This is shown through exposition, meaning what the character says and does will explain this development to the audience.

- **acts and scenes** – plays are generally divided into two or three acts (sometimes more) which in turn are divided into smaller scenes. There may be a combination of reasons of why the playwright has divided the action in this way, such as separating the action according to different locations and times, allowing for changes of scenery or costume, and/or to build up to and cool down from dramatic climaxes.

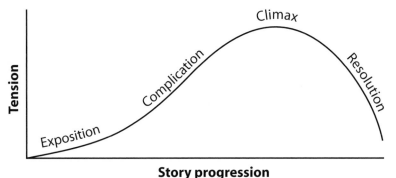

Figure 4.1: A narrative arc.

Functional skills

English speaking and listening – discussing
in class the features and categories of plays researched.

English reading – reading adverts, listings and synopses/descriptions of plays.

Did you know?

The first Greek playwright was named Thespis. The word thespian, another word for actor, comes from his name.

5.2.3 Genre

Genre is the category a play falls into on the basis of its style, content and form. Genre categories include tragedy, comedy, musical, farce, melodrama, epic, revue and multimedia. More information on these terms can be found in the glossary on p.315. Some shows may fall across more than one genre, such as *The Phantom of the Opera*, which is a melodrama as well as a musical.

PLTS

Identifying and researching the characteristics of two dramatic genres will demonstrate your abilities as an **independent enquirer** and **creative thinker**.

Functional skills

English speaking and listening – taking part in your research presentations.

English reading – reading play scripts and research information.

English writing – producing programme notes and handouts for your presentation.

Students exploring a dramatic genre.

BTEC Assessment activity 1
(P1) (M1) (D1) (P2) (M2) (D2)

Your theatre company has been asked to perform a showcase of play extracts as an introduction to drama to get young people interested in theatre.

1. Working in groups of four to six, rehearse two play extracts for performance to an invited student audience. The two extracts must be from different genres of drama (for example, comedy, tragedy, musical, experimental, melodrama). Each extract will be a key scene or event from the play.

2. You will need to research the two dramatic genres featured in your group's performed extracts and present your research to the rest of the company as rehearsal research.

This research presentation should use PowerPoint and handouts in the form of programme notes on the extracts you will perform.

You will have opportunity later to perform the two extracts to an invited audience, where you will be able to then demonstrate the dramatic characteristics of each genre.

Grading Tips

M1 Describe the key factors, providing details such as how the factors influenced the drama.

D1 Give explanations of why these key factors influenced the drama.

M2 Provide descriptions of each of the main characteristics of each drama.

D2 Explain how the characteristics are typical of each genre, backing up your explanation with specific examples.

5.3 Applying the processes of creating dramatic work

5.3.1 Starting points for drama

This unit requires you to demonstrate the process of creating dramatic work, which means you have to provide evidence of the work you do in rehearsing and developing a character and performing a play. Read the sections in this student book on acting skills and Project 7 for advice and information on rehearsal and character development. These will help you develop and apply the processes necessary for creating dramatic work.

5.3.2 Rehearsal and preparation processes

The rehearsal processes you will be assessed on will depend on the kind of play you decide to produce from your given starting point and may include any or all of the following: read-through, blocking, refining material, character development, line-learning, design, production management, technical rehearsal and dress rehearsals.

These topics are explored and guidance is provided in Unit B4 Acting Skills and Techniques and Project 7.

Rehearsals when in conversation with the director.

Assessment activity 2

Mini performance project – ten-minute devised play

As part of the Spring Arts Festival we will produce a series of devised plays, in groups, around a common theme to be decided by the company. The plays will be performed at the festival, using in-the-round staging. You will have access to basic lighting, sound and rostra for staging, Costumes and props will be sourced by each group.

1. Agree on a theme/starting point which has potential to develop into exciting drama.
2. In your group, contribute to the development of ideas inspired by the theme. Think about the style of play you are creating, staging and the intended effect on your audience.
3. In rehearsal, develop your character/role and contribute to devising the structure, content and staging of the play.
4. Perform your role in the devised work to the festival audience.
5. Keep a Drama Process Log throughout. This log will contain: notes on the starting point, development of the play, research, development of your role, annotated script or staging notes, rehearsal schedule. Some of your log can be in the form of a video diary and guided review interviews with your tutor.

Group rehearsals and devising, as well as the performance, will be recorded on DVD for assessment. Tutor observation and peer evaluation will also be used.

Grading Tips

(M) Contributions to the production must show commitment and understanding of the importance of the elements of creating drama (keeping to schedules, responding to criticism, refining and developing ideas, etc). Your Drama Process Log will reflect this in clear descriptions of the process.

(D) Contributions to the production must show confidence and detail (such as the depth and detail you have added to the devised play, refining your character, etc); your Drama Process Log will reflect this in detailed descriptions showing good understanding and explaining the importance of the drama process and techniques.

PLTS

By exploring, devising, decision making, review and development of the process of making theatre you will be able to apply skills as a **creative thinker**; and working as part of a team in the process will demonstrate application of skills as a **team worker**.

Functional skills

English speaking and listening – taking part in group discussions and reviews.
English writing – producing log book notes and review notes.

5.3.3 Acting/production skills

If you take an acting role, you will be assessed on the following skills: focus, concentration, control, imagination, communication, co-operation, observation, characterisation, movement, voice, speech and projection.

These skills and techniques are also explored in Unit B4 Acting Skills and Techniques, and Project 7: Page to Stage.

If you take a production role, you will be assessed on the following skills as appropriate to your role: design, lighting, sound, props, construction and craft skills (such as props making, costume making, mask making), set building, make-up.

These skills and techniques are explored in Unit D16 Crewing for Stage Performance and Project 5: Setting the Scene.

Joanna Cheam
An actor at work

I'm Jo, a professional actress, currently in a production of *The Crucible*. I am playing Mary Warren, one of the 'bewitched' young women of Salem.

My agent got me the audition, and I did a lot of prep – reading the play as well as books on history and witchcraft. At the audition, our director, Sian, spent a lot of time discussing the play's themes and the designs for the show.

Before the first read-through I read the play a few more times, watched TV documentaries and visited libraries and museums, to get my imagination going and soak up the world in which the play is set.

The play is very intense, especially the courtroom scene, and we did lots of exercises during each rehearsal to improve our ensemble work, energy and concentration. We also have a special voice coach, who helped us in rehearsal with the various accents. He also does work with me to help protect my voice in the scene where my character has to scream repeatedly for a long time.

Early rehearsals were great; lots of improvisations and off-text explorations before Sian did any blocking. When I finally committed my lines to memory, it didn't take long, as by then I fully understood Mary's goals and motives: why she says what she says and does what she does. We had a tight schedule, and it was no time before we were into technical rehearsals. Tech runs are bitty, needing maximum co-operation and patience, but the dress rehearsals really brought everything to life for me, as all our preparation and hard work came together for the first time with set and costume.

Think about it!

1. Why do you think Jo felt her audition preparation was necessary even before she knew if she had a part?
2. Why was the voice coach important for actors in this production?
3. Jo has a lot of different tasks and responsibilities. Make a list of the tasks and then place them in order of when they need to be done.
4. For a production you are working on, apply these tasks to your own role. Are there other tasks you need to add?

Just checking

1. Name two different stage types.
2. List two Ancient Greek plays.
3. What types of plays were performed in the Middle Ages?
4. List eight different genres.

edexcel

Assignment tips

- Good organisation is the key to success in this unit. Always keep your production log up to date by filling it in regularly. Remember also to file any documents in the correct place.

- It is important to remember that everyone contributing to the process has a vital role to play. You may think your role is not as important as that of someone else, e.g. if you are moving scenery and they are playing the lead role in the performance. But remember, the success of any production rests equally on the shoulders of all those involved.

- When working on design ideas, keep all drafts, sketches and other rough work as this will provide evidence of how you developed the final product.

- Good levels of motivation are required by anyone who works in the performing arts industry. This project is no different. To do well in this unit you must contribute fully to the tasks you have been set, demonstrating that you are fully committed to the work. In group work, make sure you play your part fully; don't sit back and let others do the work.

- Good attendance and punctuality are very important. Competition for jobs in the performing arts industry is tough, so only those who are good timekeepers succeed. You must make sure that you attend regularly and complete tasks within the deadlines that have been set.

- Always be aware of how you are communicating with other team members. Remember to treat others with respect. Criticism must always be given in a constructive manner and you must also respond to feedback from others in an appropriate way.

C13 Performing Dance

No matter what style of dancer you wish to become, you will have to attend class regularly, learn new skills and practise to improve them. This means hard work; all dancers understand the need for hard work. Dancers are often real perfectionists. They strive to dance better, stretch and bend further, turn faster and more accurately and jump higher. Much like professional athletes, they are happiest when they see their technique improving.

You will try out several dance styles, possibly some that you have never tried before. All dance styles are appropriate for this unit but most of you will explore contemporary, jazz, urban and ballet. By the end of this unit you must be able to perform at least two styles.

You will take part in regular class, keep a highly professional attitude and learn how to interpret dances and to re-create dance qualities and styles accurately. You will begin to understand how to improve your own dance for performance through rehearsal, continuing work in the dance studio, self-evaluation and finally your assessed performances.

Learning outcomes

After completing this unit you should be able to achieve the following learning outcomes:

1. Be able to participate effectively in practical dance workshops

2. Be able to use physical and interpretive dance skills

3. Be able to demonstrate dance styles and qualities in performance

4. Understand how to improve own performance in rehearsal.

Assessment and grading criteria

This table shows you what you must to in order to achieve a pass, merit or distinction and where you can find activities in this book to help you.

To achieve a pass grade the evidence must show that you are able to:	To achieve a merit grade the evidence must show that, in addition to the pass criteria, you are able to:	To achieve a distinction grade the evidence must show that, in addition to the pass and merit criteria, you are able to:
P1 attend class and rehearsal, working cooperatively **Assessment activity 1 page 101**	**M1** demonstrate a disciplined approach to class and rehearsal **Assessment activity 1 page 101**	**D1** demonstrate a high level of commitment to class and rehearsal **Assessment activity 1 page 101**
P2 demonstrate the application of physical and interpretive dance skills **Assessment activity 2a page 103** **Assessment activity 2b page 104**	**M2** demonstrate the accurate application of appropriate physical and interpretive dance skills **Assessment activity 2a page 103** **Assessment activity 2b page 104**	**D2** demonstrate the thorough application of appropriate physical and interpretive dance skills **Assessment activity 2a page 103** **Assessment activity 2b page 104**
P3 demonstrate an awareness of stylistic qualities in dance performance **Assessment activity 3 page 105**	**M3** demonstrate the assured use of stylistic qualities in dance performance **Assessment activity 3 page 105**	**D3** demonstrate excellent use of stylistic qualities in dance performance **Assessment activity 3 page 105**
P4 review the main strengths and weaknesses of own performance **Assessment activity 4 page 108**	**M4** review strengths and weaknesses of own performance with some reasoning **Assessment activity 4 page 108**	**D4** review in detail the strengths and weaknesses of own performance with considered conclusions **Assessment activity 4 page 108**
P5 show improvements in performance as a result of rehearsal **Assessment activity 5 page 110**	**M5** show improvements in performance as a result of commitment to rehearsal **Assessment activity 5 page 110**	**D5** show significant improvements in performance as a result of commitment to rehearsal **Assessment activity 5 page 110**

How you will be assessed

This unit will be assessed by your tutor observing you in all classes and workshops. Some centres may invite in other dance professionals to run workshops, and these guest tutors could feed back to your tutor on your progress.

You will also be assessed through your own Dancer's Log. This is a logbook in which you must record the work you do on all the styles you work on, making sure you objectively evaluate what you are doing and say how you plan to improve your dancing.

The work you produce may include:

- your work in class, rehearsals and performances
- your Dance Log
- reviews and evaluation of your progress during dance class and plans for ways to improve your choreography and performance
- DVD recordings of your work in class
- observations by your tutors or others.

Charlie, dancing in the festival

I first went to dance club during my second term at college. I had started studying the BTEC First in Performing Arts (Dance) in September. My best dance style was hip-hop but I knew I would have to learn a few other dance styles and within a few weeks I knew I would have to improve the way I tackled my ballet and contemporary classes.

The college spring festival was the venue for our performances of dances we'd learned over the year. I was chosen for a contemporary piece, based on a performance we saw at Sadler's Wells Theatre in London by the company Tanztheater Wuppertal Pina Bausch. This meant I had to completely forget all the set moves I'd mastered for my hip-hop dancing and get used to moving without any tension in my body. This style is called release; you use your weight, the floor and the other dancers to move around and off them. It's incredibly hard and physically exhausting, but I really liked it. The music we used was a track called *I'm Not Done* by Fever Ray and it has a flowing and incessant beat in 3/4 time. The dance was really bold and we had to do some lifts and falling off blocks and tables. We had to work on this for ages, to find out how to do it all without hurting anyone. I think it went very well – I managed my part without any mistakes – none that anyone else spotted anyway!

This has been a really useful experience and I'm going to dance part of this same piece when I audition for a youth dance group this summer.

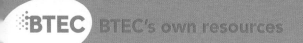
13.1 Participating effectively in practical dance workshops

13.1.1 Application

This is all about being in class and working really hard; concentrating, being totally focused on your work and being self-critical. Make plans for improving your work either by recognising what you need to do or by responding to the tutor's direction, and then showing you can do it.

Your first preparation for this learning objective is of yourself, as a dancer. All dancers are keen to look right for the style they are practising; they often spend a lot of time watching themselves working in the studio mirrors. This can mean some dancers get a bit particular about their appearance, not in wanting to look very neat and tidy when they are working, but in ensuring they look right for what they are doing.

So, it's important to come to class prepared appropriately. Hair should always be tied back and absolutely no jewellery should be worn. Jewellery is forbidden as it can cause serious injury.

In terms of clothing, for ballet, that would mean a pair of ballet flats, or shoes, plus a leotard, tights or fitted jogging trousers. Leg warmers and body warmers can also be worn to keep individual body parts warm. For contemporary styles, you will need similar clothes, or possibly a fitted T-shirt, instead of a leotard, and feet should be bare. For jazz styles you may need jazz shoes. For urban or street dance, you might be asked to wear a fitted T-shirt or vest with jogging trousers, plus light trainers suitable for dancing.

Male and female dancers all need to wear suitable, supportive underwear, in the same way as sports players have to – have a chat with your tutor or PE staff for advice.

13.1.2 Structure

The warm-up is an incredibly important part of each and every dance class

Most dance classes follow a similar pattern:

1. Warm-up.

2. Set exercises in the centre of the studio for most modern styles, at the barre for classical and modern ballet.

3. Centre practice of set steps and moves, including balances, turns and step combinations and enchainements – some styles also have floor exercises as well.

4. Travelling steps around the space, including leg lifts and kicks.

5. Jumps.

6. Dance combinations or longer sequences.

7. Cool-down.

> It is always important to stretch and warm up before class and rehearsals.

Warm-up

No matter what style you take, every class begins with a warm-up. This is essential as it allows you to slowly build up the heat in your muscles necessary for them to work efficiently. It also allows muscles to become more elastic and stretchy; this is why you should never undertake really big stretches before you have carefully warmed up your body. You will tear and pull your muscles and this will take a long time to heal. See Unit C14 The Development of Dance for more about working safely. At the end you need to cool down carefully to avoid muscle cramps and feeling stiff the following morning.

The style of warm-up you use will depend entirely on the style of dance you are working in. Ballet class starts at the barre, contemporary and jazz class starts in the centre, urban dance classes use a general warm-up to stretch, tone and isolate the body parts, much as jazz dancers do. The following activity shows a warm-up for a jazz class.

Key terms

Warm-up – a series of exercises carried out at the beginning of class or before a performance. The purpose is to carefully mobilise the body by stretching, bending and twisting muscles so they become more flexible and less susceptible to injury.

Cool-down – a gentle series of exercises to cool down muscles and help them to disperse the waste products (such as lactic acid) that build up when muscles are working hard.

Enchainement – exercises and steps linked together into a short sequence, usually used in classical ballet classes.

Activity: Warm-up jazz class

Make sure you know the elements of a jazz class warm-up. These are similar to a ballet class. They look like this:

- Stretches for the arms, trunk and legs.

- Pliés, leg and foot work, such as battements tendus, pointing and flexing feet.

- Isolations to warm up joints and start you moving in relation to the music.

- Short sequences of exercises using arms, body and legs, different directions and movement qualities.

- More energetic work on the floor, standing turns and legwork, travelling steps and combinations.

If you can put together your own warm-up and deliver it to your group, then you have the chance of showing your tutor that you really understand the basic forms and qualities of a dance style.

Dancers have to be energetic and self-driven and this kind of activity is a good way of taking responsibility. This is how professional stage dancers become dance captains for a show. They are not only excellent performers, they also help dancers new to a show to learn the choreography or improve how they are dancing it.

Rehearsal

When you have been taking class for a while you will start to learn the dance combinations that you will be asked to perform, so you will have to rehearse them. Rehearsals are called répétitions (the term is French as this is the language used in classical ballet), but repeating something is not enough for BTEC. You will be expected to evaluate your own dancing and make plans for improvement. You can use your Dancer's Log to help you record this. You should have a plan for each rehearsal that shows a clear objective for the session.

13.1.3 Range of styles

You will have to master how to dance in more than one style: maybe jazz, contemporary and street dance. The choice could also be African, South Asian or tap. Some centres offer rock 'n' roll too. For further information see Unit C14 The Development of Dance.

You will dance a number of different styles during your course.

13.1.4 Source

As part of your work for this unit your tutor or another dance professional will teach you choreography. This will mean trying out and mastering new steps and moves, sometimes taken from the professional repertoire. This can sometimes be difficult and frustrating. Even professional dancers can have trouble mastering a new style. Choreography will give you opportunities to improve your technique and really show what you can do. There might also be chances for you to make up your own dances, for yourself and each other. The dances you learn will be slowly developed and refined so that performance material emerges. Your tutor will help you to do this.

 Assessment activity 1

Teaching your own dance class

Try to put together your own class – see if you can remember what goes into each part of your regular dance class.

Start with a warm-up, then the set exercises and end with a short combination, *enchainement* or routine. (See C14 The Development of Dance for basic structure of any dance class.)

Teach this to your group.

Grading Tips

M1 Remember to show your tutor that you are both disciplined and professional in your approach to dance classes.

D1 In both classes and rehearsals you will need to show clear unquestionable commitment to your dancing.

PLTS

Teaching your own dance class will allow you to develop your skills as a **creative thinker**.

13.2 Using physical and interpretive dance skills

This learning objective is all about developing different styles of dancing. Your tutor will run classes in different styles of dance throughout your course and part of this will include chances for you to master new styles and forms. You will have to get your mind and body around new steps and moves and often learn to think in new ways about your dancing. For example, the need to move smoothly and fluently in ballet will be one of the features you want to avoid in street jazz.

There are two aspects to work on for this learning objective:

1. The acquiring and applying of physical skills related to a particular style of dance.

2. The interpretation of that style.

13.2.1 Physical skills

Start by finding out about the new style. Look on the Internet and use your centre's dance library to find examples of the style in action. This is the best way to start you thinking like, for example, a contemporary dancer. Expert dancers have a particular mindset and approach to their work.

Contemporary dancer – Merce Cunningham – knew exactly what he was doing.

When you have your first class in the new style, learn some of the names of the exercises and steps. Each style has its own vocabulary particular to that style. Contemporary dance is very concerned with the use of your body's centre. This is the area around your belly button. You will need to work on contracting this area and releasing it to create the impetus for all movements in contemporary dance.

All dance styles have common elements.

The following eight terms are considered to be key elements for contemporary dance:

- balance
- breathing
- centring
- gesture
- gravity
- moving in space
- posture
- rhythm.

BTEC

Assessment activity 2a P2 M2 D2

Learning and using a new style

Find out what the eight names for the elements of contemporary dance, above, actually mean.

Think about your regular dance class and write down which of these elements your regular exercises are working on.

For example, stretching, pointing and flexing a foot while standing on one leg, in other words a tendu, is working on centring and balance. It can also help with working on rhythm.

Grading Tips

M2 As well as applying your physical dance skills you will need to show that you can interpret movements and steps accurately.

D2 You must demonstrate the thorough application of interpretive dance skills.

13.2.2 Interpretive skills

This part of the learning objective is about performing your new style. Dance performance is an extension of the dance class. No successful dancer treats their regular class as anything other than a chance to perform, as well as their personal space for training and honing their skills. When you are taking a regular class with your tutor they will expect you to use your exercises as a way in to performance, through the way you interpret what you have been taught.

When you are carrying out a sequence of moves, or an *enchainement*, you will be expected to communicate the work to an imaginary audience. It is important to be able to copy what your tutor has taught you, or what you have learned from another dancer, very closely and accurately. This copying action is the way you develop your own interpretive skills.

The next step is to 'get' the same feeling for the movement that your tutor wants to see in your dancing. You will have to learn to appreciate the weight in a movement, the speed and emotional qualities it has. This might mean you have to develop musicality or the ability to move in rhythm with music, sound or another dancer. You will need to focus your concentration and your movement in a particular way, such as towards your audience or other performers. Your work, sometimes with music or accompaniment, will emphasise beats and movements, such as in tap dance or body popping and locking. You might also need to work on gestures and facial expressions. For example, in South Asian dance and in classical ballet, the movement of the eyes can be part of the choreography.

PLTS

This assessment activity will allow you to use your skills as a **reflective learner** as you carry out evaluations.

 Assessment activity 2b

Performing in a new style

Try to teach a short piece of dance to your partner; see if they can learn it and accurately dance it back to you.

Evaluate their work and feed back to them how well they interpreted your dance.

Reverse the process.

Dance the piece together and ask another dancer or your tutor to tell you what they think of your duet.

Grading Tips

M2 As well as applying your physical dance skills you will need to show that you can interpret movements and steps accurately.

D2 You must demonstrate the thorough application of interpretive dance skills.

13.3 Demonstrating dance styles and qualities in performance

Warm up

Stylistic qualities

Warm up

In jazz dance, isolated movements, such as shoulder twitches and rolls, are stylistic qualities specific to that style.

Think about what stylistic qualities are particular to other styles of dance, for example, contemporary, ballet or hip-hop.

13.3.1 Physical features appropriate to specific styles

Work for this learning objective will see you taking what you have learned in class and extending it towards more complicated dances for performance. The key will be how well you have absorbed the specifics of each dance style, and then gone on to interpret them accurately, but also how you put your own slant on the work.

BTEC Assessment activity 3   (P3) (M3) (D3)

Performing in a new style

Working with a partner, find a short piece of dance on video, such as a music video on the Internet or on television. Separately, learn a short section of the dance. Show it to your partner and check out the style.

Evaluate each other's work and feed back. Remember to comment on how well they interpreted the dance.

PLTS

Reflective learners will review and evaluate their work, then apply this to improving their dancing.

Self-managers will set their own targets.

Grading Tips

(M3) Remember to show your tutor that you are both disciplined and professional in your approach to dance classes.

(D3) You must ensure that your dance style is clear and that it is of a high quality. You must ensure that you are reviewing your dancing and showing improvements in areas where you are not so strong.

The assessment criteria ask for you to become assured in your use of the stylistic qualities of a dance style and then to show how well you can use them. This means you must really absorb the whole nature of a dancing style so you can learn and perform choreography made up by your tutor or even yourself.

You will have to pay careful attention in class when you are being taught new work, so get yourself in a good position to see your tutor. They will be looking for how you use the stylistic qualities of the dance and how you make them your own. You will have to practise a lot.

This unit asks for you to be able to re-create dances accurately and in the right style, using the right facial expressions, gestures, movements, on the beat and in time with the music where there is any. Your tutor will provide you with opportunities to practise this, so you gain and grow in confidence.

Dancing in performance means that there will be some sort of audience. That might mean that there are actually people who have come to see you sitting on chairs in front of the performing space, or it might be a camera that is recording your work. Whichever it is, you will have to learn how to communicate the dance, with all its individual stylistic qualities, to that audience. Although you don't get marks for how much you communicate with your audience in this unit, the fact there is one means you must be prepared to share your work. You will be marked on audience communication in other units. You will gain the confidence you need to feel comfortable with this as you go through your course.

Dancing in performance can be in costume and/or on a specific set. These things add complications that you must overcome and exploit in your performances. Costumes need to be rehearsed in so you are comfortable and confident in them. The set must be familiar to you to avoid falls and stumbles.

Are you going to be wearing a costume or mask? Have you rehearsed in it?

13.3 How to improve your own performance in rehersal

Warm up

Getting over stage fright

Dance student Usman says: 'I used to get really nervous when I performed. I even got sick once when I was about to go on stage at college. Now I make sure I take a bit of time out on my own before a show, just to do some warm-up stretches and deep breathing in the corpse pose, to make sure I'm totally relaxed and mentally ready. The corpse pose is lying down flat on your back. I learned it from a yoga teacher; she gave us some great tips for relaxing and staying calm before performances.'

Do you suffer from stage fright? Discuss with the class other good ways of overcoming this.

13.4.1 Evaluation

This is all about your own evaluation of your work as you set about working towards the performance of any dance style. The unit aims to give you the opportunity to set up good working habits. All dancers are incredibly critical of their technique; they are not happy unless they are constantly improving and moving forward.

13.4.2 Improvement

To do well in the final section of the grading criteria, use what you have done before, and then show improvements in your dancing.

This unit is really a journey, and at the end point you must show that you have travelled some distance and that you are dancing better than when you started. Your tutor will be looking for a significant commitment to rehearsals. You should have:

- gone to all classes and rehearsals on time and properly prepared
- learned all your steps, moves and combinations
- identified your targets and where your problem areas lie and have begun to rectify them yourself
- asked for, and used, help and guidance and constructive criticism.
- been supportive of the rest of your group
- kept up a positive attitude when learning and mastering new repertoire, even though you may have found it difficult.

Did you know?

All performers are nervous before they go on stage, and sometimes during the performance; this is normal. With practice you can learn to get used to these feelings and work to overcome them.

Lots of performers have routines they go through to get over stage fright. These can be very helpful but the best cure is to practise your dancing so much that it feels completely natural.

Remember – stage fright is only the hormone adrenaline helping you to get ready for something important.

Key term

Repertoire – a French word used in all forms and styles of dance. It means all the dances that are performed, sometimes relating to the work of a company or group. This might be all the major ballets performed by a ballet company, such as *Swan Lake* and *Sleeping Beauty*.

Assessment activity 4

Strengths and weaknesses

Working with a partner, make a DVD recording of your choreography. Watch it back and make a list of the following:

- What is working well?
- Where are my main strengths?
- What are my main weaknesses?
- What do I need to improve?

Make a plan for your next session in your Dancer's Log. Draw some conclusions about where you should be going next.

Grading Tips

M4 You must analyse and review all of your dance in class and performance, coming to honest and sensible conclusions about your strengths and weaknesses.

D4 When you are reviewing and analysing your dance you will need to accurately identify areas for improvement and set relevant and SMART targets.

PLTS

Working in pairs to produce a DVD recording of your choreography will allow you to use your skills as a **team worker**.

Thinking about your strengths and weaknesses and how you can improve will show that you are a **reflective learner**.

Key term

SMART – this refers to targets that are: Specific, Measurable, Attainable and Time-based.

Top tips to improve your own dance

Use the mirror

Your first way of observing and evaluating yourself is to constantly watch how you carry out all exercises, steps and moves.

Have you been watching the mirror when in class?

Ask yourself:

Am I carrying out this exercise as it has been shown to me? Check your:

- alignment

- shape

- direction.

Try to rectify faults yourself.

Ask someone else

Ask your fellow dance students to watch you, particularly when carrying out tricky moves like turns and jumps. You get a lot from watching other dancers too. In professional classes, dancers always watch each other and make comparisons with their own technique. Filming your work on DVD is a good way of checking your progress.

Ask your tutor

Always ask your tutor how well you are doing and don't be afraid to ask for advice and guidance out of lessons. If you have a workshop given by an outside dance professional, ask them for advice too.

Practice

Make sure you try to master every step and move you are taught through continual practice. When you are developing your own choreography, you will have to rehearse this yourself. This can mean coming into the studio over lunchtimes and after lessons.

Set goals for every rehearsal

Make sure that every practice and rehearsal has an objective. As well as memorising the steps you could also work on the speed, dynamics, direction, spacing and quality of movement.

Keep up your Dancer's Log

Maintain your logbook so you record everything you do, how you are doing and what you need to do to improve.

Be open to criticism

Dancers must be self-critical, but they also have to be open to constructive criticism from others. Dance is a hard business and dancers must develop a thick skin. It is essential to develop the ability to use any feedback you receive to improve your performance. Although it may not feel like it at the time, receiving constructive criticism is key to becoming a successful dancer.

PLTS

Being a **reflective learner** means taking a really hard look at the journey you have taken through your rehearsals. Use this to plan for future improvements in your dancing.

BTEC **Assessment activity 5**

Evaluating yourself and others

- Look back at where you started.
- Re-read your Dancer's Log for the first week of the course. Watch any material of you dancing you have on DVD.
- Make a comparison with where you are now.
- Ask your tutor to film you and your group in rehearsal; be critical about each other's dancing.
- Make plans for future work.

Grading Tips

M5 You must show that you have improved your performance as a result of your commitment to your rehearsals.

D5 You must show significant improvements in your dance as a result of your own evaluations from rehearsals.

Urban dance club

Leroy and Nazeen

Leroy and Nazeen are half way through their BTEC First in Performing Arts (Dance); they are both very keen dancers and want to continue their studies into further education and maybe on to dance college. They both like sharing their ideas and already run an informal dance group at college.

Leroy has learned from his younger brother that the neighbouring primary school, has lost its dance teacher on maternity leave. Leroy asks his tutor if he and Nazeen could help out by running an urban dance club there after school.

Their tutor thinks this is a great idea and makes arrangements for this to happen.

She and the school carry out the necessary risk assessments and volunteer checks, in order to make sure everything about the project is as safe as it can be. There will be a teacher on site at every dance session, but the teaching of the dancing and running of the group will be up to Leroy and Nazeen. They make plans to run a half hour session once a week after school. They will teach the pupils for a term and then arrange for them to showcase their dancing in their school's assembly.

Leroy and Nazeen then teach the pupils for seven weeks so that they are confident enough to perform in week eight. The performance is filmed.

Leroy and Nazeen were able to collect evidence for this unit by:
• asking their tutor to come and observe them regularly
• filming their work in progress
• asking for witness statements from teachers from the primary school that showed how much work they were doing
• evaluating their work in their dancer's log
• making plans for improving their work
• showing how much they had improved their work over the course of the weeks spent on the project.

Think about it!

1. If you were to run a dance club like this, what style would feel comfortable working in?
2. How would you make sure your lessons were well planned?
3. How did Leroy and Nazeen make sure they got together enough evidence for their unit assessments? Could they have done anything else?

Just checking

1. Have you noted down all the names of steps and moves learned in class?

2. Can you put steps and moves together when just given the names, without each individual move being demonstrated?

3. When you watch other dancers in class, can you spot what is good and what is not so good about their dancing?

4. Do you always take on board what your tutor says about your performance work and then make plans for future improvements?

Assignment tips

- Take an effective part in the dance workshop.

- Ballet dancers who use block shoes should make sure they are in good shape, with toes darned for strength and ribbons or tapes securely attached.

- Make sure all your dance kit is clean and ready for every class.

- If there are a lot of dancers in class, be careful where you stand. You need to be able to see and hear what your tutor is telling you, but you don't want to crowd another dancer – that's considered very rude in most studios.

- Learn to love the mirror! Dancers use the studio mirrors, not to keep admiring their look, but to check their alignment and positioning. You must learn to use the mirror as a critical friend. When you get really sure of a move you will be able to feel where you are and how you are moving. This way you will pick up and refine new styles and interpretive skills.

- Keep up your Dancer's Log, carefully noting down the names of exercises, steps and moves that you regularly use in class.

- Learn the correct terms for each step or move, so you can pick up a enchainement or combination when your tutor calls out directions.

- If you don't understand a step or move in class, ask your tutor to repeat it.

- Practise at home in front of a mirror.

- If you can, get a dance buddy to work with.

C14 The Development of Dance

This unit is all about how you build up your skills and understanding so you can enter into, and enjoy, the real world of dance. You will be looking into the social and historical roots of dance as well, so that you understand how dance has developed and some of the ways dance is used in society. The work you do in the studio, the rehearsal room and onstage will be rooted in the way you approach and develop within this unit.

Any street jazz artist, ballerina or chorus member in a West End musical will have begun their career through hard work and dedication to practice, practice, practice. It's the only way to gain the skills, to understand how to get your body to execute a difficult manoeuvre and to have the ability and fitness level to rehearse and perform.

When you work on this unit, you will be exploring the world of the real dancer. There will be lots of learning and interpreting of steps and moves, plenty of rehearsing and working on your own body and technique, and many chances to create and perform your own work.

Learning outcomes

After completing this unit you should be able to achieve the following learning outcomes:

1. Know social and historical contexts in the development of dance and dance styles
2. Be able to respond to the choreographic process
3. Be able to review the choreographic process.

Assessment and grading criteria

This table shows you what you must to in order to achieve a pass, merit or distinction and where you can find activities in this book to help you.

To achieve a pass grade the evidence must show that you are able to:	To achieve a merit grade the evidence must show that, in addition to the pass criteria, you are able to:	To achieve a distinction grade the evidence must show that, in addition to the pass and merit criteria, you are able to:
P1 identify the social and historical factors that have influenced the development of dance and dance styles **Assessment activity 1 page 120**	**M1** describe the social and historical factors that have influenced the development of dance and dance styles **Assessment activity 1 page 120**	**D1** explain in detail the social and historical factors that have influenced the development of dance and dance styles **Assessment activity 1 page 120**
P2 identify a variety of dance styles and their particular features **Assessment activity 2 page 122**	**M2** describe a variety of dance styles and their particular features **Assessment activity 2 page 122**	**D2** explain in detail a variety of dance styles and their particular features **Assessment activity 2 page 122**
P3 create dance material that demonstrates key elements of the choreographic process. **Assessment activity 3 page 123**	**M3** create dance material that demonstrates key elements of the choreographic process clearly and creatively **Assessment activity 3 page 123**	**D3** create dance material that demonstrates key elements of the choreographic process with confidence and creativity **Assessment activity 3 page 123**
P4 present, with guidance, a review of the choreographic process. **Assessment activity 4 page 128**	**M4** present, with guidance, a sound review of the choreographic process. **Assessment activity 4 page 128**	**D4** present, with minimal guidance, a thorough review of the choreographic process. **Assessment activity 4 page 128**

How you will be assessed

This unit will be assessed through a series of internal assignments that will be designed and marked by the tutors at your centre. You will be assessed on how much you know about your chosen styles through discussing and writing about them, demonstrating them in class, the way you learn and develop choreography in a particular style and how you set about learning and mastering steps or dance combinations.

The work you produce may include:
- your work in class
- a log book or diary
- a choreography notebook
- information you have found out through personal research
- evaluations of your progress during dance classes and plans for ways to improve your choreography and performance
- DVD recordings of your work in class
- observations by your tutors or others.

Chloe, 16-year-old dance student

I belong to a street dance crew and I go to dance club every week, but until I started taking regular dance classes at college I had no idea how many types of dancing there were and knew nothing about how they had come about.

I found out about jazz dance and how it started in America and that there are many different types. I really enjoyed trying out some different styles, like rock jazz, where we learned a dance choreographed for us by our tutor. We danced this to some music she gave us. I made up a section for me and my dance partner and we put it together with some steps made up by another group. Then we pulled all our ideas into one long dance routine. We performed this at a showcase for learners taking a BTEC First in Performing Arts at our college.

Our tutor made a film of us dancing. This was really helpful as I can now see where I am really strong and where I need to improve my dance technique. I am keeping a log and I try to record how well I am doing in class and what I need to practise some more at home. I have done research into some professional dance crews as well and I gave a short talk about one of them. I showed some moves that I learned by looking at a DVD. That was really scary, but really fun.

I have learned a lot about how jazz dance had been used to develop new styles of dance and this has helped me really improve my dancing. I can dance much better now at dance club and have brought some of my new moves into our choreography there and at college.

14.1 Social and historical contexts in the development of dance and dance styles

How did that dance style come about?

See what you can find out about your favourite form of dance. Where did the style first get performed?

Who are the people making dance in that style?

Put together some ideas for a workshop session on your favourite dance form that you can lead in your centre or show your group.

14.1.1 Social and historical influences

All dance forms are influenced by what is going in on at the time they are developed – the social, political and cultural goings-on of the day.

For example, court dancing in Elizabethan times was incredibly formal because people were often dancing in front of influential people – including the queen – whom they wanted to impress. They wanted to show off both to their betters and to the opposite sex how athletic and talented they were. Many Elizabethan dances gave opportunities for energetic young men to shine, and for both sexes to show off their skill with complicated sequences and dramatic flourishes.

Elizabethan dance was formal and demanded great skill.

Today some modern dance styles are influenced by DJs. There has been a huge rise in the numbers of young people developing dance styles by pursuing famous DJs around clubs both here and abroad. This in turn has led to a genuine new movement associated with tourism development, where dance and music lovers go to places on holiday specifically so they can hear and dance to the kinds of club music they like. Some styles that are danced in clubs are street, hip-hop and break dancing and, even though people generally just dance how they feel like dancing, there is a definite style that develops in different clubs.

Both of the examples show how cultural and social factors can influence dance.

- In Elizabethan times it was the need to show loyalty to a leader, while taking the chance to be seen in public.

- In the contemporary European club dance scene it is the availability of cheap air travel that has allowed young people to pursue their love of dance and music.

Any kind of dance you take part in has a history and a purpose, from the ritual African dances performed at funerals, to the Flamenco, originally danced by Spanish gypsies and now danced across all of Spain.

Activity: The purpose of dance style

Choose a dance style and answer the following questions about it.

1. Where did it come from?
2. Why was it originally developed, for instance, for enjoyment, celebration or to express something?
3. How has the style developed over time?

14.1.2 Dance styles

There are many different dance styles, all of which you should approach slightly differently in class in terms of what to wear and how to prepare yourself. This is incredibly important. No matter what style you take up, classes are organised in a similar way so that you have time to get really warm before you exert yourself, you have a chance to learn and explore new moves, you have challenges built in though the way your tutor puts steps together, and you have a chance to move around the space. After all classes, no matter what style, you should cool down to avoid any cramping and stiffness the next day.

Go to Unit C13 Performing Dance page 98 to check what clothing you should have ready for each style of class, as well as more information about the importance of warm-ups.

Why and how do dance styles develop?

Wherever you look, dance comes about because something needs to be said. All forms of dance begin with someone needing, or wanting, to express something. Take classical ballet, for example. This style developed in the 17th century in the court of the French King Louis XIV. Based on an Italian dance form, it allowed people to have fun and enjoy themselves together, but in a style that was very controlled. That's why all the words used for steps and positions in classical ballet are in French. It's also why the style is still very formal and precise and has to be danced very carefully with great attention to technique. By contrast, folk dancing was for the ordinary people, not royalty or the rich. It was a chance for the community to get together and for young people to have contact, and was much less formal and controlled.

Contemporary dance developed as a contrast to the rigorous techniques of classical ballet. Dance pioneers, such as Isadora Duncan in the early 20th century, wanted to break away from a set technique and set steps. Despite this, modern dance today can still be very organised and contemporary styles have created their own language of moves and positions that are just as strictly adhered to.

Jazz dance originated in African folk dance in the late 19th century and developed right through the 20th century. It was associated with tap dance in its early days. But the influence of choreographers, such as Bob Fosse (choreographer of the musical *Cabaret*) in the 1960s and 1970s, and Arlene Philips (choreographer of music videos and popular dance groups) in the 1980s and beyond has developed this style along new routes. You might study both African and jazz dance styles so you can follow how one has led to another.

Urban dance has, in its turn, developed from jazz dance and become a form in its own right, with its own new and usually young choreographers. Street jazz, locking and popping, and hip-hop are all fairly new styles of urban dance.

Have you taken urban dance class before?

Exploring dance styles

Your tutor will probably choose the dance styles they want you to explore. These might be a particular form of contemporary dance, such as Graham technique, and something more up to date, like urban dance. You will probably have to take classes in the styles chosen so you become familiar with them and develop your own technique in each. For this unit you have to produce at least two pieces of dance, each two to three minutes long, as well as evidence that you know about the development of your chosen styles. This could mean an essay, a talk, a PowerPoint presentation or a workshop that you lead to show how much you have learned. All of these will need a lot of research.

Make sure you find out about some styles of dance that you have not come across before. Go on the Internet and put in the name of a style you like the sound of. There are plenty of dance companies that put up video clips and articles about their dances. They also tell you when and where they are going to be performing. You may be lucky and find something going on your area. It's always a good idea to try to see dancers in performance, both professional and amateur.

Getting started on your project

The choice of the dance styles you will explore for this unit may be left up to you or may be decided by your tutor. Their decision will depend on the experience and skills of the whole group, as well their own expertise in particular dance styles. You may find that your whole class will look at the same style, but this doesn't mean that you won't have to carry out your own research. Every learner will have to produce their own portfolio of work for this learning objective.

How you present the evidence of your research may also depend on what your tutor decides. For instance, you may be asked for an essay, a talk from notes, a PowerPoint presentation or to run a short workshop – on your own, with a partner or in a group. But if you are given a choice, make sure you choose a method you feel you can really do best in.

Where can I find out about dance?

Your tutor will be running regular class so that you will find out about particular dance styles through experiencing them, gradually learning new moves and steps. For example, if you are researching contemporary dance your tutor will probably give a class in the style of dance pioneers such as Martha Graham or Merce Cunningham. Other dance styles you may experience are Limón or one called Release – a relatively new style all about using your own breath and energy to move very smoothly and fluidly.

Activity: Release

See what you can find out about the style called Release. There is quite a lot on the Internet about it. Search for contemporary dance, then Release.

If you have a free choice about which styles you are going to look into, you might choose ones you already know well. Lots of dance companies and dance colleges have very good websites with plenty of information on them – but remember, don't just download pages off the Internet, or even copy them, as that is not proper individual research. You must make sure you use what you find to write or record your own ideas. You could also look in your centre's library and in dance magazines for writing about dance styles and forms.

Key terms

Technique – means the set of things you can do that relate to a particular dance style. For example, if you are taking ballet class, your technique will include how much you can turn out your legs and feet,to get into second position or master a grand plié, how well your body is aligned as you move, jump and turn. For street jazz your technique will include how well you can isolate parts of you body and move them around the beat of the music.

Choreography – the way dance is created, how steps and moves are put together.

Did you know?

The Place is a very famous dance school in London and its website has lots of useful information about dance makers and styles.

PLTS

Working as a member of the group when you are devising dance is an excellent opportunity to develop your personal learning and thinking skills by working confidently with others as a **team worker**.

Working on your own ideas for dance will give you opportunities to develop your own individual creativity. You will be able to show that you can create dances from first ideas demonstrating your skill as a **creative thinker**.

When you are carrying out research into dance styles and can identify the social and historical factors that have influenced the development of dance and dance styles this shows you are an **independent enquirer**.

 BTEC **Assessment activity 1**   P1 M1 D1

Researching and record keeping

During your work on this unit you should keep a record of your activities and researches.

First decide which dance style you are exploring, then get started with your research file by attending regular class in that dance style. This could lead to you writing an essay, giving a talk, a PowerPoint presentation or leading a workshop to show how much you know.

Keep up your log, recording how you are getting on. Remember to include details about:

- the structure of the class, the order of any set exercises
- how easy or difficult you are finding the class
- improvements you make, or don't make, as you progress with your research
- setting goals for your future improvement.

Record all the information you find out about the history of your chosen style, for instance, details about pioneers of the style, famous performances that have taken place, who was dancing in them and where they happened.

Grading Tips

M1 Remember to include details about:

- the structure of the class
- how easy or difficult you are finding the class
- how the history of the dance has influenced the way it is danced.

D1 Remember to include details about:

- the structure of the class, the order of any set exercises
- how easy or difficult you are finding the class
- improvements you make, or don't make, as you progress with your research
- how the social and historical factors have influenced the development of the style. Try to show this understanding in your dancing, as although this might look a bit indirect, it is very clear evidence that you understand the dance style you are working in. This is a way of illustrating practically what you are working in. This is a way of illustrating practically what you have learned. You will also show your understanding when answering questions by your tutor or another learner, writing an essay, giving a talk or presentation, or leading a workshop.
- set goals for your future improvement.

Here is an exercise you and your class could use to find out as much as you can about the work of Martha Graham. The best way of really understanding a dance form and how it developed is to find out practically. Remember, this unit is not all about theory and you can explore a dance form practically in the studio.

Activity: Dance research – Martha Graham

Prepare for a short presentation, including some practical dance, showing how Martha Graham's work has influenced contemporary dance today.

Include who she trained and danced with, what her dances were like and the influences she has had on dance today.

Preparing to present your work

When you have begun to explore a dance style through research, start trying to master how the style works in class. Be bold and take some risks. You will have to decide how you want to present your findings, and some form of demonstration might make up part of your presentation. Your tutor will advise you.

If you are going to write an essay, make notes first and prepare a draft version so you can check it or add things to it. You could add some pictures or sketches if you want to show who the pioneers of your style were, or how some of the steps and moves work.

If you are going to construct a PowerPoint presentation you will have to get all your ideas together and organised before you write your slides.

If you are taking a more practical approach, you will have to organise what aspect of the technique you are going to share with your group. Remember that a warm-up is a good way of beginning your practical session, followed by a selection of exercises or an enchainment or combination.

Key terms

Enchainment – a series of steps organised into a short dance, used for practising how steps go together. Usually used in classical ballet.

Combination – a similar idea to enchainment, but usually used in more modern dance styles, such as jazz dance, or street jazz.

PLTS

Exploring dance styles through work in the studio and taking risks with your dancing shows you are a **creative thinker**.

Did you know?

Much of the technique for jazz dance has developed from ballet so it uses many French terms. It can be a struggle to remember these names so it's a good idea is to try to learn the name for a step or move every day.

 Assessment activity 2 (P2) (M2) (D2)

Showing what you know about a dance style

This is an activity about showing what you know about a dance style. Your tutor will be watching you in class as you are learning – this is called continuous assessment and it will help you gain marks for both LO1 and LO2.

You should always try to work to the best of your ability in all your dance classes. This will help your tutor to see how well you are progressing.

You should learn the names of new moves and steps. For example, in classical ballet each step, move, direction and how you perform them, has a name. You must get into the habit of using the correct names for all the dance exercises you do and showing your tutor how much you know. You could record this information in your log as written evidence of your knowledge. You may be asked to write an essay, give a talk, a PowerPoint presentation or lead a workshop to show how much you know.

Your tutor will probably set you enchainments or combinations to perform by giving you the names of the steps they want to see, and how they want you to perform them. You may then need to perform them to the group. How you use these terms in class will provide very clear practical evidence of your understanding of the styles you are dancing. This will back up your answers to questions from your tutor, interviews by your tutor or another learner or written evidence about the different features of dance styles and will be very important if you find writing and giving presentations difficult.

Grading Tips

(M2) You need to show understanding of more than one style. Look for some clear features that mark each one out. Try to take a combination you know and develop it into a different style e.g. take a piece of jazz dance and turn it into street jazz. Write an essay to support this evidence, give a talk, a Powerpoint presentation or lead a workshop to show how much you know.

(D2) You should be able to dance well in more than one style. You will have to get to grips with two styles in this unit. Try to learn the way your tutor carries out the class warm-up so that you can practise on your own, or with a partner. If you feel confident, ask your tutor if you can run the warm-up for a class – bring in some music, decide what you want to say and do and practise it. Write an essay explaining the features of your dance styles, give a talk, a Powerpoint presentation or lead a workshop for the group to back up and show how much you know.

14.2 Responding to the choreographic process

The process of making a dance is gradual. Your tutor will start you off with set pieces they want you to learn. Then they may want you to choreograph new work for a particular purpose, such as a show. This will mean you have the chance to create your own work.

Once you have been given an idea for a piece of dance, you must be bold and experimental. You must also be prepared to throw ideas away if they don't quite work out.

PLTS

Working imaginatively to create and respond to choreography shows you are a **creative thinker**.

BTEC **Assessment activity 3**

Choreographing a short dance sequence

Your tutor will show you a picture. Study it carefully. Ask yourself what is going on in the picture.

Try to copy the shapes that you see.

Where there is more than one person or shape in the image, try moving from one shape to the other.
This is the start of your dance. Now you have two shapes and moves in between. Now try the following:

- Change the size of your shapes and moves. Try making them smaller or larger.
- Dance them slower or faster.
- Decide how to organise these changes. You might speed up the sequence or gradually slow it down.
- Change the speed of your dance – this is called changing the dynamics.
- Decide which versions work best and decide on your final dance.

Remember, you will need to record your choreography as you do it, so don't forget that you must keep up your log. You could use drawings of stick people to record your moves by drawing them on the computer or film yourself as you work.

Grading Tips

M3 You must show that you understand the key elements of choreography. Remember to approach your interpretation creatively, forming links between the movement selection, the use of dynamics and relationships.

D3 If you combine your ideas from the photo dance with motif development, you are showing real understanding of more than one of the main ways of creating choreography. Taking the exercise above, you can achieve D3 by showing that you really understand the idea of developing something abstract from something real – the photograph. Your work must be creative, confident and bold, using a broad range of movements.

14.2.1 Constituent features

To be a successful dancer, you will have to become familiar with how choreography is danced – to music, or not – and how dancers move around the space. These are the constituent features:

- aural setting
- action
- timing
- group size
- design
- space
- dynamics
- physical setting
- relationships.

14.2.2 Creating

How does choreography get made?

Choreographers all have their favourite ways of creating and devising dances. For example, some take a movement idea while others use improvisation. Here is a list of the types of choreography you are expected to understand and be able to use:

- stimuli
- improvisation
- unison
- canon
- motif development.

You will also have to decide on which material to use and which not to use. This is called 'rejection of material' and is a vital part of the choreographic process.

Together with the constituent features, rejection of material is the choreographic theory you will need to become familiar with and use.

Your tutor will probably give you opportunities to work on each of the elements and choreographic processes, either in turn or together.

Key terms

Canon - a sequence of steps danced by different dancers or groups of dancers but each dancing a different part of it at any one time.

Choreographic theory – the rules that govern the way dances are made.

Dynamics – speed of the moves and steps in a dance.

Motif – a series of steps organised into a short sequence that can be developed into a longer and more complex dance. A motif can be used over and over again during a long piece of dance so it becomes familiar and more enjoyable for the audience as well as more straightforward for dancers – you don't have to keep on inventing absolutely new steps and moves.

Unison – a group of dancers dancing the same series of steps together – i.e. at the same time.

Activity: Creating a dance

Choose a piece of music that you like.

Make up a short sequence of dance steps in your chosen style, such as the one you are working on in class.

Add some more moves, maybe in a particular set of directions, such as in the shape of a square or in circles.

This is how you improvise dances. You have also added a stimulus, in the music, and another element, space.

14.2.3 Working on constituent features and creating elements

Creating a canon

If you want to create a canon in dance, you need to work with some other dancers. This will also bring in one of the other features, group size. For a canon you need to create a short sequence; this is danced by one person who keeps it going, then at a certain point it is started by the next dancer and so on. Eventually the whole group is dancing the sequence, but each is dancing a different part of it. Here you have used relationships between the dancers. This can make your dance appear much more complicated than it really is. Lots of choreographers use this technique as it makes the audience think they are seeing something much trickier to create than it really was. It doesn't have to be complicated to appear very complex to an audience.

If you decided to take a point in your canon and get everyone to begin the piece again all at the same time, you would be dancing together in unison.

Dynamics, timing, setting and space

Your tutor may ask you to think about ways of improving your work, such as through thinking about its dynamics or timing. Here they are asking you to think about the speed at which you dance and the energy levels you are using in a particular section.

They might also ask you to stage it in a particular way. For example, you could use some stage blocks for some of the group to begin the dance on, or you could perform it all facing out from a circle or in a line. This is how you work on the physical setting and the space. If you were to take the dance a stage further, towards performance, you might want to design a more complicated work, using props and sets on the stage, coming on from a particular direction or going off at the end.

Always think about the staging of your dance.

These are all ways that professional choreographers create dances that often appear to be very long and complicated – they build up ideas in the same ways as you have done. What you see as an audience member is often seamless and hides the processes the dance maker went through to get to what you are looking at on stage or in the studio.

Why not try putting these elements together for yourself?

Activity: Developing a piece of choreography for a group

Decide how many dancers you want in your group. Two dancers allows you to mirror and contrast movements. Three dancers gives you the chance to make canons and moving chains – you can go over and under each other. Four dancers allows for circles, lines, canons, pairs.

Try out your choreography in all of these groupings. What can you do with the movement to make it more interesting for your audience?

14.3 Reviewing the choreographic process

As you start to make your own dances in the studio, you must review and evaluate your own and other dancers' work. You have already started recording what you are working on in your log – this is an extension of that process.

You must find a way of recording your dance ideas as they evolve; this might be by writing down the names of the steps, drawing them, photographing them or filming them and how they go together. Whichever you choose, this is a serious part of the work and you must keep it going all the way through the unit. Work for this section builds up to a third of the unit marks.

It's a good idea to try out different ways of recording your choreography to find the one that suits you best.

Professional choreographers sometimes use a special form of recording the steps and moves in a dance on paper – see if you can find out what these written forms are called. In the main, though, choreographers use DVD to record their work as it develops. You can do the same.

Your tutor might want you produce an essay, some notes, or a talk in which you review how your choreography has come together.

When you have worked in groups have you made canons or working chains? Make the most of dancing in a group.

Whichever you do you have to think about how well you have:

- interpreted any stimulus material either given to you, or that you have chosen yourself

- selected the right steps and moves for your dance

- used the performance space creatively

- had good working relationships with other dancers

- managed your time

- rehearsed your dance

- recognised your own strengths and weaknesses

- made plans to improve your work.

Evaluations

The work that you produce over the course of the term will be the foundation for your future development as a dancer. It will be vital that you take a critical view of all you do because this is how dancers improve their performance. Dancers are well known to be incredibly critical about their work, and striving to improve is a way of life for all dancers. Your log is a vital way to record what you are doing in class and workshops and how well you are doing. In your evaluations you can use what your tutor says about your work, what others say about it, the results of mini and more formal assessments, and what any other people who come to work with you say about you.

Remember

If you can record all of these details, making sure you are objective in the way you look at your own performance, right through the unit, as well as making practical plans for your future work, you can achieve a high grade.

PLTS

Taking time to think carefully and reflect on what you have done, then make plans for the future demonstrates you are a **reflective learner**.

 BTEC Assessment activity 4 **P4** **M4** **D4**

Reviewing a piece of choreography

In this activity you must record all your choreographic processes, from first stimulus or ideas, through to the end. You must comment at the end of each stage on how well you did, what worked out and what didn't, and explain why. You need to:

- explain all the changes you made on the way, with reasons
- use the correct terms for all the changes you made, what ideas you rejected or accepted. e.g. did you change the dynamics, the space you used, the groupings of the dancers?

At the end of the choreography write a final evaluation of the dance, explaining its success, or otherwise. Use drawings to illustrate what you mean.

Show this to your group and ask for feedback.

Prepare a talk and demonstration for the whole group, called 'Dance Making in Action'.

Grading Tips

M4 You must write and present a review of your choreography. In it you should try to identify the strengths and weaknesses of your approach and results. You should offer some suggestions on how you could develop as a choreographer in the future.

D4 You must write and present a thorough review of your choreography. You should explain the strengths and weaknesses and use them to identify areas for improvement. You will need to offer some suggestions on how you can develop as a choreographer in the future. Remember, you must work on your own to achieve a distinction.

First Auditions

Carrie

Carrie is a young dancer who has put herself forward for her first professional job as a member of the chorus for the pantomime Sleeping Beauty.
Carrie has had to choreograph her own dance routine, ready for the audition. She wanted to show the panel how well she can dance, so she chose a style she feels really comfortable in – jazz dance.
She picked a piece of music she knows very well – a track from an album by Madonna. She already knew a dance to this music, but it was too long. She took the chorus sequence and worked out a way of repeating it twice, each time changing the turns at the end, so that it finished on the floor.

She practised it over and over again until she could dance it confidently, without any mistakes.
What Carrie has done here is to take a piece of choreography and develop it, so it ends up quite different from the original idea. She has taken a motif, and altered it to suit a new purpose. This is a method often used in choreography, in order to develop longer and more complicated dances.
Carrie has had to work hard to make sure her dance is perfect and polished in time for the audition.

Think about it!

1. What style of dance and music would you choose if you were going to an audition like Carrie's?
2. Put together a two-week schedule of how you would spend your time to make sure you were ready for the audition. Don't forget to allocate a little time to making sure you have the right clothing and equipment as well.

Just checking

1 Where did Flamenco originate?

2. How has urban dance developed to become what it is today?

3. What is an enchainment?

4. What is a canon?

5. What is a motif?

6. Who is Martha Graham and how did she helped the development of dance?

edexcel

Assignment tips

- Good organisation is one of the keys to success. Always keep your log up to date by filling it in regularly.

- It is important to always be looking out for ideas for your dancing. Pick up pictures and photos of anything that makes you think about movement. Save recordings of pieces of music you like. Watch other dancers in action to see how movement works.

- Effectively organise rehearsals of your work so that all those involved in your choreography know when they are supposed to be rehearsing.

- Plan your rehearsals so you don't waste time.

- Make sure that you fully understand key features of a number of different dance styles

- If you are using costumes, keep any draft sketches or ideas you might have for them.

- Talk to the lighting and sound technicians to pick up ideas for accompanying your own choreography.

- Always have your music or accompaniment with you so you can listen to it – the better you know the music, the easier it is to choreograph.

- Be bold and practise, practise, practise your work.

- Give and accept constructive criticism throughout your work.

- Make sure you evaluate all of the work you do. This will be useful for setting targets for future dance work.

- Remember to use the correct choreographic words.

Credit value: 10

D16 Crewing for Stage Performance

There are many varied and interesting job opportunities for those who choose to work behind the scenes in the theatre, television and film industries. Unit D16 Crewing for Stage Performance will give you an insight into what backstage work is all about and a grounding in the knowledge and skills required.

The backstage crew is the team of people who have the skills and knowledge to make the show actually happen. They begin their work at the get-in, then they perform the fit-up, following instructions to build and dress the set, rehearse scene changes in the technical and dress rehearsals, and ensure that the set works properly throughout the run. At the end of the show they will do the 'strike', that is the de-rigging of the equipment, and complete the get-out.

Working backstage is a high-risk occupation. Therefore you must learn about, and apply, health and safety practices in all of your backstage work.

As a performing artist you will work with greater confidence and skill if you appreciate and understand the work of the backstage crew.

This unit will introduce the essential skills and knowledge that a member of the backstage team will need to become an effective crew member.

Learning outcomes

After completing this unit you should be able to achieve the following learning outcomes:

1. Know the roles, responsibilities and terminology involved in general stage operations

2. Be able to operate as a member of the crew preparing for and during a performance

3. Be able to implement safe working practices when carrying out processes and using tools and equipment.

131

Assessment and grading criteria

This table shows you what you must to in order to achieve a pass, merit or distinction and where you can find activities in this book to help you.

To achieve a pass grade the evidence must show that you are able to:	To achieve a merit grade the evidence must show that, in addition to the pass criteria, you are able to:	To achieve a distinction grade the evidence must show that, in addition to the pass and merit criteria, you are able to:
P1 identify at least six backstage/ production roles and their responsibilities using appropriate terminology **Assessment activity 1 page 138**	**M1** describe at least six backstage/ production roles and their responsibilities using appropriate terminology **Assessment activity 1 page 138**	**D1** explain at least six backstage/ production roles and their responsibilities using appropriate terminology **Assessment activity 1 page 138**
P2 produce a scale drawing with sufficient accuracy to be usable **Assessment activity 2 page 141**	**M2** produce a detailed scale drawing with sufficient accuracy to be usable in which secondary elements are present and accurate in the same standard **Assessment activity 2 page 141**	**D2** produce a complex scale drawing with accuracy suitable for the task in which secondary elements and annotations are accurate and professionally presented **Assessment activity 2 page 141**
P3 carry out get-in/out, fit-up and strike under direction **Assessment activity 3 page 146**	**M3** carry out get-in/out, fit-up and strike, taking some responsibilities for processes implemented **Assessment activity 3 page 146**	**D3** carry out get-in/out, fit-up and strike, taking responsibility and implementing and instigating processes **Assessment activity 3 page 146**
P4 set up basic scenery/set/ props to supplied plans under direction **Assessment activity 3 page 146**	**M4** set up basic scenery/set/props to supplied plans with some direction **Assessment activity 3 page 146**	**D4** set up basic scenery/set/props to supplied plans without direction **Assessment activity 3 page 146**
P5 follow cues and react satisfactorily **Assessment activity 3 page 146**	**M5** follow cues using industry terminology, reacting correctly **Assessment activity 3 page 146**	**D5** follow cues using industry terminology, reacting correctly and professionally **Assessment activity 3 page 146**
P6 demonstrate safe working practices in pre-production and production, showing an awareness of relevant health and safety regulations. **Assessment activity 4 page 151**	**M6** demonstrate safe working practices in pre-production and production, showing a clear awareness of relevant health and safety regulations. **Assessment activity 4 page 151**	**D6** demonstrate safe working practices in pre-production and production, showing a consistent and acute awareness of relevant health and safety regulations. **Assessment activity 4 page 151**

How you will be assessed

This unit will be assessed by internal assignments that will be designed and marked by your tutors. The early assignments will be more theory-based. They will require you to show your understanding of backstage roles, theatre terminology and how to make a scale drawing. Later assignments will be based on practical work. They will require you to show that you can apply crewing skills in a practical situation. All assignments will include an assessment of your understanding and application of health and safety.

Peter, 17–year–old backstage crew member

This unit really opened my eyes to all of the different backstage jobs. I can sort of do the acting side of things, but I like working backstage more. I was surprised at how much there was to learn about being a member of the crew: there's the terminology, different roles, teamwork and, of course, we are never allowed to forget the health and safety.

First we learned in class about the different roles and then we visited our local theatre where the stage manager talked to us. This really helped me to see that backstage work is actually quite skilled. There were loads of practical tasks that helped me to get my head around what I was being taught. Whenever there was a show in school I did a different job in the backstage team.

Finally, we crewed for our end-of-course show – we were a brilliant team. Everyone turned up and worked hard, and we all did what we were meant to. Our tutor was pleased with us and gave us a big tin of chocolates. There were some fun moments, but I had to keep remembering about health and safety and make sure that I didn't mess around. I was a bit fed up because my mum didn't notice me, but I guess that means I was doing my job properly!

A big message that I learned is that production work is about teamwork – we had to make sure that we worked as a team, just like they do in the industry.

Over to you

- Have you ever thought about working backstage?
- What areas of backstage work do you think you might enjoy?

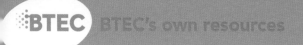
16.1 Know the roles, responsibilities and terminology involved in general stage operations

Warm up

What does 'general stage operations' mean?

Go on a backstage tour of your local theatre. Take a camera (remembering to ask permission to take photos first) and prepare a list of questions.

Have a look at the onstage and offstage space. Make sure that you have a good look at the set that is on the stage.

Take a note of how many people are in the backstage team. What are their job titles?

Using this information, imagine that you are about to put on a show at your local theatre and that you have a set to work with:

* How many people will you need to change the set around and make sure that everything is in place for each scene?
* What will their jobs be?
* Discuss your ideas with your group and list all of the things that will need to happen backstage for the show to run properly.

16.1.1 Roles

To understand backstage roles you need to understand what is involved in putting on a production. Each stage in the process of putting on a show has a different name.

Production process	Show preparation period
Production week	Last week before the show opens
Get-in	Set and equipment brought into the theatre
Fit-up	Set put up in performance space, lighting and sound rigged
Technical rehearsal	All technical cues finalised
Dress rehearsal	Final run-through in costume
Run	Every performance to an audience
Strike	Set and equipment taken down
Get-out	Set and equipment removed from the theatre

This table shows you how the work of the backstage crew fits into the whole production process.

Team	Production work	Run	Post production
Lighting	Rig equipment as directed	Check equipment before performance	De-rig and store equipment
Followspot operator	Focus as directed	Operate followspot as cued	
	Attend technical and dress rehearsals		
	Attend director's notes		
Sound	Rig equipment as directed	Check equipment before performance	De-rig and store equipment
Stage crew	Support sound team as instructed	Assist sound check	
	Attend director's notes		
Stage management	Dress the set and set props as instructed	Check cue lights working	Get-out props, set dressing and furniture
Stage management crew	Attend lighting and sound plotting	Respond to cues to run the show	Return hired and borrowed items
	Attend technical and dress rehearsals		
	Attend director's notes		
Stage crew	Get-in and fit-up	Carry out set changes in response to cues	Get-out set
Flying crew	Rehearse scene changes as directed	Operate flies in response to cues	Restore performance space
	Attend technical and dress rehearsals		
	Attend director's notes		

Larger companies will have many backstage staff; smaller companies will have smaller teams who do a wider range of jobs.

Activity: Local theatre businesses

Identify one of each of the following theatre types in your local area:

- repertory theatre company
- small-scale theatre company
- receiving house.

1. Find out how many backstage crew they employ.

2. What can you infer from the size of their backstage crews?

16.1.2 Responsibilities

When you work backstage you are part of a team in which people have different responsibilities. A key player in this team structure is the stage manager. The following diagram shows the reporting lines.

As a member of the backstage team you will have the following responsibilities:

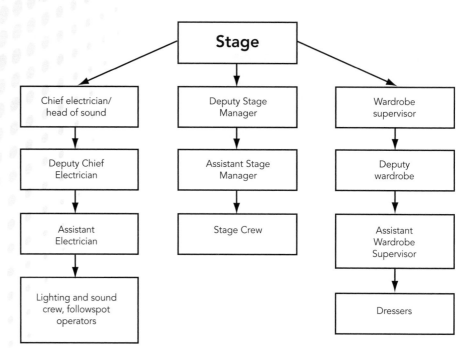

Figure 16.1: Backstage reporting lines.

Activity: Adverts for backstage work

Find as many adverts as you can in the press or on the Internet for backstage jobs. From the information given in these adverts, what can you find out about:

- training needed for stage-management work

- teamwork skills required for backstage work

- the hours backstage crew members have to work?

What	Who	When
Following cues	All backstage crews	During the performance you will be cued by the deputy stage manager to operate the followspot, move the set or operate the flies.
Management of self and others	All backstage crews	You need to be punctual, reliable, appropriately dressed and complete all tasks as instructed. You should also be aware of, support and at times manage the others in your team.
Handling flats, scenery and flying lines	Stage crew and flying teams	You will be responsible for manoeuvring and securing the flats during the fit-up, strike and get-out and also sometimes during a scene change. The flying crew is also responsible for attaching the flown elements to flying lines and flying them in and out when cued.
Managing props	Stage management crew	You will use the props lists to ensure that props are correct and in position for performance. Dangerous props must be handled correctly e.g. fake guns must be stored securely when not in use onstage.
Health and safety	All backstage crews	Health and safety is everyone's responsibility. You will consistently and strictly apply health and safety procedures in all of your work.

16.1.3 Terminology

Theatre has its own universal terminology used throughout the industry. The glossary (page 315) and key terms throughout this book give descriptions of words you will need to become familiar with. Even the stage itself has nine different terms that you must learn for use when working on it. The diagram below represents a plan view of the stage. Notice that the left and right are as if you are standing on the stage and looking out into the auditorium.

Key terms

Flats – any flat elements of the set. These can often be large and unwieldy.

Flies – space above the stage where flown scenery is stored and then moved on stage (flown in) or moved off stage (flown out) using lines and winches.

Upstage Right Left (USR) (USL)	Upstage Centre (USC)	Upstage
Centre Stage Right Left (CSR) (CSL)	Centre Stage (CS)	Centre Stage

Apron

Figure 16.2: Do you know your stage right from your stage left?

PLTS

As you research roles and responsibilities of backstage roles using effective research approaches you will be developing as an **independent enquirer**.

Functional skills

English speaking and listening: making a contribution to team research activities.

English reading: reading and responding to written information.

Assessment activity 1

Backstage roles

Research six different backstage roles. Use your research to compile a presentation for the rest of your class. The presentation should explain the roles and responsibilities of each member of the team. The roles that you research could include:

- followspot operator
- stage manager
- deputy stage manager
- assistant stage manager
- chief electrician
- flying crew.
- stage crew

After you have watched the presentations, produce a guide to working backstage. The guide could include:

- the work of the six backstage roles that you explored earlier
- the job responsibilities for each role
- the correct terminology with definitions.

Grading Tips

M1 Your research will cover at least six backstage production roles. You will describe the roles and responsibilities for each of the targeted production roles. You may use annotated photographs, diagrams or written descriptions to help to describe your understanding. You will use the correct theatre terminology.

D1 You will explain the roles and responsibilities for each of the targeted production roles. Your research may include both primary and secondary sources. You may show your depth of understanding by using annotated photographs, interviews, diagrams or clearly written explanations. You will use the correct theatre terminology.

16.2 Operating as a member of the crew preparing for and during performance

Warm up

Paper trails

This section looks closely at production paperwork. If you are lucky enough to have a repertory theatre near you, they may let you have past production paperwork or materials. The education officers at some of the larger theatres can also be very helpful in providing information. You may also use your centre's library or the Internet. Using these sources, try to find examples of at least three of the following:

- scale groundplans
- props lists
- lighting plans

- scale elevations
- get-in lists
- strike plans.

16.2.1 Processes

To work as a member of the backstage team you will need to use production paperwork as listed above. The purpose of production paperwork is to communicate all production details to the team accurately and efficiently because production periods are short and pressurised and misunderstandings slow the process down.

Plans

Scale drawings are used so that all measurements, dimensions and the placing of the set can be worked out accurately before the show gets into the theatre.

The scales that are used most often in the theatre are 1:50 or 1:25.

> A 1:25 scale is shown on a ground plan like this

1:25

This means that

1 unit on the ground plan	: represents	25 of the same units in real life

Key term

Scale drawing – line drawing giving a birds-eye view of the performance space. The plan will show the area of the stage and the position of the set on the stage. It is used by the stage manager to position the set onstage and by the lighting designer to plan the lighting.

Make sure you have the right equipment to draw your groundplans.

To translate a real-life measurement into a scale measurement you divide the real-life measurement by 25. For example:

Measurement	Doing the maths	Scale measurement
225 cm	225 ÷ 25 = 9	9 cm
560 cm	560 ÷ 25 = 22.4	22.4 cm

To find out a real-life measurement from a plan you reverse the process. You multiply the scale measurement by 25. You could also use a scale rule to work out the measurements; this is a ruler that has scaled measurements.

A scale groundplan will always include:

- a centre line (marked CL) showing the centre of the performing space and marked by a series of long and short dashes

- a setting line (marked SL), which runs at right angles to the centre line and shows the farthest downstage acting area.

You need to get used to working to scale, so measure some objects in the room that you are working in and then work out what their scale measurement would be:

- in a scale of 1:25

- in a scale of 1:50.

Groundplans also show exactly where each set piece will be onstage. There are common ways of representing these on a plan.

Activity: Features on a groundplan

Find out how the following are commonly represented on a groundplan:

- rostrum

- trucked rostrum

- door

- flat

- staircase.

Because every set is different, there may be something unusual that you have to represent on a groundplan. The designer has to pick a symbol that represents the object and then explain in a key what that symbol represents.

Assessment activity 2

Drawing a scale groundplan

As a class, create a set in your performance space. Measure the stage area and all of the objects on it, making sure your measurements are accurate.

Working individually, use the measurements to draw a scale groundplan of the space with the set in it. You can choose to work in either 1:25 or 1:50.

- Mark a setting line.
- Mark a centre line.
- Mark your set onto the plan.
- Include a key.

Grading Tips

M2 Ensure that correct terminology is used throughout. Include all relevant annotations and explanations.

D2 Ensure that your plan is clear, accurate and well presented; that all representations of the set are clearly drawn and identified in the key. You should aim to emulate plans produced by a professional. Make sure you draw any set changes clearly by using a different fine-line colour.

PLTS

Working as a group to make and translate measurements develops your skills as a **team worker**.

Functional skills

Mathematics: using measuring, estimation and calculation to work out and draw scale measurements.

Key terms

Key – a list of all the symbols used on a plan and what they represent.

Key box – an accepted way of communicating key information on a plan.

Production	
Venue	
Scale	
Drawn by	

Pre-production process

The pre-production period is usually the longest part of the production process. It is when all of the planning and making happens for the show. The production manager monitors the process, oversees the budget and keeps the team on task. During this period, the stage crew will be booked.

At the end of the first planning phase, the designs are finalised, the actors go into rehearsal and the set, props and costumes go into production. The lighting and sound designers plan for the get-in.

The pre-production process will mostly involve the stage management team as they are in charge of the rehearsal space and they will find and supply rehearsal props and costumes. They will also mark out the set on the rehearsal room floor.

During the rehearsal, the deputy stage manager (DSM) will carry out the blocking and record all rehearsal decisions in the prompt copy (also known as 'the book'). This is what the DSM will use to call the show. The DSM will also communicate new requirements to the production team in the rehearsal report on a daily basis.

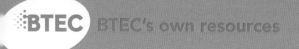

The get-in

The get-in day is timetabled and managed by the stage manager. Everyone has time onstage to get the performance space ready.

This table shows a typical get-in day

Time	Lighting crew	Stage crew	Sound crew
9.00 am	Bars in to rig lanterns Gel in lanterns	Take delivery of the set, props and costumes Organise, sort and plan ready for get in	Collect any hire equipment Begin sound rig away from stage
10.30am	Advance bars and off stage bars rigged, all lanterns patched Rig and patch followspot	Begin get-in: Lay floor Flying backcloths and all flown set, including projection screen, installed Erect flats Dress set, e.g. curtains, decoration Position set furniture Set up prop tables Organise wing space	Begin to rig onstage speakers in agreement with the stage crew Organise radio mics Organise backstage mics
2.00		Finish set; any painting touch ups or repairs	Sound rig onstage
4.00	Focusing onstage; the stage is in darkness so no one else can have access to it	DSM briefing	Check that all equipment is working
6.00	Production meeting	Production meeting	Production meeting
6.30	Focusing continues until the task is completed		

Focusing and plotting

Focusing is the process of pointing the lanterns in the right direction and ensuring that they are correctly adjusted to prevent spill. A 'walker' is used as lanterns must be focused onto a person and not an empty space. The walker can be a member of the stage management crew.

Plotting is the process of agreeing and programming each lighting state. Members of the backstage crew may be needed to move the set around on the stage.

See if you can find out whether the followspot operator or flying teams are needed for the focusing and plotting.

Key terms

Programming – selection of lanterns and levels for a particular lighting effect. When selected the lanterns and levels are programmed into the lighting desk and given a cue number.

Spill - when light falls where it is not wanted, e.g. on the audience, on the proscenium arch.

Technical rehearsal

During the technical rehearsal, every technical cue is finalised and recorded. This includes every lighting change, sound effect, set change and prop movement.

- The final position of the set is marked on the stage floor with LX tape so that the crew can see where to position the set in each scene change.

- Lighting and sound managers make a careful note of all of their cues on cue sheets.

- All cues and stand-bys are numbered and marked in the prompt copy by the DSM.

- Stage crew members note set and prop moves and manage the prop table and wings.

This can be a long process, so you have to be patient. Remember that the technical rehearsal is for the technical team; it is your chance to make sure that everything has been thoroughly planned so that you know exactly what you are doing during the run. After the technical you will listen to the director's notes.

Afterwards, the technical backstage crew may have an opportunity to practise any difficult set changes before the dress rehearsal.

Dress rehearsal

The dress rehearsal is called by the DSM. The dress rehearsal is the first time that the show is performed as if there is an audience; this means no stopping for the actors or the technical team. As a member of the backstage team you will respond to the cues that were set in the technical rehearsal. It is useful to draw up your own crew sheet to remind you of your jobs. After the show you will get director's notes.

Crew also have a costume. Often this means wearing all black so you will not be obvious when moving set and other things about. But it may be that the designer has given you a particular costume to wear. Whatever you are wearing, don't forget your steel toecaps – these will protect your feet from crush injuries if you drop items of set or scenery.

Run

On performance nights you must arrive at the theatre on time. On arrival, report to your team manager to find out your pre-show jobs. Make sure that you are in position and ready as instructed by the DSM calls. If there are long gaps when you do not have a job, you may be asked to wait in the green room rather than in the wings. Don't forget sightlines – if you can see the audience then they can see you.

At the end of the show, check for damage or breakages, before setting back.

Remember

Keep every bit of paper that you make notes on and take photographs so that you can use them for assessment.

Key terms

Props table – table for holding props, usually situated at the side of the stage and managed by the stage management team. Props are taken from here for use onstage and then returned to the table after they have been used in performance.

Director's notes – notes taken by the director during the technical and dress rehearsals. At the end of the day the director discusses the notes with the whole company. It is important to have a notepad and pen so that you can record what you have been asked to do.

Setting back – setting up the stage for the next performance.

Did you know?

Professional theatres sometimes have open dress rehearsals. This means that people can go to watch a final dress performance. See if you can go and watch an open dress rehearsal.

Strike and get–out

The strike and get-out is the process of removing all of the lighting and set elements from the stage, the wings and the flies and storing them or removing them from the theatre. The strike will usually happen directly after the final performance.

There will be a strike list that details jobs and responsibilities. Make sure that you know what your responsibilities are. This a reverse of the get-in and fit-up so what went up last comes down first. It is important that the strike is not rushed as this can lead to accidents, injury and damage.

The get-out then includes the storing of the set and equipment, either in the theatre or off site, and return of any hired or borrowed items. Any elements of set that are not re-useable should be recycled or disposed of responsibly. When the stage is empty it will be swept and restored to its pre-show state.

16.2.2 Stage scenery

To be able to operate as a member of the backstage team you need to understand what the following terms mean, and who does what.

	Activity	Backstage team
Setting	Follow plans to ensure that scenic elements and props are in the correct position as intended by the designer and agreed in the technical rehearsal.	Stage, flying and stage management crews
Handling flats	Flats, which could include backdrops, are usually quite large. They often require two members of the crew to move them. Terms related to flats include: • Flat floating – a member of the crew says this loudly as the flat is released to fall on the floor. • Walking up a flat – one member of the pair puts a foot at the bottom of the flat the other member holds the top of the flat and pushes the flat up until it is standing vertically. • Securing the flats – using a brace, tying flats together with cleats or attaching fling lines.	Stage and flying and crews

Key terms

Scenic elements – all pieces of the set e.g. flats, backdrops, set furniture, drapes, ground row, treads, rostra, staging systems.

Ground row – a flat that is placed horizontally on the floor upstage. It often has a profile of hills, trees, etc.

Activity: Practising

To be able to complete get-ins, fit-ups and strikes you will need to practise the following:

- manipulating flats
- securing flats
- preparing scenery for flying
- flying scenery.

Research what needs to be done for each of the above.

16.2.3 Cueing

The stage management team give cues to communicate with the backstage team. The DSM knows when to give a cue by following cueing instructions in the prompt copy established during the technical rehearsal. Each backstage team will also have a cue sheet that records every detail of every cue.

The DSM will be watching the performance and following the prompt copy. Most cues will be linked to actors lines, although sometimes they will be visual cues. In this case, the DSM will give the cue after the performer has completed a certain movement. Can you think what sort of performances might use visual cues?

Every lighting, sound and set change happens after the DSM has given a cue. Each cue has its own number. The DSM will give a standby cue that warns the backstage team that a cue is coming up. The DSM will then give a go cue at the exact point where the change will happen.

The DSM will communicate the cues through a talk back or cans system, which is a headset and transmitter pack.

Key terms

Cue sheet – a grid that records the details of each lighting and sound cue.

Visual cue – a cue based on an actor's action rather than a line of speech.

Standby cue – a 'get-ready' signal to alert the operator that the next cue is only a few lines away.

Talk back/cans – a headsets system that enables the backstage crew to communicate and run the show from their separated backstage positions. Usually the DSM will call the show over the cans system.

PLTS

Working with others to carry out the get-in, fit-up, strike and respond to cues shows how you are developing as a **team worker**.

Organising your time and resources, following cues and reacting to unforeseen circumstances tests your skills as a **self-manager**.

Reflecting on your experiences in your log demonstrates that you are a **reflective learner**.

Working well with others, completing tasks as agreed and being a reliable team-member makes you an **effective participator**.

BTEC Assessment activity 3 (P3) (M3) (D3) (P4) (M4) (D4) (P5) (M5) (D5)

Working backstage

Your practical work is the main focus for this assessment.

You will be able to choose whether you are a member of the stage crew, the flying crew or a followspot operator. Your responsibilities may include:

- completing get-in and fit-up tasks
- following plans to set up scenery and props
- completing technical and dress rehearsals tasks and responsibilities
- responding to cues in the dress rehearsal and performances.

Because everyone is doing a different job, it is not always possible for your tutor to be aware of everything that you do. You must therefore keep your log up to date, making sure that it contains:

- a detailed account of each new skill learned
- an explanation of your responsibilities and how well you have fulfilled them
- details of how you have set up the scenery, props or lighting, explaining the tools and processes used
- reflections on how well you have demonstrated new skills and on your ability to operate as a backstage crew member
- reflections on your use of terminology and ability to respond to cues
- explanations of your understanding of health and safety issues and how you have dealt with them throughout the process.

Your log can be presented in bullet points, annotated photographs, diagrams, videos, mind maps or storyboards. It can also include other people's opinion of how well you have worked.

Grading Tips

(M3) As you complete your backstage role, show that you can be reliable and complete the tasks that you are set and assume some responsibility. Record your experience of the process with descriptions and annotated photographs. Describe how you have completed your role in your log.

(D3) Make a valuable contribution to the get-in/out, fit-up and strike in your practical work. Complete tasks set independently and show responsibility by directing others. In your log, reflect on how you have been influential in completing tasks and leading and managing the others in the team.

(M4) Show that you can read plans to set up scenery and props with some direction. Describe how you completed this task in your log.

(D4) Show that you can read plans to set up scenery and props independently without direction. Explain how you completed this task in your log.

(M5) Understand and respond to cues and use the correct terminology during the run. Give descriptions of how you have managed this process in your log.

(D5) Respond to cues promptly and use the correct terminology throughout the process. Demonstrate a professional approach during stressful situations where any problems occur, give clear explanations, either to your tutor or in your log.

16.3 Safe working practices when carrying out processes and using tools and equipment

Warm up

Keeping safe

The theatre performance and backstage areas are high-risk zones. You are using electricity, a variety of tools, working at heights, manual handling and manipulating large pieces of scenery. Think about all the various health and safety hazards there are in a theatre. Make a list of as many as you can think of and compare with your group.

16.3.1 Safe procedures

The health and safety of all backstage workers must be taken into full consideration at every stage of the production process. The health and safety of employees is legally protected, meaning that employers must look after the people who work for them.

The law states that the employer must make sure that:

- the workplace is free from risks to health
- machinery and equipment are safe
- people are trained in the use of the equipment and consistently follow safe working practices.

Employees also have a responsibility to themselves, their employer and their colleagues. They must agree to:

- consistently ensure their own safety and the safety of others
- co-operate with their employer on health and safety matters
- use equipment and machinery correctly
- ensure that they do not misuse anything that is provided for the health and safety of workers.

The Health and Safety Executive (HSE) produces a leaflet outlining the things that employers and employees should know about health and safety law. To download the leaflet, please see the hotlinks section on p2 and discuss in pairs how the law affects a school performance space and a professional theatre.

Did you know?

You can find out about manual handling techniques by visiting the Ergonomics 4 Schools website. To access this site, go to the hotlinks section on p.2

Lifting

As member of the backstage crew you will be asked to lift heavy and, at times, awkwardly shaped objects. Your back is precious and easily damaged, so it is very important that you follow correct manual handling processes. The key considerations of manual handing are outlined in the table below.

Assess the risk	How heavy is it? Will you be able to lift it on your own? Should you get someone to help you?
Is the route clear?	Check that there are no trip hazards on your route. Check that there is a clear space to put the object down.
Lift properly	Bend your knees not your back. Hold the object close to you. Ensure that you can see over the object.
Moving with the object	Concentrate on the task and move slowly. If you are lifting the object with someone else, make sure that your communication is clear.
Putting the object down	Bend your knees not your back.

Working with electricity

Electricity is used by the lighting team, the sound team and the crew. It must be used with respect and vigilance; misuse could lead to electric shock or fire.

Activity: Electrical safety

Find out the following;

- What does PAT testing mean?
- What rules should you apply when using electricity?
- What does an electric shock do to your body?
- What should you do if someone is receiving an electric shock?
- Who is your centre's first aider?

Fire

Every effort is made to avoid the risk of fire backstage, for instance, by fireproofing the set. Find out what fire regulations exist for your performance space.

Working at heights

Working at heights is an integral part of backstage work. Lighting and sound equipment and elements of the set are often rigged at height. Working at heights presents hazards both to those doing the actual work and to anyone below. Find out what is your centre's policy for working at heights.

Did you know?

Fire extinguishers have different colours. Find out why.

Activity: Getting up high

To access heights you might use:

- a tallescope
- a scissor lift
- a scaffold tower
- a ladder or stepladder.

Research these pieces of equipment. What precautions should you take in order to minimise risk when using this equipment?

Key terms

Risk – the level of the danger that exists in the work space.

Hazard – a specific object or action that may pose a danger.

COSHH – Control of Substances Hazardous to Health. Standard guidelines from the Health and Safety Executive.

Identifying the risks

Every school, college and performance venue carries out risk assessments for every activity. A risk assessment identifies possible risks and hazards and puts procedures in place to minimise them.

When undertaking a risk assessment you need to look at the following:

- **Access** – can everyone get into and out of the performance space safely? This includes the actors, the backstage crew and the audience. Don't forget to consider disabled access.

- **Slip and trip hazards** – everything must be carefully stored and tidied away. Cables should be taped down and spillages mopped up immediately so that there is no risk to anyone by tripping or slipping.

- **Storage** – all stored items must be safely put away so that they will not fall. They must also be stored at accessible heights.

- **Fire exits** – must be well signed and access kept clear at all times.

- Hand and power tools – everyone must be trained in the safe use of tools

- **Set-building materials** – all paints and glues will have a COSHH assessment which tells you what to do if you have an accident with the materials. This must be kept visible and accessible in the set-building workshop. The workshop space must be well ventilated and dust masks should be worn when cutting certain set-construction materials. Care must be taken when lifting or moving heavy objects.

- Risks to the performer – it must be safe for the performer to move around the set in the different lighting states. All set must be secured and all raised areas should have a handrail. All backstage areas should be clear and all cables taped down.

- Risks to the backstage crew – all backstage areas should be clear and all cables taped down. Other risks include lifting and manoeuvring heavy or large objects, working in subdued lighting, using hand and power tools, dealing with electricity.

Activity: Assessing risks

Consider some backstage activities and rate their risk, give a high-risk activity a high score and a low-risk activity a low score.

Carry out a health and safety audit of your performance space, considering:

- access

- slip and trip hazards

- storage

- fire exits

- hand and power tools

- risks to the performer

- risks to the backstage crew.

Compile a list of health and safety rules that would make the performance and offstage spaces safe places to work in.

Invite your centre's health and safety representative to discuss your health and safety rules.

Look at the publication *Five steps to risk assessment* published by the HSE. To access the website, please see the hotlinks section on p.2 . Use this to help you draw up a risk assessment for working backstage. Identify the different areas of risk and undertake a risk assessment for one backstage activity.

16.3.2 Tools and equipment

The backstage crew must know how to use hand and power tools safely. Your centre will train you in their safe use and make sure that you are aware of the centre's guidelines for using tools.

You may be asked to operate some stage machinery, such as the front-of-house tabs, the dock door, flying winches, etc. It is important that you receive specific training in the use of these before you use them. Record your training in your log.

Followspot operators must have the correct training. The followspot is powered by electricity. It is heavy and challenging to manipulate. It is often dusty. If you operate the followspot, be well prepared and ensure that your working space is clear and that your cans are working. Do not eat or drink while you are operating.

Activity: Hand and power tools

What sort of hand and power tools might you use during a fit-up? Make a list and then find out your college's procedure for using these tools.

BTEC Assessment activity 4

Health and safety

There are two parts to this assessment activity: the theory and the practical.

Research health and safety procedures and legislation. Produce a booklet that details correct approaches and action for the backstage crew. This booklet should be clear enough to give to a new member of the backstage crew. The booklet must include:

- the get-in and fit-up
- the technical and dress rehearsals
- the run
- the strike and get-out.

As you carry out your practical backstage work (including Assessment activity 3) you will be observed by your tutor at certain points. Peer assessments will also be used to see what your team members thought of your approach to health and safety. After the run your tutor will ask you questions about your practical work.

Grading Tips

M6 Consistently show that you understand and can apply health and safety procedures and can act appropriately if required. Explain how you apply your health and safety practices in your log.

D6 Consistently show that you know how to apply the correct health and safety procedures and react quickly to any problems. Make links between your knowledge of health and safety legislation and your practical work in your log.

PLTS

Researching roles and responsibilities of backstage roles and reading and using plans shows you are an **independent enquirer**.

Collaborating with others to run the show, carry out the get-in, fit-up, strike and get-out requires you to be a **team worker**.

Organising time and resources to follow cues, managing interpersonal interactions throughout stressful periods of the production process and reacting positively to unforeseen events throughout the production period and the run are skills shown by a **self manager**.

Functional skills

ICT: selecting and using a variety of sources of information for a complex task. Researching health and safety information and legislation on the Internet.

Mathematics: understanding routine and non-routine problems in a wide range of familiar and unfamiliar contexts and situations. Using estimation and calculation to work out if planned stage sets or structures can fit into the performance space.

16.3.3 Documentation

Throughout this unit, references have been made to documentation and paperwork that is used by the backstage crews. As you work through a production as a member of the backstage crew you will use the following paperwork.

Paperwork	Purpose	Used by
Risk assessment	Completed before the production process, this identifies risks and details processes and procedures that will minimise risks and hazards	All backstage crews must read the risk assessments and be aware of how to avoid dangers
Cue sheet	Lists the exact detail of all cues. Each team has its own cue sheets	Stage management crew Followspot operator Backstage crews
Props list	A list of each prop, when it is used, by whom and on which side of the stage it is stored for performance	Stage management team
Set change list	A list detailing the movement of each piece of set during each set change	Stage crew and flying crew
Show report	Completed by the DSM after each show. This is an objective account of the show including comment on the running of the show	All teams may contribute to this in particular circumstances, but it is often completed by the DSM only

Woody Peterkin
lighting designer

Woody began studying performing arts as a BTEC First Diploma student. After a successful year he progressed onto the BTEC National Diploma course where he developed his set-building, crewing, lighting design and operation skills further.

Woody was a key member of the production backstage crew during his three years at college, taking particular responsibility for the lighting box: organising it, keeping it tidy and generating shopping lists for any new equipment needed.

College productions were staged at the local 600-seat theatre. During his first year Woody asked the chief electrician at the theatre whether there was any casual backstage work.

He got work there for the rest of his time at college. His duties included followspot operator, stage crew and eventually lighting-board operator.

After he had completed his National Diploma Woody worked for a London-based lighting company. The company hired out lighting and did lighting installations for performances and festivals. Woody worked with the company for two years.

Woody was then offered a job as lighting-crew member for three large theatres at a well-known holiday camp. Woody worked hard and is now responsible for a 3000 seat venue and in charge of a stage crew himself.

Think about it!

1. Draw up a list of the types of job that Woody might be responsible for during a typical week. Remember that there may be multiple acts with different requirements.

2. Woody manages a backstage crew. What do you think the crew might have to do for the following shows:
   - an afternoon magic show in one of the smaller performance spaces for 50 children
   - an evening performance of a band in the 3000 seat venue
   - a variety performance that uses a set and has a cast of eight for a three-night run in the 750 seat venue?

Just checking

1. What paperwork is used in backstage work during a production, and why?
2. What technical and personal skills does a backstage crew member need?
3. How can you make sure that you are safe when you are working as a member of the backstage team?
4. What is the difference between a fit-up and a get-in?
5. What are the manual handling risks during a get-in?
6. What should you do before using any piece of electrical equipment?
7. What are the guidelines for working at heights?
8. What procedures should you use for manipulating flats safely?
9. What procedure should the DSM follow if there is a suspected fire?

Assignment tips

- Keep every bit of paper that you create or use and make regular entries into your log, describing what you have done, how you have done it, why you have done it, and what you have learned.

- Ask a fellow team member to give you feedback about how well you did on each task and ask them to be as objective as possible. Evaluate your ability to demonstrate each new skill.

- Use diagrams, sketches, mind maps, bullet points, photographs, witness statements, self evaluations and video clips of your practical work. These may be kept in your log to demonstrate your understanding and skill development.

- Always use the correct terminology.

- Try to keep up to date with the latest health and safety regulations. Rate your application of health and safety in your log giving reasons.

- Get someone to take a photo of you putting health and safety into practice.

- When drawing scale plans:

  - Always work on a clean flat surface with clean hands and drawing tools when drawing plans.

  - Use a metal rule and set square to make sure all lines and angles are neat and accurate.

  - When the plan is complete, ink it in with a black fine-liner.

  - DO NOT write in measurements or label your groundplan.

E31 The Development of Music

Nothing is ever created in a vacuum. All creative work is influenced by, and becomes part of, the world in which it is produced. This unit will enable you to understand the role of music in society. You will explore how social, political and historical factors can influence developments in music and how music itself can affect the world in which we live.

This unit will also give you the opportunity to find out about developments in musical instrument making and the emergence of completely new musical instruments, such as the clarinet in the 18th century and the electronic synthesiser in the 20th century.

During this unit you will be introduced to a range of musical styles. While you might be familiar with some, others will be new to you. It is important that musicians have a broad knowledge of the characteristics of a range of different musical styles, and of the audiences for these styles, in order to inform their own work. This unit will enable you to broaden your knowledge of musical styles and demonstrate your understanding through performance.

Learning outcomes

After completing this unit you should be able to achieve the following learning outcomes.

1. Know some of the factors that have influenced developments in music
2. Know some of the characteristics of different musical styles
3. Be able to illustrate characteristics of a chosen musical style.

Assessment and grading criteria

This table shows you what you must to in order to achieve a pass, merit or distinction and where you can find activities in this book to help you.

To achieve a pass grade the evidence must show that you are able to:	To achieve a merit grade the evidence must show that, in addition to the pass criteria, you are able to:	To achieve a distinction grade the evidence must show that, in addition to the pass and merit criteria, you are able to:
P1 identify some of the political, social and cultural factors that have affected the development of different styles/genres of music **Assessment activity 1 page 164**	**M1** describe some of the political, social and cultural factors that have affected the development of different styles/genres of music **Assessment activity 1 page 164**	**D1** explain some of the political, social and cultural factors that have affected the development of different styles/genres of music **Assessment activity 1 page 164**
P2 identify some of the technological developments that have influenced music **Assessment Activity 2 page 167**	**M2** describe some of the technological developments that have influenced music **Assessment activity 2 page 167**	**D2** evaluate how technology has had positive and negative influences on the development of music **Assessment activity 2 page 167**
P3 identify some of the characteristics of different styles/genres of music **Assessment activity 3 page 175**	**M3** describe some of the characteristics of different styles/genres of music **Assessment activity 3 page 175**	**D3** comment critically on some of the characteristics of different styles/genres of music **Assessment activity 3 page 175**
P4 perform one piece from musical history, demonstrating some of the characteristics of the music associated with the related style. **Assessment activity 4 page 176**	**M4** perform one piece from musical history, demonstrating an accurate interpretation of some of the characteristics of the music associated with the related style. **Assessment activity 4 page 176**	**D4** perform one piece from musical history, demonstrating a clear and accurate interpretation of all the main characteristics of the music associated with the related style. **Assessment activity 4 page 176**

How you will be assessed

This unit will be assessed by an internal assignment that will be designed and marked by the tutors at your centre. You will be assessed on your contribution to a project that involves the organisation and planning of a performing arts event. You will need to show that you can work as part of a team, to make decisions about what needs to be done and to put the plans into action.

The work you produce may include:
- written pieces, such as a magazine articles or reports
- PowerPoint presentations
- podcasts
- video or audio recordings of a musical performance.

Jim, a jobbing musician

On my first day at music college, I remember my tutor telling us all to 'check our musical tastes in at the door'. The other learners and I were an odd bunch with a range of musical tastes and favourite bands. To begin with we found it difficult to put as much effort into playing stuff we didn't like as we did when working in musical styles that we were into.

Eventually we learned the difference between being a music fan and a musician. As a music fan I was very particular about what I would listen to and play and there were styles of music that I wouldn't go near. To become a musician I had to be more open-minded about the kinds of music I listen to and play, and while I still have my favourites I know that the broader my knowledge of different musical styles, the better I will be as a musician.

Over to you
- What styles of music do you enjoy?
- What styles do you want to find out more about on this course?

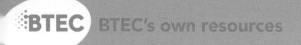
31.1 Factors that have influenced developments in music

Warm up

My kind of music

What kind of music do you like? Is it the same kind of music that your parents, aunts and uncles listen to? Is it likely to be the same type of music as someone your age living in Japan likes? What about someone who was a teenager 50 years ago?

Divide into small groups and discuss the ways in which the place and time we live in, particularly as young people, affects the type of music we listen to and enjoy.

In the first section of this unit we will explore four types of factor that have influenced the ways in which different styles and genres of music have developed.

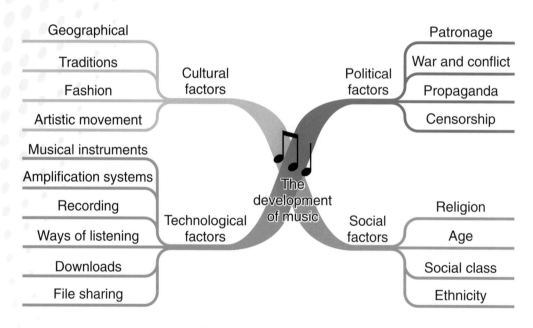

Figure 31.1 : Types of factor that influence the development of music.

31.1.1 Political factors

The way in which a country is governed can have a huge effect on the music that is created by its composers. During the 17th and 18th centuries in Europe, for instance, composers were directly employed by the ruling classes – from kings downwards. This system is called patronage.

In the present day, think about how music is used in modern political campaigns. Governments often use music to promote messages and political propaganda. In 1997, for example, the pop song 'Things Can Only Get Better' by D:Ream was adopted by the Labour party for its election campaign. Governments may also restrict access to certain types or pieces of music that are considered subversive – threatening to the establishment or dangerous to those in power. This is known as censorship, and while it can sometimes stifle the development and popularity of certain types of music, it can also have the opposite affect.

Protest songs

Music, like other art forms, is a form of expression, and musicians often use their music to comment on political issues, to protest against things that they think are wrong in society or to rebel against authority. This is particularly true during times of war, conflict or unrest.

A style of music known as the protest song developed out of the need to express views about what composers/musicians saw as wrong with the political situation in their country.

Examples of protest songs can be found from the 18th century onwards. However, it was in the mid 20th century in the USA when the form really began to blossom. Artists such as Bob Dylan, Marvin Gaye and John Lennon all wrote protest songs to comment on, and raise awareness of, issues such as the war in Vietnam War, the civil rights movement and the nuclear arms race.

Political unrest in the USA in the 1960s led many musicians to write protest songs about the situation.

Activity: 'Eve of Destruction'

The song 'Eve of Destruction' was written by Phil Sloane in 1964 and recorded by Barry McGuire in 1965. The song criticised the US government on the war in Vietnam, the nuclear arms race and the civil rights movement. Despite being banned by many radio stations, it reached number one in the US charts.

Listen to 'Eve of Destruction' or a similar protest song from the 1960s. Discuss how the song communicates its message through:

- the lyrics
- the style of vocal performance.

Now listen to a range of other protest songs from the 1960s and 1970s. For each song discuss:

- the message of the song
- how the message of the song is communicated.

Ideas for further research: The Music of the First World War

Many songs were written during the First World War to be sung both on the battlefield and at home. Examples include:

- 'Pack Up Your Troubles in Your Old Kit Bag'
- 'Keep the Home Fires Burning'
- 'Take Me Back to Dear Old Blighty'.

Investigate why these songs were written and the purpose they served.

31.1.2 Cultural factors

Culture is a difficult thing to define. It includes the traditions and customs of a country as well as the tastes of its people. Music is an essential part of the culture of a country. It both affects and is affected by its country's traditions. Most countries have a national anthem as well as other traditional/national songs that are sung at public events, such as sporting fixtures.

The United Kingdom has 'God Save the Queen' as its official anthem but England, Ireland, Scotland and Wales also have their own traditional patriotic songs, as shown on the next page.

Fashion is also affected by music and vice versa. For example, the 1970s saw a rise in the popularity of punk music, and in turn, punk fashions became popular.

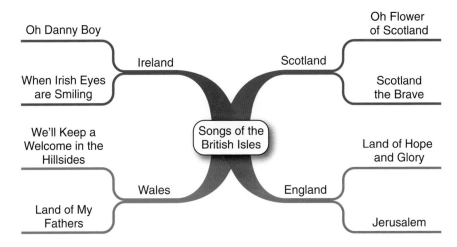

Figure 31.2: Traditional songs of the British Isles.

19th–century nationalism in Europe

Nationalism was a musical movement of the 19th and early 20th centuries. It was a reaction by composers against the dominance of the German classical tradition in music that had developed in the 18th century.

Composers wanted to re-engage with the musical traditions and cultures of their countries by:

- using traditional or folk music in their compositions
- using stories from folklore in their operas and programmatic compositions
- aiming to evoke the landscape and features of their country in their compositions.

Most European countries had their own nationalist composers. The table below shows some of the more famous of them, as well as the important pieces they wrote.

Norway	Edvard Grieg's *Peer Gynt* was the incidental music for the play by Henrik Ibsen, which was based on a Norwegian fairytale.
Finland	Jean Sibelius wrote the symphonic poem *Finlandia* in celebration of his country.
Spain	Issac Albéniz wrote a collection of piano pieces called *Iberia*, which represented various parts of Spain.
Czechoslovakia	Antonin Dvorák included Bohemian themes in many of his compositions including his *Slavonic Dances*.
Russia	A group of Russian composers known as 'The Five' dominated the Russian nationalistic style. They were Mily Balakirev, César Cui, Modest Mussorgsky, Nikolai Rimsky-Korsakov and Alexander Borodin.

Key terms

Programmatic – music that tells a story or represents moods, emotions or physical places.

Symphonic poem – an extended piece for orchestra that is programmatic. Also known as a tone poem.

In the early 20th century the nationalistic style continued to develop and was found in America through works by composers such as Aaron Copeland and Charles Ives.

Did you know?

Folk music was not written down in the way that classical music was - it has been passed on through word of mouth over centuries.

Activity: Comparisons

Listen to an orchestral piece of nationalistic music from the 19th century and a piece of classical music written by either Mozart or Haydn in the previous century.

- Discuss the two pieces in terms of their similarities and differences.

- Mozart and Haydn composed at a time when music composition was bound by specific rules regarding the form and structure of a piece, as well as the way melodies were constructed and harmonies added. Composers in the 19th century began to abandon these rules. Does this come across in the music? If so, how?

- By the mid to late 19th century the orchestra had grown in size with more brass and percussion instruments added and string and woodwind sections also larger in size. How well does the nationalistic piece make use of these increased resources?

Ideas for further research: Traditional music from the British Isles

Britain has a rich tradition of folk music that has been passed down from generation to generation.

- Find out about the folk traditions of your region. Explore the features of the music and the instruments it is played on.

31.1.3 Social factors

The social groups in which we live have an effect on the music produced in our society. A person's musical taste will have much to do with their age, where they live, and to some extent, the social class they come from. A person's religious views and ethnicity may also affect the type of music they listen to. For example, Bhangra is a form of music and dance that developed from a Sikh folk dance created to celebrate the coming of spring. The form became popular in the 1990s among Indian and Pakistani youths as well as ethnic communities in the UK.

In the 18th century, classical music tended to be composed for the aristocracy and the church. The ruling classes would engage composers to produce music to be played at social and celebratory events. The church would also employ composers to produce music for services. Johann Sebastian Bach, for example, spent a number of years producing music for St Thomas Lutheran Church in Leipzig.

Rock 'n' roll and the rise of the teenager

In the 20th century, a social factor that had a profound and lasting affect on music was the rise of the teenager. After the Second World War Britain went from an era of hardship to one of prosperity. Young adults in particular benefited from relatively high incomes. Teenagers had money to spend, and both music and fashion developed to meet what they wanted as consumers.

Before the 1950s young adults were just that. They were younger versions of their parents who wore the same sort of clothes and listened to the same kinds of music. In a social revolt against the styles and interests of their parents, teenagers developed their own way of dressing and their own styles of music.

Rock 'n' roll had developed by the mid-1950s with American artists, such as Bill Haley, Chuck Berry, Jerry Lee Lewis and Elvis Presley. British musicians, such as Billy Fury, Marty Wilde and Cliff Richard then began producing their own versions. The development of music at this time was also fuelled by technological advances including the electric guitar and the jukebox, which allowed young people to listen to their favourite songs in the many coffee bars that opened.

Teenagers began to develop their own style in the 1950s.

Activity: 'Shake Rattle and Roll'

Listen to an example of 1950s rock 'n' roll, such as 'Shake Rattle and Roll' or 'Rock Around the Clock' (both recorded by Bill Haley & His Comets)

- Why do you think this type of music appealed to young people in the 1950s?

- What are the similarities and differences between this type of music and what is popular with young people today?

Ideas for further research: Brass bands

In the mid 19th century, brass-band music developed in working-class communities where people were living in larger social groups due to industrialisation. Brass bands were sponsored by collieries and factories and provided the workers with a pastime and the wider community with entertainment.

- Investigate the development of brass bands and the types of music they played.

PLTS

Researching the development of music styles is a good way of improving your personal learning and thinking skills as an **independent enquirer**.

Functional skills

ICT could be used to find and select relevant information when researching the development of music styles.

Remember

During your research work you should aim to:

- identify questions to answer and problems to resolve

- analyse and evaluate information, judging it's relevance and value

- support conclusions, using reasoned arguments and evidence.

BTEC **Assessment activity 1**   P1 M1 D1

Produce an article for a music magazine in which you discuss the political, social and cultural factors that affected at least two important developments in music.

Grading Tips

M1 When writing your article, you must ensure that you describe the political, social and cultural factors you have identified.

D1 In your article you must explain why the political, social and cultural factors you have identified have affected the development of the different styles/genres of music you discuss.

31.1.4 Technological factors

One of the most important factors to influence the development of music styles is advancing technology. From improvements in the manufacture of orchestral instruments in the 18th and 19th centuries to the move to digital recording systems in the late 20th century, technology can affect the types of music being produced and the ways in which we listen to and consume music.

The pianoforte

The development of the piano in the 18th century was an important musical landmark. Previous keyboard instruments, such as the harpsichord and clavichord, had been popular with composers but they didn't have the range of volume or the ability to sustain a note that the piano has. In a clavichord, the strings are struck by metal blades called tangents. The harpsichord produces a sound when the strings are plucked by quills.

The mechanism of the piano made it a more expressive instrument. The player altered the volume by exerting more or less force when depressing the keys, hence the name 'pianoforte' (which means 'soft-loud' in Italian). The system of dampers also allowed notes to be sustained.

Activity: Inside a piano

Under the supervision of your tutor take a look inside a piano.

Identify the following parts of the instrument:

- keys
- strings
- hammers
- dampers
- pedals.

Discuss what happens inside the instrument and the sound that is created when:

- a key is pressed
- a key is released
- the left (sustain) pedal is held down

- the right (soft or *una corda*) pedal is held down
- (on some a grand pianos) the third (*sostenuto*) pedal is held down.

Try each of the pedals and discuss the resulting sounds.

Ask a pianist to play something and watch how all the piano parts work together.

Ideas for further research: Your own instrument

Undertake an investigation into the development of your own instrument.

- When did the instrument (or instruments) you play first start to be used?

- Have advances in technology improved the instrument? What impact has this had on the music written for the instrument?

- If you are a singer, look at the development and impact of the microphone.

The Electronic Age

A technological invention that had a huge influence on the development of popular music styles in the 1970s and 1980s was the synthesiser – an instrument that produces sounds electronically rather than acoustically. The first analogue synthesiser (or analog synth), a device that allowed musicians to create and alter sounds using electrical oscillations, was developed in the 1970s. Robert Moog designed a number of models including the Mini Moog, the first portable version. In the 1980s synths grew in popularity and digital versions such as the Yamaha DX7 became popular.

In the late 1970s a form of music known as 'synthpop' emerged. It was dominated by the use of electronic instruments and abandoned the drum kit, a key instrument in pop music since the 1950s, in favour of the electronic drum machine. Successful groups included Kaftwerk, Devo, The Human League, Soft Cell, Tubeway Amy, Yazoo and Pet Shop Boys.

Activity: Synthpop

Listen to an example of 1970s/80s synthpop such as:

- 'Are "Friends" Electric' – Tubeway Army
- 'Love Action' – Human League
- 'Only You' – Yazoo
- 'Tainted Love' – Soft Cell
- 'The Model' – Kraftwerk.

Discuss the use of electronic instruments in the piece. Are they being used to make sounds and create effects that acoustic instruments are not capable of?

What are your feelings towards this kind of music?

Ideas for further research: Songwriting or recycling?

Sampling – taking a section or extract of one song and re-using it in another – has been popular with recording artists since the 1990s. An example is 'I'll be Missing You' by Puff Daddy, featuring Faith Evans, used samples from the Police hit 'Every Breath You Take'.

- Is this a form of songwriting or simply recycling someone else's hard work and ideas?
- Investigate some more examples of songs based on samples and consider whether this is a good or a bad thing.

Key terms

Unsigned – bands not signed up to a particular record label to produce, promote and distribute their work.

Distribution – how we listen to music

The way in which we listen to music has been greatly affected by developments in technology throughout the 20th and into the 21st century. From the invention of the jukebox to MP3 players and downloads, the way in which we buy and listen to music has had particular effects on the popular music industry. In the 1970s a young person would need to save up to buy the entire album from their favourite band. Today's teenagers can just download an album a track at a time, not bothering with tracks they don't want. The Internet has allowed unsigned bands to release songs to promote themselves and sites such as YouTube allows free access to music videos.

Activity: Music and the Internet

How has the downloading of music affected the music industry?

Does file sharing (passing on a downloaded track to another listener who has not paid for it) really harm the music industry? Think about it and discuss it with your class.

 Do you have an MP3 player that you download music onto?

 Assessment activity 2 P2 M2 D2

Prepare an oral presentation on the influence of technology on the development of music. Make sure you include specific examples.

Grading Tips

M2 Remember to give descriptions of the examples you include showing that you understand the uses of each.

D2 Your presentation should include an evaluation of how technology can have both a positive and negative influence on the development of musical styles.

 PLTS

Researching technological developments that have influenced music is a good way of improving your personal learning and thinking skills as an **independent enquirer**.

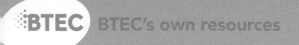

31.2 Characteristics of different musical styles

Warm up

What makes a piece of music what it is?

What is the difference between a piece of orchestral music by Mozart, a song from a musical by Andrew Lloyd Webber and a Brit Pop song by Blur?

Divide into small groups and identify the characteristics that make one style of music different from another.

Make a list and discuss with the rest of your class.

In this section of the unit we will explore the characteristics of a number of different musical styles by examining what makes one particular style recognisable and distinguishable from another. It is designed to help you understand these characteristics so you can apply your understanding to your performance work.

31.2.1 Features

When considering the characteristics of a musical style or genre you should begin with its key features, including:

* the type of instrumental and/or vocal ensemble the piece is specifically written for

* the intended purpose of the piece and the type of venue in which it will be performed

* the structure of the piece.

Instrumentation

Different styles of music are typically composed for particular groups of instruments. The instruments and voices used in a 1950s rock 'n' roll song, for example, are very different from those used in a classical symphony. Certain combinations of instruments are typical of certain styles of music. In a rock song you would expect to hear lead and rhythm guitars, bass guitar, drums and vocals. The combination of different musical instruments and/or voices, and therefore types of sound produced, is sometimes referred to as the 'texture' of a piece.

A composer can use instruments to create different textures by combining them in different ways. Having all the instruments playing together, for example, may produce a thick texture, which can be contrasted with sections within the music where only one or a few instruments play to create a thinner texture.

Activity: Instrumental and vocal ensembles

Listen to some pieces of music that are written for different types of ensemble.
Here are some pieces you could try:

• a piece of classical chamber music for strings, such as 'Eine Kliene Nacht Music' by Mozart

• a rock anthem, such as 'Free Bird' by Lynyrd Skynyrd

• a choral piece, such as the 'Chorus of the Hebrew Slaves' from the opera Nabucco by Verdi.

Discuss the type of musical ensemble used in each case and comment on the musical textures you can hear.

Venue and purpose

The intended performance venue and the purpose for which the music
has been written may affect the choices a composer makes in terms
of the ensemble of instruments and/or voices used. Chamber music,
for example, is written for smaller ensembles than full-scale orchestral
pieces. This was because chamber music was intended to be performed
in small spaces i.e. rooms (chambers) rather than large concert halls.
The string quartet, an ensemble made up of two violins, a viola and a
cello, has been a popular combination in chamber music from the 18th
century onwards. Composers writing music for large-scale events now
use different resources from in the past. Today, for instance, especially
for rock and pop music, powerful amplification systems can reduce the
number of players needed. Composers writing before amplification was
available had to use large numbers of players and singers to fill a large
venue with sound.

Activity: Zadok the Priest

'Zadok the Priest' is a coronation anthem composed by George Frideric Handel for the coronation of
George II in 1727. It has been played at every coronation since.

To produce a piece that would fill the venue, Westminster Abbey, as well as befitting the importance of the
occasion, Handel used a large Baroque orchestra, including oboes, bassoons, trumpets, timpani, strings and
a harpsichord, as well as a large choir.

The UEFA Champions League Anthem is based on Handel's composition. You may have heard it, as it is used
to introduce television coverage of matches.

• Listen to 'Zadok the Priest' and discuss Handel's use of instrumental and vocal resources.

• How is the importance of the ceremony conveyed in the piece?

• How does Handel gradually build the piece to the first entrance of the choir?

Structure

The structure or form of a musical composition is also a key feature of its style. Many styles of music are composed using conventional or tried and tested structures.

Most musical structures include elements of both repetition and contrast. One of the most simple structures is the binary form which includes two contrasting sections A and B, both of which are repeated.

A section	A section	B section	B section

Ternary form also uses an A and a B section, arranged in a slightly different order.

A section	A section	B section	A section

Rondo form includes several contrasting sections with the familiar A section being repeated again and again.

A section	B section	A section	C section	A section	D section	A section

Strophic or verse/chorus form is used in many types of song.

Intro	Verse 1	Chorus	Verse 2	Chorus	Chorus	Outro

Activity: Musical structure

Listen to a selection of pieces that use simple structures like one of those listed above. With you tutor discuss:

- the pattern of the form e.g. A A B A

- the number of bars in each section

- how the different sections contrast with each other e.g. does the B section move to a different key or use a different combination of instruments?

- whether the piece includes an intro and/or outro

- whether the piece includes any linking or bridging passages between the main sections.

Key terms

Repetition – where passages are repeated for a particular musical effect.

Contrast – juxtaposition of different passages (in terms of melody, instruments or voices used, key, tempo or dynamics) for musical effect.

Case study: 'Everyday' by Buddy Holly

'Everyday' was written by Buddy Holly and Norman Petty and was recorded and released in 1957. The structure of the piece is as follows:

Intro	A section	A section	B section	A section	A Section	A section	B section	A section	Outro
2 bars	8 bars	8 bars	8 bars	8 bars	8 Bars	8 bars	8 bars	8 bars	4 bars

This makes the structure of the piece ternary form (AABA) with an extra AABA added to make the piece longer.

The B section contrasts with the A section because is uses a different chord structure.

The piece begins with a short introduction and ends with a four-bar outro, which is made up of the last four bars of the A section.

31.2.2 Types of instruments

The attributes of different musical instruments used in a composition will contribute to the style and mood of the piece. While we might describe how instruments and voices are combined as the texture of the music, individual musical instruments each have a unique sound or timbre of their own.

Strings

The traditional string section is made up of violins, violas, cellos and double basses. These instruments can produce a sound in two ways:

1. by a bow being drawn across the strings (arco)

2. by the strings being plucked (pizzicato).

Generally, orchestral compositions make use of bowed strings more than plucked. However, some pieces, such as Johann Strauss's 'Pizzicato Polka' make greater use of pizzicato playing. The double bass when used in jazz ensembles also tends to be plucked.

Woodwind

Woodwind instruments can be found in both classical and popular styles of music. The oldest examples are flutes, which produce sound when air is blown across the edge of a hole, and the oboe and bassoon, which have double reeds made of two small pieces of cane between which air is forced. The clarinet is a later invention. It was developed during the time of Mozart and has a single reed that is held against the mouthpiece of an instrument with a cuff called a ligature. The saxophone produces a sound in a similar way to the clarinet. Invented in the mid 1800s by Adolphe Sax, it comes in a variety of sizes and is found in orchestral music and many forms of popular music.

> ## Key term
>
> timbre – the character of the sound.

Key terms

Pitch bending – sliding from one note to another.

Vibrato – a pulsating effect.

Flutter tonguing – where the performer flutters their tongue while blowing into the instrument to create a 'frrrr' sound.

Dynamics – changes in volume.

Activity: The saxophone

The saxophone is a very versatile instrument found in a range of musical styles such as big band, jazz, ska, soul and rock 'n' roll. In the hands of an accomplished player it can be a very flexible and expressive instrument.

The saxophone is commonly used as a solo instrument, as well as part of a larger horn section that includes trumpets and trombones.

Listen to some examples of music for the sax. Examples could include:

- 'Baker Street' – Gerry Rafferty

- 'Will You' – Hazel O'Connor

- 'Sir Duke' – Stevie Wonder

- 'Young Americans' – David Bowie

- 'Baggy Trousers' – Madness.

For each example you listen to, discuss the following:

- Can you hear one saxophone or a section?

- Does/do the player/s use any techniques, such as pitch bending, vibrato or flutter tonguing?

- How are dynamics used in the piece?

Brass

Brass instruments are essentially lengths of metal tubing that flare out in a bell shape at one end and have a cupped or conical mouthpiece at the other. A brass player produces a sound by buzzing their lips against the mouthpiece as they blow. The pitch and quality of sound produced will depend on:

- the length of the tube

- the width of the tube

- whether the tube is mainly cylindrical or conical.

Percussion

Percussion instruments include anything that is hit. Percussion instruments can be either:

- tuned – they sound at a definite pitch or pitches, such as a bell or xylophone

- untuned – they sound at an indefinite pitch like a tambourine or side drum.

Electric instruments and amplified vocals

The use of electrically amplified instruments from the 1950s revolutionised the way in which music was written and performed and led to a range of new popular musical styles.

The standard make-up of a rock or pop group, however, has remained unchanged since the 1960s. The line-up of one or two electric guitars, bass guitar and drum kit is found in a range of different musical styles. Sometimes the only addition is vocals – the lead vocalist sometimes being joined by backing vocalists, using microphones so they can be heard. Additional electronic instruments, such as synthesisers, may be included. In some forms of popular music, acoustic instruments may be used alongside electric and electronic ones. Horn sections of several players are common as are string sections.

Activity: Call and response vocals

The relationship between lead and backing vocals is an important feature in many styles of popular music. The backing vocalists often repeat or respond to a phrase the lead vocalist has sung. This is known as 'call and response' vocals and is found across a number of pop music styles.

Listen to and discuss one of the following examples of call and response vocals:

- 'Can't Help Myself' – The Four Tops

- 'Twist and Shout' – The Beatles

- 'Midnight Train to Georgia' – Gladys Knight & the Pips

- 'My Generation' – The Who.

31.2.3 Musical styles

The way in which the characteristics we have now looked at are put together is what makes a particular style or genre of music what it is.

The history of music is a wide and complex subject but here is a brief look at the main musical periods and styles you should be aware of.

The Renaissance

The Renaissance is roughly defined as the interval from 1400 to about 1600 in Europe when there was a great development in music, learning and the arts. Musical styles that developed during this time include vocal music, such as the madrigal and the motet.

Key terms

Avant-garde – new and unusual or experimental ideas in the arts.

Mode – a series of pitches used to create a piece of music.

Instrumental ensembles, known as consorts, also emerged made up of instruments such as the recorder and the viol (a stringed instrument played with a bow). Music was composed using a system of modes, which developed towards the end of the period into the major and minor scales we still use today. Composers writing at this time included William Byrd in England and Giovanni Palestrina in Italy.

Baroque

The Baroque style was popular from the late 16th century until the early 18th century. It is a style that was seen in all areas of the arts and was characterised by a love of ornamentation, whether it be highly decorated facades on buildings or complex interweaving melodies in musical compositions.

Classical

The Baroque style gave way to the classical period in the early 18th century. Classical music tends to be less complex than the highly decorated pieces written previously. The period was an era of beautiful melodies during which Mozart, Haydn and, towards the end of the period, Beethoven were composing. The period also saw the development of a number of key musical styles, such as the symphony, the solo concerto and the string quartet.

Romantic

As the term suggests, Romantic composers produced music that was expressive. The period covers music written from around 1820 until the end of the 19th century. Programmatic music was prevalent and the growth of the orchestra meant that composers had huge instrumental resources to work with. As we have already seen, the period was also a time of nationalism in musical composition.

20th Century

The last century was a time of furious development in music. Some musicians abandoned traditional musical styles to create experimental and avant-garde compositions.

The United States saw huge developments in music. Through African–American communities in the South, Blues music was created. Jazz music originated in New Orleans in the early part of the 20th century, and was first popular in African–American communities before becoming more widespread. Country music gained popularity, having developed from traditional folk songs.

Ska and reggae developed in Jamaica in the 1950s and 1960s and is still popular today.

Other 20th-century styles/genres, some using elements of styles already mentioned, include pop, rock and the musical.

Activity: Musical timeline

Listen to and discuss a range of music from the Renaissance through to the 20th century. In each case you should identify:

- when the piece was written. Is it typical of a particular style/genre?

- what was the intended purpose of the piece?

- what was the intended venue for performance?

- what type of ensemble is playing/singing?

- which instruments or voices are particularly prominent?

- does the piece have any noticeable structure, and if so, what?

BTEC Assessment activity 3

Prepare an audio recording or podcast in which you discuss the characteristics of two different musical styles. You should refer to specific examples of both musical styles and include extracts of the pieces you are discussing.

Grading Tips

M3 Remember to describe the musical characteristics.

D3 Your recording should analyse the characteristics of the styles comparing and contrasting the two examples you give.

Functional skills

English speaking – your audio recording or podcast will highlight your speaking skills.

Make sure you listen to a range of musical styles.

31.3 Demonstrating characteristics

Now it's your turn! Having spent time listening to and analysing a range of musical styles it is now time to demonstrate your understanding of the key features of a particular musical style through performance.

31.3.1 Context

When planning your performance it is important to consider the context in which it will take place. You may wish to perform as a soloist or in an ensemble. You may decide to put on an evening concert for your friends and family or a more informal performance for your peers. Whatever you decide to do, you must consider a number of factors carefully.

- Choose a piece appropriate to your level of ability. You may have the urge to perform a Jimmy Hendrix guitar solo but if you are a relative beginner you should choose something simpler.

- If you are considering an ensemble piece, take into account the other people involved. For example, you can't perform in a string quartet unless you have another violinist, a viola player and a cellist who can join you and play at a comparable level.

- Choose a piece that demonstrates the key features of the musical style it represents, whether it is a protest or rock 'n' roll song, a synthpop anthem or a piece of Renaissance recorder music.

31.3.2 Realisation

Realisation describes the process of rehearsing and performing a piece of music. When rehearsing your piece, aim for a musically accurate performance in terms of pitch and rhythm. Also, be aware of the conventions of the style of music you are performing. A protest song, for example, may require a certain type of vocal performance to get the message across to the audience. This type of singing is different from the vocal style used in a ballad or a musical. Listen to examples of the style you are performing and try to emulate them in your performance.

BTEC Assessment activity 4

Rehearse and perform a piece of music demonstrating the characteristics of the style of music chosen.

Grading Tips

M4 Your performance must be an accurate interpretation of some of the characteristics of the style.

D4 Your performance should be an accurate interpretation of the piece that demonstrates the key characteristics of the chosen style of music.

Jenni
professional trombone player

Jenni is a professional trombone player. She has been asked to talk about how her interest in the trombone began, and how her playing led to a career in music.

I started playing the trombone at school when I was 11. The brass teacher had room for more pupils and I was lucky enough to be chosen. After a while I was good enough to play in the school wind band, which was made up of brass and woodwind instruments as well as percussion, and that is when I really started to enjoy my playing.

The trombone is different from other brass instruments as it uses a slide to change the pitches of notes rather than valves that you have to press.

It seemed quite complicated when I began to learn but with practice I soon got the hang of it. Looking back I sometimes can't believe how far I've come. At 15 I was asked to join the City Youth Orchestra and by that time I was also playing in a ska band with some of my friends.

I now earn my living by playing the trombone both in live concerts and the recording studio. The trombone is such a versatile instrument that I get to play a wide range of music including orchestral, pop, jazz and big band.

Think about it!

1. Jenni played in more than one sort of band as she was learning her instrument. How do you think this may have helped her to develop her skills?
2. Which other instruments can be used to play such a wide range of musical styles?

Just checking

1. Name some of the factors that can influence the development of music.

2. What is censorship?

3. How did the war in Vietnam and the nuclear arms race impact on the development of music in the USA in the 1960s?

4. In the 19th century, many European composers used traditional folk tunes from their countries in their compositions. What was this called?

5. What effect did the increased spending power of young people have on the development of music in the 1950s?

6. Why was the piano seen as a landmark development in the design of keyboard instruments in the 18th century?

7. What is a Mini Moog?

8. Name three groups that were important in the rise of synthpop music in the 1970s and 1980s.

9. What type of instrument is a saxophone and when was it invented?

10. What is the difference between tuned and untuned percussion?

11. Put these musical periods into chronological order:

   Classical – Renaissance – Romantic – Baroque.

edexcel

Assignment tips

- Become an active listener.
- Try to spend some time each week listening to music you haven't heard before. Your local library may have a listening section that allows you to borrow CDs. You could also spend a little time each week listening to a range of different music radio stations.
- Make notes about the music you listen to in your log. Make sure you list the key features of each piece you listen to.
- Try to make connections between the different styles of music you listen to by comparing and contrasting them.
- If you come across a piece of music in a style you are not familiar with, discuss it with your tutor.

E32 Working as a Musical Ensemble

If you are going to make your living as a musician, the chances are you will spend a lot of time playing in ensembles.

A professional musician might play in a wide range of different musical ensembles. A trumpet player, for example, might play in an orchestra, a brass quintet, a wind band or in a brass section for an R 'n' B group. A singer might be a member of a choir as well as working as a backing singer for a recording artist.

Regardless of the size of the ensemble and the style of music played, the skills required are generally the same. Musicianship skills are vital to the ensemble player to ensure that the music is performed to the highest possible standards. Reliability, respect for others and patience are also vital in an industry where competition for jobs is fierce.

This unit will allow you to explore and develop the skills required by musicians in ensembles. It will provide you with an understanding of what it is like to be an ensemble player and give you the opportunity to be part of a musical team working towards a practical group project.

Learning outcomes

After completing this unit you should be able to achieve the following learning outcomes:

1. Know the roles and responsibilities of members of musical ensembles
2. Be able to prepare for performances as a part of an ensemble
3. Be able to present effective ensemble performances
4. Be able to demonstrate employability skills through participation in musical ensemble activities.

Assessment and grading criteria

This table shows you what you must to in order to achieve a pass, merit or distinction and where you can find activities in this book to help you.

To achieve a pass grade the evidence must show that you are able to:	To achieve a merit grade the evidence must show that, in addition to the pass criteria, you are able to:	To achieve a distinction grade the evidence must show that, in addition to the pass and merit criteria, you are able to:
P1 identify roles and responsibilities of members musical ensembles **Assessment activity 1 page 187**	**M1** describe roles and responsibilities of members musical ensembles **Assessment activity 1 page 187**	**D1** justify roles and responsibilities of members musical ensembles **Assessment activity 1 page 187**
P2 demonstrate some of the processes required in the effective preparation of musical performances, as a member of a musical ensemble **Assessment activity 2 page 192**	**M2** demonstrate all the processes required in the effective preparation of musical performances, as a member of a musical ensemble **Assessment activity 2 page192**	**D2** demonstrate all of the processes required in the effective preparation of musical performances as a member of a musical ensemble with confidence and commitment **Assessment activity 2 page 192**
P3 demonstrate the musical, presentation and musical communication skills required in ensemble performances **Assessment activity 3 page 196**	**M3** demonstrate the musical, presentation and musical communication skills required in effective ensemble performances with confidence **Assessment activity 3 page 196**	**D3** demonstrate the musical, presentation and musical communication skills required in effective ensemble performances, with confidence and creativity **Assessment activity 3 page 196**
P4 demonstrate some employability skills in ensemble activities. **Assessment activity 4 page 198**	**M4** demonstrate a range of employability skills in ensemble activities. **Assessment activity 4 page 198**	**D4** demonstrate a wide range of employability skills effectively in ensemble activities. **Assessment activity 4 page 198**

How you will be assessed

This unit will be assessed by an internal assignment that will be designed and marked by the tutors at your centre. You will be assessed on your ability to demonstrate your understanding of the roles and responsibilities of members of a musical ensemble and your ability to prepare for and present an ensemble performance.

The work you produce may include:
- a written or oral presentation
- a project log
- videos of discussions, rehearsals and performances.

Joel, member of an up-and-coming band

When I started my BTEC First in Performing Arts I thought I knew all there was to know about playing in a band. I had been with my band for a year and we had even had a few gigs.

It wasn't until I began the course and started working with my music tutor that I realised that there was so much more to learn about being a member of a musical ensemble. Our rehearsals tended to be chaotic and we didn't really understand how to get the best out of the time we spent practising. We were also badly organised when it came to arranging our gigs.

While on my BTEC course I studied a unit called Working as a Musical Ensemble. It was really useful as I learned about the roles and responsibilities within a group and how to plan and prepare properly for performances.

We now make much better use of our rehearsal time, and as a result, our gigs go better. We now have a regular spot at a local pub and we are also planning to record a demo soon.

Over to you
- What experience, if any, do you have of being a member of an ensemble?
- How confident are you about your ensemble skills?
- What kind of ensemble playing would you like to take part in while completing this unit?

32.1 The roles and responsibilities of members of musical ensembles

Warm up

A team sport

Who is the most important member of a rock group? Is it the:

- lead singer
- drummer
- lead guitarist
- rhythm guitarist
- bass player?

The answer is, of course, that they are each as important as the other.

Why is teamwork so important in a musical ensemble?

Musical ensembles come in all shapes and sizes, from 50-strong symphony orchestras to duos and trios. Whatever the size of the ensemble and the type of music it plays, the roles and responsibilities of its members will be largely the same.

32.1 Roles and responsibilities

The conductor/ensemble leader

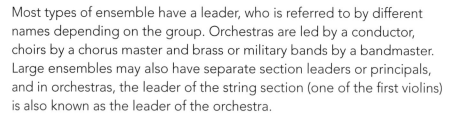

Did you know?

In the 17th century, conductors often used a large stick, called a staff, to keep time. The staff was moved up and down and sometimes would be banged on the floor. The composer and conductor Jean-Baptist Lully managed to stab himself in the foot while conducting. The wound became gangrenous and Lully died as a result.

Most types of ensemble have a leader, who is referred to by different names depending on the group. Orchestras are led by a conductor, choirs by a chorus master and brass or military bands by a bandmaster. Large ensembles may also have separate section leaders or principals, and in orchestras, the leader of the string section (one of the first violins) is also known as the leader of the orchestra.

The conductor or ensemble leader is responsible for preparing and running rehearsals. They will prepare rehearsal schedules of when and where rehearsals are to be held and who is called. In large ensembles, separate rehearsals may be organised for different sections of the ensemble before the piece is put together.

The conductor or leader is also responsible for making decisions about the musical interpretation of the pieces being rehearsed and performed. They will make decisions about the tempo of the piece and how dynamics and articulation will be approached and then guide the ensemble in this as they conduct.

Conducting is the method of directing and leading the musicians by a series of gestures, often made using a small wooden stick known as a baton. This enables the musicians in a large ensemble to keep together.

Activity: Beating time

Practise beating time to a piece of recorded music. Follow the appropriate pattern a professional conductor would use, depending on the number of beats in a bar.

For duple time (two/four) the pattern is as follows:

For triple (three/four) time you should follow this pattern:

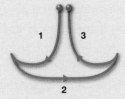

For quadruple (four/four) the pattern is as follows:

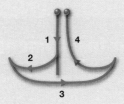

A conductor leads the orchestra using a series of gestures.

Did you know?

In some types of ensemble, the leader may direct from the piano, keyboard or other instrument. In this case, the leader may conduct for the first and last few bars of a piece to ensure the correct tempo is set and everyone starts and finishes together. For the remainder of the piece, the leader will play along with the other musicians in the ensemble.

Musical director

Many large orchestras and other established musical ensembles have a musical director who is in overall charge of the ensemble. The musical director will make decisions about the repertoire of the ensemble and the overall vision for the concerts they take part in and recordings they make. The musical director may appoint conductors for particular projects and will also be responsible for auditioning, hiring and firing. In smaller ensembles, the roles of musical director and the conductor/leader may be undertaken by the same person.

Key terms

Tempo – the speed at which the piece is played.

Dynamics – variations in the volume of the piece.

Articulation – how musical phrases are played e.g. smoothly or with notes separated.

Key term

Repertoire – the range of musical works played by an ensemble.

Performers

The term 'performer' refers to anyone who plays an instrument or sings. In an orchestra, the performers are divided into sections: strings, woodwind, brass and percussion. Some sections of the orchestra are then subdivided into smaller groups e.g. first and second violins. Similarly, in a brass band the cornet section is divided into solo, repiano, second and third cornets. Generally the solo or first players will play a higher-pitched part.

In a choir, singers are divided in terms of the pitch and range of their voices e.g. soprano, alto, tenor and bass. In pop and rock music, singers are often designated as lead or backing singers. The lead singers will sing the main portions of the songs and will also front the band while the backing singers provide harmonies.

Your kit

Music teachers up and down the country will have had rehearsals disrupted and delayed by drummers who have forgotten their sticks, guitarists with leads that don't work and brass players with sticky valves.

The most basic requirement of any member of a musical ensemble is to arrive at rehearsals with their instrument in good working order. This means you should spend some time each week maintaining your instrument and check that you have all the relevant equipment with you for rehearsals. This may also include carrying spare reeds for woodwind instruments, valves, valve oil and mutes for brass instruments and strings, plectrums or spare bows and rosin for string instruments.

Activity: Your instrument

Consider the maintenance requirements of the musical instrument you play.

Make a list of these requirements along with any spares or supplementary equipment you should take to ensemble rehearsals.

Preparation and individual practice

Rehearsals are not a time to practise your individual part in a piece. An ensemble rehearsal is an opportunity for the players to fit all the individual parts of the piece together and to work to perfect the piece of music as a whole according to the interpretation of the conductor. To ensure this happens, each player must be familiar with their own part. Each member of the ensemble should arrive at the rehearsal confident that they can play their part from beginning to end without errors. It is therefore vital that each member of the ensemble undertakes individual preparation and practice prior to the scheduled rehearsal; working through their part section by section to ensure that they are confident with the notes and tempo.

Case study: Practice makes permanent

Jim has a difficult guitar solo to master and is practising it in advance of a rehearsal of his band. The solo is 32 bars long and has two tricky phrases. Jim plays the 32 bars again and again and is frustrated that he makes the same errors with the two difficult phrases each time. The more he practises, the worse it gets.

The reason why Jim isn't making any headway with the solo is that he is practising the errors, making them permanent. Practice only makes perfect if you practise in the correct way.

1. What would be a better way of approaching the solo?

2. Think about how you practise your instrument. Are there any improvements you need to make to your practice technique?

Activity: The three pennies method

A good way of practising and perfecting tricky passages in a piece of music is by using a technique called the three pennies method.

Choose a difficult passage or phrase of no more than two bars in length and practise it as follows.

1. Place three coins in a pile on the right side of a table or music stand.

2. Play the phrase slowly and carefully once. If you play the phrase correctly, move one coin to start a new pile on the left and move to step three. If you play the phrase incorrectly, leave the coins as they are and begin step two again.

3. Play the phrase slowly and carefully once more. If you play the phrase correctly, move another coin to the pile on the left. If you play the phrase incorrectly, move one coin from the left pile back to the pile on the right.

4. Continue the process until all three coins have been moved to the left pile, i.e. until you have played the phrase correctly on three consecutive occasions.

Ensemble rehearsals

Rehearsals, like any other activity involving a group of people, requires co-operation from all the participants. During an ensemble rehearsal you, the performer, require a number of skills and attributes.

Rehearsing as a member of an ensemble is a skill that has to be learned and perfected if you want to get the best out of the time you spend working together.

- **Playing or singing skills** – careful preparation and individual practice before the rehearsal should ensure that you will play or sing your part accurately.

- **Listening skills** – you must listen carefully to instructions from the conductor or leader of the ensemble as well as listening to your musical part or line in relation to what the other performers in the ensemble are playing.

- **Concentration and patience** – rehearsals can sometimes be tedious, particularly if the conductor or leader spends time going over and over a passage with another section of the ensemble. It is vital, however, that concentration is maintained throughout the rehearsal so when your moment comes you are not half asleep or daydreaming about what's for tea that evening!

- **Self-discipline** – the successful rehearsal's biggest enemy is lack of discipline. Players who chatter and play or fiddle with their instruments at inappropriate times disrupt the rehearsal. Conversation must be focused on matters relating to the rehearsal.

- **Communication skills** – members of an ensemble may be required to take part in discussions to decide what needs to be worked on and set targets for a rehearsal. You might also take part in discussions during and after the rehearsal to consider what is going well and less well and suggest how pieces might be improved. This is particularly the case in a small ensemble that performs without a conductor or designated leader.

Activity: Observing a rehearsal

Observe a rehearsal of a professional orchestra or other ensemble.

(This can be done by sitting in on a rehearsal by a local ensemble or by viewing a rehearsal on DVD).

Make a note of how the following skills are used by the members of the ensemble.

- Playing/singing skills.
- Listening skills.
- Concentration and patience.
- Self-discipline.
- Communication skills.

Assessment activity 1

Roles and responsibilities of ensemble members

Produce a brochure entitled 'Working with Music' that identifies the roles and responsibilities of ensemble members.

Grading Tips

M1 You must also describe the roles and responsibilities.

D1 Your brochure should explain why the responsibilities of the roles you have included are necessary to the success of the ensemble.

32.2 Preparing for a performance as a member of an ensemble

Preparing for a performance as a member of a musical ensemble can involve a range of tasks and activities related to the planning, preparation and rehearsal of the event.

In this part of the unit you will have the opportunity to consider these processes and put them into action by working to prepare an event of your own.

32.2.1 Initial considerations when devising a performance

The venue

When planning a musical event, one of the first considerations is the venue in which it is to take place. Music venues vary greatly in size, layout and style and include:

- arenas
- concert halls
- arts centres
- pubs and clubs
- open-air venues
- church halls and community centres.

An ensemble will need to find a venue suitable to their needs and the type of performance being planned. They will need to take into account the size and capacity of the venue as well as the equipment and facilities available. Cost may also be an issue.

Key term

Capacity – the size of audience that a venue can hold.

Activity: Venues in your region

Undertake some research into the music venues in your region. What sorts of venue are available?

Find out about the types of musical events being staged at them.

The potential audience

When planning a performance, a musical ensemble must have a clear idea of its audience. It must tailor its performance to this audience to ensure it gets the ticket sales and that the audience enjoys the performance (you don't want people asking for their money back!). The audience needs to be considered at every stage when preparing for a performance. For example, when you are considering a time and venue for your performance you must think about where your audience will feel comfortable and when they will want to hear the music. The audience for a string quartet may feel out of place in a pub at 11.30 at night and those coming to see an indie band may not be as attracted to a gig in a church at four o'clock on a Sunday afternoon!

For a performance to be financially viable it must make more money from ticket sales than is spent on the cost of the venue hire, equipment, travel and any wages. Professional ensembles must therefore sell a certain number of tickets for the performance to be worthwhile. It is therefore essential that they consider their audience at every step of their preparation. They must ensure that the venue and timing are suitable, the repertoire is appropriate – established groups may have a fan base or following that expect a particular type of experience – and the publicity is effective. It's no good putting on the perfect show if nobody knows about it.

Timescales and deadlines

When planning a musical event there is much to organise so it is vital that the timescale and deadlines for the event are taken into consideration in the planning process. A large-scale event may take months to plan and enough time must be allowed for the rehearsal of the music as well as all the other preparations.

Personnel

The ensemble itself will also be a major consideration in the planning of an event. For some events, an ensemble may need to be put together specifically and this will involve auditions and interviews to ensure the appropriate performers are engaged.

Repertoire

The type of music to be played will, of course, be a prime consideration when planning an ensemble performance. The repertoire must be suitable for the ensemble as well as the type of event and the intended audience.

Activity: Intitial thoughts

As a group, consider ideas for a musical event that features ensemble performances.

You should discuss the following:

- the venue for the event
- who your intended audience would be
- the time needed for rehearsals and other preparations
- who would be involved in the ensemble(s)
- the repertoire for the event.

32.2.2 Planning, preparing and rehearsing

Organising an ensemble performance requires careful planning and preparation both in and out of the rehearsal room.

Equipment and resources

When organising any musical event you will need to consider the resources and equipment needed. Specialist technical equipment, such as PA systems for singers, and other materials, such as music stands, staging and musical scores may be needed.

The resources required will depend on the type of ensemble involved, the style of performance being planned and the facilities available at the venue. It is vital, therefore, that requirements are considered and lists drawn up at the outset of the planning process. It is much easier to plan a performance around the facilities available than to have to try and get hold of them (and possibly pay for them) at the last minute, or even worse to have to change the performance because a vital piece of equipment is missing.

Schedules and plans

Rehearsal schedules will need to be drawn up to ensure all pieces are ready for performance within the deadlines. A rehearsal schedule should state what is to be rehearsed, by whom, when and where.

Case study: St Mary's Grove

The learners at St Mary's Grove are preparing for an ensemble musical performance at their centre's arts festival. Having decided on the repertoire for the performance they are using weekly schedules to organise their rehearsals.

Mary's Grove Community College Musical Ensemble Project Rehearsal Schedule – week beginning Jan 8th			
Piece(s) to be rehearsed	Personnel involved	Location	Date and time
'Fields of Gold' 'Scarborough Fair'	Jenny, Kel, Maggie, Jonathan, Lewis	Music Room 3	Monday 9.15–10.15
'I Dreamed a Dream' 'Can you feel the Love Tonight?'	(Vocalists only) Maggie, Jenny, Kym, Belle, Justine	Music Room 3	Monday 1.00–1.45
'Circle of Life'	Jenny, Kel, Maggie, Jonathan, Lewis, Ben, Marc	Music Room 2	Tuesday 3.00–4.00
'I Dreamed a Dream' 'Can you feel the Love Tonight?'	(Full ensemble) Maggie, Jenny, Kym, Belle, Justine, Jonathan, Lewis, Ben, Marc, Kel	Drama Studio	Thursday 9.15–10.15

Additional plans will also need to be made to ensure other necessary preparations are undertaken. For example:

- booking and setting up rehearsal spaces
- hiring or purchasing resources and equipment
- publicising the event
- selling tickets
- organising transport to the venue for musicians and equipment.

1. Why do you think the students decided to rehearse 'I Dreamed a Dream' with only the vocalists before rehearsing the full ensemble?

2. Why is it important to draw up a new schedule each week rather than planning the whole rehearsal schedule at the beginning of the rehearsal period?

Responsibilities

With so much to do it is vital that each member of the ensemble understands their responsibilities in the planning and preparation process. In large, professional ensembles, responsibilities will be delegated to specialist personnel, such as administrative and technical staff, tour managers and stage crew. In smaller groups, however, these responsibilities may be undertaken by members of the ensemble, who will carry out both organisational and musical roles.

Rehearsals

Once a schedule has been drawn up, rehearsals will form the main activity in preparations for a performance. The rehearsal techniques employed will need to be appropriate to the material being rehearsed and the type of ensemble. Larger groups may need to undertake section practices before pieces are put together. Whatever techniques are employed, however, rehearsals should enable the ensemble to work on the accuracy of the pitch and rhythmic features of the pieces as well as the blend and balance between the musical parts, expression and musicality.

BTEC Assessment activity 2

Your class has been asked to plan and take part in a musical event that includes ensemble playing.

You should take an active role in the planning, preparation and rehearsal process for the event. You will be required to keep a project log for the event in which you will provide details of your contribution to planning, decision-making, assessment of technical requirements and other resources, and participation in rehearsals.

Recordings of milestone rehearsals and other preparation activities should also be made to provide evidence of your contribution.

Grading Tips

M2 You must be fully involved in rehearsals and other preparations.

D2 You should display enthusiasm and commitment to the project working confidently during rehearsals and other preparations.

32.3 Presenting effective ensemble performances

An effective ensemble performance relies on a range of musical, presentation and communication skills from the players within the group. Professional performers will produce performances that are slick and often appear effortless. This is, however, the result of hard work both in rehearsals and individual practices.

32.3.1 Musical skills

Pitch, intonation, rhythm and timing

Musical accuracy is a vital element of any effective musical performance. Ensemble members must ensure that they are able to play the rhythmic, melodic and harmonic elements of their musical parts accurately. In terms of the pitch of notes, good intonation or tuning is vital when playing with other musicians. Care must be taken at the beginning of all rehearsals and performances to ensure all instruments are in tune with each other. Timing is another important element. During rehearsals the ensemble must work on keeping together.

Balance and blend

The balance and blend of different musical instruments and/or voices is what makes an ensemble effective. Individual players/singers need to use listening skills to ensure they blend with others rather than drowning them out. The conductor/leader also has a role in ensuring a balance between the different parts is achieved.

Musicality and expression

Musical performance is about so much more than just the notes being played accurately. The way in which they are played can make the difference between a flat and uninteresting performance and an expressive, exciting and communicative one.

Did you know?

At the beginning of an orchestral concert, the leader of the orchestra will get all players to tune their instruments to an 'A' played by the oboe. This is done because the pitch of the oboe is considered to be secure and the penetrating sound can easily be heard above the sound of the other players tuning their instruments.

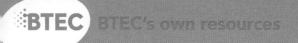

32.3.2 Presenting a performance

The way a group of musicians present themselves is often what sets it apart as a professional ensemble.

Visual aspects of a performance

The visual aspects of a performance can be an important part of the experience for the audience. Some musical performances have certain dress codes associated with them. Brass bands, for instance, often wear uniforms, and orchestras may wear evening dress for certain events. Pop and rock bands also dress in a particular way in keeping with their image. For some groups, lighting and other visual effects, such as pyrotechnics, are an important aspect of the show.

The way in which the performers sit or stand on the stage often follows certain conventions, which have been developed to enhance both the sound and the look of an ensemble. A symphony orchestra, for example always sits in the same formation.

Lighting and other visual effects are an important part of many pop and rock events.

Stage presence, communication and projection

Playing the right notes is obviously very important in ensemble playing. What truly makes a memorable performance, however, is the way in which the music is played. Stage presence, communication and projection are needed to ensure the meaning or mood of the piece is captured and communicated to the audience.

Stage presence is the quality that makes a musician or singer watchable. It comes from self-confidence and experience and is a vital skill for anyone fronting an ensemble, such as a lead singer. A performer who lacks stage presence could be boring or even embarrassing to watch.

For a singer, projection is a term that is used to describe the way in which the voice is produced to ensure all the audience can hear it. If you are performing in a large space without amplicification you will need to work on your vocal projection to ensure you can be heard, even at the back of the hall. The term is also used to describe the way in which musicians communicate the meaning or mood of a piece to an audience through the use of musical expression.

Confident communication with the audience is a vital aspect of any musical performance both during pieces and in between. In a concert featuring several pieces, someone may need to talk to the audience to introduce each piece and fill in while the players are preparing for the next musical item.

Entrances and exits

A performance begins as soon as the members of the ensemble take to the stage and it does not end until the last one has exited. A professional ensemble will ensure that entrances and exits are undertaken in an organised and tidy manner and it is important that the arrangements for getting onto and off the stage are understood and, if possible, rehearsed.

32.3.3 Musical communication within an ensemble

A good ensemble will operate like a well-oiled machine in performance. This is due mainly to good levels of musical communication between the members of the ensemble and the conductor/leader.

Working with the conductor/leader

Ensemble members will need to keep an eye on the conductor or leader whose job it is to keep the group together during the performance. This is particularly important at the beginning of each piece when the conductor will set the tempo, and as a piece ends, when the conductor ensures that the final moments have the desired impact to create a lasting impression for the audience. The conductor is also there to help the ensemble maintain the pulse during the piece.

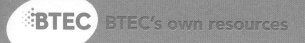
Working with other performers

Members of the ensemble will also need to use both musical and physical communication skills during the performance, listening and responding both musically and through their body language to ensure the balance and blend is effective.

 Assessment activity 3

Take part as an ensemble player in the musical event your class has been planning. During the performance you should demonstrate the musical, presentation and communication skills required by a member of an ensemble.

A recording of the event will be made to provide evidence of your contribution.

Grading Tips

M3 Your performance should show effective and confident use of musical presentation skills.

D3 Your performance should demonstrate creativity in the use of the required skills by ensuring the mood and meaning of a piece are carefully communicated to your audience.

Make sure you take note of any information and advice the conductor gives you.

32.4 Demonstrating employability skills through participation in musical ensemble activities

Being an outstanding performer does not necessarily mean that a musician is employable. There are many other skills that must be learned before anyone can become a fully rounded musician. These skills are what employers look for in team members, both in the music industry and all other types of business.

32.4.1 Employability skills

Reliability and time keeping

The music business is an incredibly competitive industry with many more musicians than jobs. For this reason, reliability is a vital attribute for the budding musician. If you are late or do not turn up to a rehearsal or gig, there are plenty of musicians ready and waiting to take your place. People who are unreliable or poor time keepers will quickly be replaced. In many cases, musicians will find work through word of mouth or may be offered a role because they have a good reputation. A reliable musician who is known for their good time keeping is much more likely to find themselves with work than a musician who has let others down in the past.

Attitude, focus, enthusiasm and motivation

A positive attitude is also a key attribute. Musicians often have to work together in close proximity for long periods of time, and a member of the group who is unenthusiastic or has a negative attitude to the work can stifle the creativity and focus of an ensemble.

Making a contribution to the set tasks

Like many other professions, employment in the music industry involves contributing to tasks within the context of a team. Making a positive contribution by pulling your weight is vital.

Respect for others

We may like some of the people we work with and enjoy their company. Others we may be less keen on and would not choose as friends in a social setting. Whether or not we would choose our colleagues as friends, they must be treated with respect. This means that their opinions should be treated fairly and disagreements should be resolved through reasoned discussion rather than argument. Think about how you would like to be treated and spoken to and act in this way to others even if their approach frustrates you. As musicians you must work as a team. Being supportive in the rehearsal room and during performances is vital to a good performance.

Responding to feedback and taking advice/direction

Nobody enjoys being criticised. For a musician, however, this comes with the job. The leader or conductor is there to provide feedback to members of an ensemble highlighting where they are on track as well as the aspects of their performance that need work. This is not a personal attack but rather a reflection of their desire to make the performance the best it can be. It is important that all ensemble members respond to this advice/direction in a positive way using the feedback to improve their playing.

BTEC **Assessment activity 4**

During preparations for and performances of ensemble work you should demonstrate employability skills.

You should then take part in a group forum discussing the employability skills required for working as an ensemble musician.

A recording of the discussion forum will be made to provide evidence of your contribution and your teacher/tutor will provide an observation report on your demonstration of employability skills during rehearsals and performances.

Grading Tips

M4 You must demonstrate a range of employability skills e.g. at least five of the following: reliability, good time keeping, positive attitude, focus, enthusiasm, motivation, contribution to set tasks, responding to direction, respect for others, negotiation, taking advice.

D4 You should effectively demonstrate the majority of the employability skills listed above in ensemble activities.

Iain Smyth
The Lions Community Wind Band

The Lions Community Wind Band has been together for 14 years. Iain Smyth is the bandmaster, and has been leading the group for the last six years.
The band is an ensemble of 32 players, including brass and woodwind players, as well as a drummer and a bass guitar player. The Lions perform at many community events each year, including the annual Crowford Summer Carnival. The Lions will be required to provide a 75-minute spot in the main marquee in the early evening. The band will prepare for some months before their performance.

Although the band has a wide repertoire of pieces, Iain still needs to decide what pieces, they will play and make sure the chosen ones are fully rehearsed and their performance is polished to a good standard.
As well as ensuring that the performance will go smoothly, Iain has a few other things he must do. He needs to make sure that all 32 members of the band know where they need to be and when, as well as reminding them that their uniforms should be correct and smart. He also needs to liaise with the organisers of the event to confirm information and ensure that the equipment and resources the band require are in place for their performance.

Think about it!

- Other than the players' own instruments what other equipment and/or resources might the Lions need?
- What information will Iain need to confirm with the organisers of the carnival in advance of the event?

Just checking

1. How does a conductor lead an ensemble during rehearsals?

2. How are the singers in a choir generally divided?

3. What is the leader of a brass or military band called?

4. What kind of supplementary equipment should a trumpet player carry?

5. Why is individual practice important before a rehearsal?

6. Why is self-discipline an important skill for the ensemble player?

7. A conductor makes decisions about the interpretation of a piece. What does this mean?

8. What are the differences between the responsibilities of a conductor and a musical director?

9. Why does the potential audience for an event need to be taken into account when planning the repertoire for a concert?

10. Why is a rehearsal schedule necessary in the planning of an ensemble performance?

11. What is stage presence?

12. Why are employability skills vital for a musician?

edexcel :::

Assignment tips

• Hard work and patience are key to success in this unit. A consistently focused contribution to all aspects of preparations, rehearsals and performances is what will help you achieve the higher grades.

• It is important to remember that everyone contributing to an ensemble has a vital role to play. You may think your role is not as important as that of someone else e.g. if you are playing third trombone and they are the principal trumpet player, but in fact, the success of any ensemble performance rests equally on the shoulders of all those involved.

• Complete your practice log on a regular basis i.e. at the end of every session. Don't neglect it and try to catch up later.

• Good attendance and punctuality are very important. Competition for jobs in the music industry is tough so only those who are good time keepers succeed. You must make sure that you attend regularly and complete tasks within the deadlines that have been set.

Project 1 Devising a Songbook Musical

Unit B6 Devising Plays

Unit B8 Musical Theatre Performance

In recent years, the songbook or jukebox musical has become a popular form of entertainment. This is a form of musical theatre performance that uses previously written music, often by a specific artist or group, around which a story has been woven. Popular examples include *Mama Mia*, *We Will Rock You* and *Buddy*.

In this project you will devise a one-act musical using existing songs from a chosen artist, group or musical style.

You will be required to work as a group to choose appropriate songs, come up with a plot and devise the dialogue that will link the songs together. You will then need to rehearse the musical developing your own role in it. Finally you will need to perform your role in the musical combining acting, dancing and musical performance skills.

Learning outcomes

After completing this project you should be able to achieve the following learning outcomes:

Unit B6 Devising Plays

1. Be able to explore and develop material for a devised play
2. Be able to use a range of drama forms and techniques

Unit B8 Musical Theatre Performance

3. Be able to use acting skills
4. Be able to use dance skills
5. Be able to use music performance skills
6. Be able to perform a musical theatre work.

Assessment and grading criteria

This table shows you what you must to in order to achieve a pass, merit or distinction and where you can find activities in this book to help you.

To achieve a pass grade the evidence must show that you are able to:	To achieve a merit grade the evidence must show that, in addition to the pass criteria, you are able to:	To achieve a distinction grade the evidence must show that, in addition to the pass and merit criteria, you are able to:
Unit B6 Devising Plays		
P1 contribute some ideas an suggestions that are relevant to the work **Assessment activity 1 page 206** **Assessment activity 2 page 207** **Assessment activity 3 page 209**	**M1** develop ideas and suggestions which are clearly focused on the drama and attempt to shape the structure of the work **Assessment activity 1 page 206** **Assessment activity 2 page 207** **Assessment activity 3 page 209**	**D1** develop ideas and suggestions that make a positive contribution to the shape and form of the work with effective results **Assessment activity 1 page 206** **Assessment activity 2 page 207** **Assessment activity 3 page 209**
P2 select and use some drama forms and techniques as part of the development process. **Assessment activity 2 page 207** **Assessment activity 3 page 209**	**M2** select and use a range of forms and techniques with some invention as part of the development process. **Assessment activity 2 page 207** **Assessment activity 3 page 209**	**D2** experiment creatively with different forms and techniques as part of the developmental process. **Assessment activity 2 page 207** **Assessment activity 3 page 209**
Unit B8 Musical Theatre Performance		
P1 demonstrate acting skills with technical control **Assessment activity 4 page 211** **Assessment activity 5 page 212**	**M1** demonstrate acting skills in ways that show a good degree of technical control **Assessment activity 4 page 211** **Assessment activity 5 page 212**	**D1** demonstrate a strong technical command of acting skills **Assessment activity 4 page 211** **Assessment activity 5 page 212**
P2 demonstrate musical skills with technical control **Assessment activity 4 page 211** **Assessment activity 5 page 212**	**M2** demonstrate musical skills in ways that show a good degree of technical control **Assessment activity 4 page 211** **Assessment activity 5 page 212**	**D2** demonstrate a strong technical command of musical skills **Assessment activity 4 page 211** **Assessment activity 5 page 212**
P3 communicate a simple interpretation in performance through the application and combination of musical theatre skills **Assessment activity 5 page 212**	**M3** communicate intentions in performance with attention to detail and success in the consistent application of skills across the three disciplines **Assessment activity 5 page 212**	**D3** communicate intentions in performance clearly and effectively through the imaginative and consistent application of skills across the three disciplines **Assessment activity 5 page 212**

To achieve a pass grade the evidence must show that you are able to:	To achieve a merit grade the evidence must show that, in addition to the pass criteria, you are able to:	To achieve a distinction grade the evidence must show that, in addition to the pass and merit criteria, you are able to:
P4 review the main strengths and weaknesses of own performance. **Assessment activity 5 page 212**	**M4** review strengths and weaknesses of own performance with some reasoning. **Assessment activity 5 page 212**	**D4** review in detail the strengths and weaknesses of own performance with considered conclusions. **Assessment activity 5 page 212**

How you will be assessed

This project will be assessed by an internal assignment that will be designed and marked by the tutors at your centre. You will be assessed on your ability to play an active part in the devising process and contribute to the performance of a one-act songbook musical. The work you produce for assessment could include:

- tutor and peer observations
- DVD recordings of classes, workshops, rehearsals and performances
- your logbook of the devising and rehearsal processes
- audience feedback.

Ashley, professional actor

I first took up acting as a hobby when I was 15 and joined my local youth theatre. The youth theatre produced loads of musicals, including *West Side Story*, *Sweet Charity* and *Caberet*. I really enjoyed them, so decided to do a BTEC National in Performing Arts. After doing that I still wasn't sure what I wanted to do, and even contemplated becoming a carpenter! However, I decided to apply for one drama school in London just too see how much talent they thought I had and got in! I gained a 2.1 in Professional Acting. They were the best three years of my life, and although life as an actor is sometimes uncertain as jobs can be hard to find, I can't imagine doing anything else!

I think the most important thing to realise as an actor is that you have to be ready to take a few knocks – you'll be turned down from more auditions than you're successful in, but when you do get a job it feels so great – I'm about to tour the country doing *A Midsummer Night's Dream*.

Songbook musical

The scenario

In this project you will devise, create and perform a one-act songbook musical. The project will be made up of a series of workshops and rehearsals where you will research and explore a chosen musical genre and create your own show. You will devise and develop a plot that links the songs you have chosen. You will then rehearse and perform your final work to an audience. But first, you need to know a bit more about the structure and form of the musical.

The musical

Musicals combine the three disciplines of music, drama and dance. There are two general styles:

- sung-through
- musical numbers linked by libretto.

Sung-through musicals do not include any spoken dialogue. Many of Andrew Lloyd Webber's musicals are 'sung-through' e.g. *Joseph and the Amazing Technicolor Dreamcoat*.

Some musicals include spoken dialogue (the libretto) to link the various songs (known as musical numbers) together. Most classic American musicals, such as *Oklahoma!* and *The Sound of Music* are in this style.

Key term

Libretto – the spoken dialogue sections of a musical.

Songbook musicals are now a popular form of entertainment.

Songbook musicals

A songbook or jukebox musical uses popular songs as a basis for the musical. These productions can be either sung-through or have a libretto. One of the earliest examples of a songbook or jukebox musical is *Buddy*. Based on the life story and untimely death of the musician Buddy Holly it uses a range of songs by Holly and other early rock 'n' roll musicians. It ran in London's West End for 12 years from 1989 and had a successful run on Broadway in New York. Professional productions still tour regularly.

Return to the Forbidden Planet also opened in 1989. Directed by Bob Carlton, the show takes its inspiration from Shakespeare's *The Tempest* and a 1950s science fiction film *Forbidden Planet*. The musical score uses a range of 1950s and 1960s rock and pop songs. This musical is now a popular choice with school and college musical theatre groups.

Two of the most popular songbook musicals of more recent years are *Mama Mia*, based on the songs of Swedish pop group ABBA and *We Will Rock You*, which uses the music of the rock band Queen. Unlike *Buddy*, neither of these musicals has plots based on the careers of the musicians who made the songs popular. *Mama Mia*, for example, tells the story of a young girl searching for the identity of her father on the eve of her wedding.

Activity: Watching a musical

Watch an extract from a songbook musical on DVD.

Discuss how the elements of acting, music and dance are combined in the extract.

Discuss how the songs relate to the plot of the musical.

Finding your starting point

The starting point of most songbook musicals is the songs themselves. You need to begin by choosing the songs for your musical. You could use songs:

- written by a specific songwriter or artist e.g. Elton John or Lily Allen

- made popular by a specific group e.g. Coldplay or Travis

- from a specific musical genre or style e.g. 1970s disco or Brit pop.

BTEC **Assessment activity 1** **Unit B6**

Choosing your score

1. Divide into small groups and discuss song ideas for your musical. Avoid simply choosing songs from your favourite group.

2. Produce a shortlist of two ideas for artists, groups and/or musical styles along with examples of three or four songs for each.

3. Discuss your ideas with the class and your tutor.

4. Draw up a shortlist of the most popular and appropriate ideas. Look at each idea in turn, discussing the potential of the songs. Remember to consider:

    *   how easily you can weave a plot around your songs

    *   the ability of the group to successfully perform the songs

    *   how your ideas might fit in with the costumes and props you have available

    *   a theme or a situation that ties your songs together

    *   characters in any of your songs who you might like to include in your musical.

5. Use these criteria to make a final choice with the guidance of your tutor.

Evidence

Your logbook – Make detailed notes on this activity in your logbook describing what has been discussed and the decisions made.

Grading tips

(M) Remember to take an active role in the discussions and make sure you contribute to discussions with ideas that are clearly focused on the work you are developing.

(D) You will need to make a prominent contribution to the discussion. You should contribute well thought-out ideas that impact positively on the final piece that is created.

Structuring your plot

Musicals often use plots with simple structures, such as 'boy meets girl – boy loses girl – boy wins girl back'. This structure can be applied to a number of popular musicals. The plots of *Oklahoma!*, *Guys and Dolls*, *The Boyfriend* and *Grease* all follow this pattern.

Even when love is not central to the plot, the basic dramatic three-act structure is common. It begins with everything being fine, builds tension through some form of conflict that eventually comes to a head and ends with the tension being resolved.

This structure has a clear exposition (beginning), complication (middle) and resolution (end) and is sometimes known as a story arc.

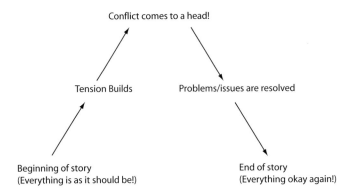

Figure P1.1: A story arc.

Assessment activity 2 — Unit B6

Exploring the key points of a plot

Research the plots of your favourite musicals. Use this research to help you to come up with ideas for a plot for your own musical.

- For each plot idea, identify the key points in the story. Does it follow the pattern of the story arc?
- Write your plot as a series of key moments using no more than five bullet points (one for each moment).
- Create a still picture that illustrates each bullet point.
- Practise moving from one still picture to the next, holding each picture for a count of ten.

You may have to revise your ideas a few times to explore what will work. Discuss the ideas you have explored and with the guidance of your tutor make decisions about the final plot of your musical.

Evidence

Your logbook – Make notes on this activity in your logbook describing what has been discussed, the decisions made and why certain plot ideas where rejected.

Grading tips

M2 You should work as a member of the group to develop ideas and suggestions that make a positive contribution to the shape and form of the musical you are developing.

D2 You should demonstrate that you are able to experiment creatively with your own ideas and those of other group members using different drama forms and techniques in a creative manner.

Moving the work on – devising

Now that you've decided on the songs you will use in your musical and have mapped out an outline for your plot, care has to be taken to use project time effectively. You will be working to a deadline, and it is easy to waste precious time because rehearsals have not been planned, for example, so you end up sitting around wondering what to do next.

Your devising sessions should be structured as follows:

1. Quick warm-up – games as well as a physical and vocal warm-up.

2. Plan of attack – go over the aims for the devising/rehearsal session.

3. Practical work on the material including:

- discussing the shape and structure of the musical
- improvising to explore material and generate dialogue
- working on material suggested or scripted by group members
- discussing and evaluating work created so far
- developing and improving material already produced
- agreeing what needs doing, and setting aims for next session.

The chorus.

The chorus

The chorus is an important element in musicals. The term 'chorus' was originally used in the theatre of ancient Greece to describe a group of performers who were separate from the principal actors. They were used to create spectacle, to give the principal actors a break (in order to change costume for example), to provide background information and to comment on the action. While the use of a chorus has become less popular in plays without music, forms of drama with music continued to use them. For example, Italian operas of the 19th century often have very large choruses and the operettas of the late 19th and early 20th centuries also used them. This has led to the chorus becoming a common feature of the modern musical.

Members of the chorus may be required to both sing and dance – the big chorus numbers are often central to the success of the show. Chorus members also have to act. They may not have dialogue, but are often on stage in the background during spoken scenes. The director must ensure that the chorus is engaged in the action in a meaningful way when they are present on stage.

Activity: The role of the chorus

There may be a chorus in your musical. Discuss who they are in relation to the main characters and what their purpose is in the world of your musical.

If chorus members do not have a particular identity, e.g. group of sailors (South Pacific) or nuns (The Sound of Music) they will need to be given an identity and a purpose for being there e.g. a married couple out for a walk, a policeman walking his beat, a drunk slumped in a doorway or a group of office girls on their lunch break.

Assessment activity 3   Unit B6

Developing a libretto

Take part in devising sessions to develop a libretto (script) for your musical.

Evidence

Your logbook – Keep a record of the devising activities you take part in including the following:

- notes on progress made in each session – include your personal views and responses
- research notes
- ideas – it is vital to record your own ideas and those of others
- director's notes (given to the performers by the director)
- action plans and 'to do' lists.

Tutor observations – Your tutor will be observing your work during these sessions and will produce a report to provide evidence of your contributions.

Rehearsals

Initial rehearsals for a musical theatre piece may begin with separate sessions for music, dance and dialogue.

 Activity: Rehearsal schedule

As a group, draw up a rehearsal schedule for your musical. You should include:

- who is required at each session
- whether the session is a music, dance or dialogue rehearsal
- what will be rehearsed.

Musical numbers

Musical theatre performers have to be able to learn songs quickly and accurately. As your musical is based around popular songs, it is likely that you will already know many or all of the melodies. But it is still important to go through the songs in detail to ensure that every performer is able to sing the pieces accurately.

A musical theatre song is a piece of dramatic dialogue set to music. The music and the lyrics (words) combine to create the mood. It is vital that the performer understands the meaning of the words they are singing. Lyrics must be carefully read and the timing of the song within the musical considered. The process is similar to the work an actor undertakes when preparing a speech or scene from a play.

The mood or character of the song, sometimes known as the musical setting, must be taken into account by the performer. When an actor performs a monologue, they are free to alter the pace and rhythm of the speech as they wish. When performing a song, however, the singer must work with the musical setting the composer has provided.

Always think about the words you are singing.

Dance routines

Skill in both singing and dancing are vital in musical theatre and their combination is what makes the musical theatre performer different from a pop or rock singer.

Musical theatre performers have to be able to learn dances quickly and accurately. The audition process often involves dancers being taught a routine by the choreographer so their ability to pick up a routine can be judged. Professional dancers will take pride in the fact that they can pick up a complicated routine rapidly.

When teaching dance routines, the choreographer will usually begin by teaching the dancers the steps while counting the beats. Short phrases will be repeated again and again until everyone gets it right. The music will only be added when the routine has taken shape. It is vital that dancers develop a good movement memory so that they can pick up movement phrases quickly and are able to reproduce them accurately.

Further guidance on rehearsing dance routines can be found in Unit C13 Performing Dance.

The dialogue/libretto

When you are rehearsing the dialogue sequences for your musical it is vital to remember that these sections are just as important to the show as the song and dance numbers. Dialogue is used to move the plot along and the audience may only understand the story properly if the spoken scenes are performed well. It is important that enough time is allowed for thorough preparation and rehearsal of these scenes.

A dialogue scene in a musical needs to be rehearsed in much the same way as a scene in a play. Directors may use a variety of methods when approaching the rehearsal of dialogue. These may include the use of games and off-text exercises as well as working with the libretto.

Any speech or conversation that leads directly into a musical number will require meticulous rehearsal to ensure the entrance of the vocal is properly timed. This may take a lot of practice.

Further guidance on rehearsing passages of dialogue can be found in Project 7 Page to Stage.

Putting it all together

There comes a point in the rehearsal period when all elements of the musical must come together. The first time this happens is known as the 'stagger through'. This is where the show is run in sequence for the first time. At this point, the dance routines and songs will have been learned and performers with dialogue will be off book.

Key terms

Stagger through – first run through rehearsal of a production when all the separate dance, music and drama elements are put together.

Off book – when actors know their lines and no longer use their script.

 BTEC **Assessment activity 4** **Unit B8**  P1 M1 D1 P2 M2 D2 P3 M3 D3

Take part in the rehearsal of the musical numbers, dance routines and dialogue sections for the show.

Evidence

Your logbook – Keep notes on the rehearsals you attend in your logbook describing the activities undertaken and the progress you make.

Recorded evidence – Your tutor will video a number of milestone sessions to provide evidence of your contribution.

Grading tips

M1
M2   During rehearsals you must show that you can develop new skills and hone existing ones.
M3   Your use of musical performance, acting and dance skills should demonstrate that you have a good degree of technical control.

D1
D2   You will need to show that you are eager to improve and keen to try to rise to any challenges you are set. You will also need to show confidence in using the new skills you have learned, demonstrating a strong technical command of musical performance, acting and dance skills.
D3

Final preparations

Depending on the scale of the musical you have devised and the venue and equipment you are working with, final preparations may include technical and dress rehearsals.

Information and guidance on these processes can be found in Unit A3 Performing Arts Production Process.

Curtain up

The opening of any show, whether in the West End or the theatre of a school or college, is an exciting and nerve-wracking time for all involved. It is the culmination of all the hard work that has been undertaken and the time when the director and choreographer must step back and allow the performers to get on with the show.

The presence of an audience can change the pace of a show. Applause may follow musical numbers so those with dialogue immediately after the end of a song or dance must be responsive to this, pausing if necessary to allow the applause to subside before speaking the line.

If the piece is a comedy, the audience should be laughing at appropriate moments. Sometimes they may laugh in unexpected places. Again, performers must remain focused at all times and be prepared to respond to this, pausing slightly should this happen.

 Assessment activity 5   **Unit B8**

Take part in the performance of your songbook musical demonstrating the use of acting, dance and musical performance skills.

Evidence

Your logbook – add a final entry to your logbook commenting on your use of skills during the performance and your ability to communicate the intentions of the piece to the audience.

Grading tips

M4 Communication with the audience is vital to the success of the show. During performances of the musical theatre piece you have devised you should demonstrate the ability to communicate the intentions of the piece and the role you are playing with some confidence and attention to detail. You should also show consistent use of musical performance, acting and dance skills.

D4 You should remain focused and engaged throughout the performance. You should also aim to use skills across the three disciplines of music, acting and dance to communicate your intentions in performance effectively and with imagination.

Project 2 Dance Festival

Unit C10 Contemporary Dance

Unit C11 Exploring Urban Dance Styles

Unit C13 Performing Dance

This project is all about creating and performing in a dance festival – a showcase of your work to be performed for an audience.

There will be opportunities to develop dances in a range of different styles so that you can be assessed across two style units, but you will also be able to work in a more general way towards some of the learning outcomes for Unit C13 Performing Dance.

The project will not cover the whole of the three units, but will allow you to gain marks from assessments for some of the learning outcomes for each of them.

Learning outcomes

After completing this project you should be able to achieve the following learning outcomes:

Unit C10 Contemporary Dance

2. Be able to apply physical skills in class
3. Be able to absorb and reproduce patterns of movement

Unit C11 Exploring Urban Dance Styles

1. Be able to perform the key features of urban dance

Unit C13 Performing Dance

1. Be able to participate effectively in practical dance workshops
2. Be able to demonstrate dance styles and qualities in performance
3. Understand how to improve own performance in rehearsal.

Assessment and grading criteria

This table shows you what you must do in order to achieve a pass, merit or distinction, and where you can find activities in this book to help you.

To achieve a pass grade the evidence must show that you are able to:	To achieve a merit grade the evidence must show that, in addition to the pass criteria, you are able to:	To achieve a distinction grade the evidence must show that, in addition to the pass and merit criteria, you are able to:
Unit C10 Contemporary Dance		
P3 show application of physical skills in the execution of movement phrases/exercises **Assessment activity 1 page 217** **Assessment activity 3 page 219** **Assessment activity 4 page 223**	**M3** show a consistent application of physical skills in the execution of movement phrases and exercises **Assessment activity 1 page 217** **Assessment activity 3 page 219** **Assessment activity 4 page 223**	**D3** show a high degree of competency in physical skills in the execution of movement phrases and exercises **Assessment activity 1 page 217** **Assessment activity 3 page 219** **Assessment activity 4 page 223**
P4 reproduce simple technique phrases with occasional errors demonstrating awareness of action, dynamic, rhythmic and spatial content **Assessment activity 1 page 217** **Assessment activity 4 page 223**	**M4** reproduce simple technique phrases in action, dynamic, rhythmic or spatial content **Assessment activity 1 page 217** **Assessment activity 4 page 223**	**D4** reproduce simple technique phrases accurately and confidently **Assessment activity 1 page 217** **Assessment activity 4 page 223**
Unit C11 Exploring Urban Dance Styles		
P2 perform key features of urban dance **Assessment activity 2 page 218** **Assessment activity 3 page 219**	**M2** perform key features of urban dance accurately **Assessment activity 2 page 218** **Assessment activity 3 page 219**	**D2** perform to a high standard key features of urban dance accurately and with flair **Assessment activity 2 page 218** **Assessment activity 3 page 219**
Unit C13 Performing Dance		
P1 attend class and rehearsal, working co-operatively **Assessment activity 1 page 217** **Assessment activity 2 page 218**	**M1** demonstrate a disciplined approach to class and rehearsal **Assessment activity 1 page 217** **Assessment activity 2 page 218**	**D1** demonstrate a high level of commitment to class and rehearsal **Assessment activity 1 page 217** **Assessment activity 2 page 218**

To achieve a pass grade the evidence must show that you are able to:	To achieve a merit grade the evidence must show that, in addition to the pass criteria, you are able to:	To achieve a distinction grade the evidence must show that, in addition to the pass and merit criteria, you are able to:
P3 demonstrate an awareness of stylistic qualities in dance performance **Assessment activity 4 page 223**	**M3** demonstrate the assured use of stylistic qualities in dance performance **Assessment activity 4 page 223**	**D3** demonstrate excellent use of stylistic qualities in dance performance **Assessment activity 4 page 223**
P4 review the main strengths and weaknesses of own performance **Assessment activity 5 page 224**	**M4** review strengths and weaknesses of own performance with some reasoning **Assessment activity 5 page 224**	**D4** review in detail the strengths and weaknesses of own performance with considered conclusions **Assessment activity 5 page 224**
P5 show improvements in performance as a result of rehearsal. **Assessment activity 4 page 223**	**M5** show improvements in performance as a result of commitment to rehearsal. **Assessment activity 4 page 223**	**D5** show significant improvements in performance as a result of commitment to rehearsal. **Assessment activity 4 page 223**

How you will be assessed

This project will be assessed by your tutor observing you in all classes and workshops. Some centres may invite other dance professionals to run workshops, and these guest tutors could feed back to your tutor on your progress during their workshop.

You will also be assessed through your own logbook that you should keep going all through the course. You must record the work you do in all the styles you work on, making sure you objectively evaluate what you are doing and say how you plan to improve your dancing. You can refer to any evidence you have of your work recorded on DVD or video.

The work you produce for assessment could include:

* tutor observations
* peer observations
* witness statements from visiting professionals
* DVD recordings of classes, workshops and rehearsals
* DVD recordings of performances
* your logbook.

Dance showcase

The scenario

For this project, the scenario is that you have been asked to perform in a showcase Festival of Dance to be produced by your centre and performed at the end of term.

Your work will not be primarily about learning new technique. The main focus will be on coming to class well prepared and ready for the work in hand, to learn and rehearse dances, review and evaluate your dancing to ensure that your work progresses and finally to perform your dances.

You may have already been working on your dance for a while, so will have taken class in, for instance, both contemporary and urban styles. You may also have been going to workshops in some other styles, such as South Asian dance. The festival is an opportunity for you to be assessed on part of three dance units. You can't gain all the possible marks for the three units, because the assignment is not long enough for that. This work will be a chance to consolidate some marks you have already gained in the studio and small performances you have been giving at the end of class, at dance club and so on.

Use your skills in urban dance in your showcase.

Dance festival timetable

The dance festival must be carefully planned to ensure that there is enough time to:

- select the dances
- choreograph the dances (this could be done by your tutors, by you and your tutors or you and other learners on your own)
- teach the dances
- practise the dances and re-work if necessary.

Your tutor will look after the timeline for the festival and guide you through the process. Once you are given the timeline make sure that you make a note of important dates – such as the first full rehearsal and the performance – as it is your responsibility to make sure that you follow the schedule and complete the necessary classes and rehearsals.

Planning your dances

The first few weeks of the festival timetable will focus on selecting the dances – one contemporary dance and one urban dance. Your tutor may invite you to make suggestions or you may be assigned a dance. Your tutor may choreograph the dances for you or you might be invited to choreograph a whole dance or some dance elements. Your urban dance classes could take very different forms due to the range of styles available. It could include hip hop, funk or break-dancing.

Did you know?

Your logbook should include:
- plans for what you are going to do in class, names of assignments, details of performances
- ongoing review and evaluation of your own progress
- areas to work on at home or in your own time in the studio
- peer review and comments
- objective self-reflection.

Health and safety

If you are working on break-dancing you must ensure that you are learning safely. There are moves that can be dangerous if they are not performed correctly. Examples include head spins and kneeling turns. Ask your tutor before you try a new move, especially when you are putting weight on a small part of your body, for example, your knees, head, elbow or hand.

Did you know?

Break-dancing is one of the most popular forms of urban dance. Look on YouTube for examples of experienced break-dancers. They will show you how to do a six step, a glide or many different turns.

 Assessment activity 1 Unit C10 (P3)(M3)(D3)(P4)(M4)(D4)
Unit C13 (P1)(M1)(D1)

Learning contemporary dance

You will work on contemporary dance with your tutor, learning movement phrases, sequences and dance pieces. To complete this assessment you will need to make sure that you attend all classes and rehearsals and that your attitude is always positive.

Evidence

Your logbook – Record all your sessions in your logbook. Note any problems or feedback and any improvements you or your tutor observes.

Tutor observations – These will also build up as part of your evidence for assessment.

Grading tips

Unit C10

(M3) You must master the key features of the contemporary style, particularly those that make this style different from any other, as you dance through movement phrases. These might include use of contraction or parallel leg positions. Make sure that you work hard to learn the choreography and dance it well.

(D3) Your use of the stylistic qualities will be clear to see; you will be able to reproduce movement phrases very accurately and confidently.

(M4) You will reproduce dance steps and moves accurately, moving at the correct pace, in the right rhythm, using the space that choreographer intended.

(D4) Your work will show that you fully understand the rhythm of the piece, have good spatial awareness and understand the dynamics of the material.

Unit C13

(M1) You must be disciplined in rehearsal. Take another look in Unit C13 page 98 for tips on approaching class with the right attitude and always make sure that you have the correct dancewear and shoes with you, if you need them.

(D1) High levels of commitment to class and rehearsals mean getting there on time, with the right equipment and props, and with steps learned and practised. You must take objective criticism well and then set targets for improving your own dancing.

Case study: Leroy's work schedule 1

Leroy is working towards a dance performance at his centre's Festival of Dance. These Worked Example boxes follow his progress, and linked activities will take you through the same processes.

Week 1	
Activity	Notes
Classes	Usual class in contemporary and urban dance.
	My two dances will be:
	Main contemporary piece called 'Pictures at an Exhibition'
	Urban dance piece called 'East Meets West'.
Kit	Make sure I turn up at class with all my dance kit clean and ready to go:
	Contemporary kit – leotard, tights, leg warmers/socks for warm-up. Hair tied back
	Urban kit – vest, jogging bottoms or leggings, trainers.
Aims and objectives	Go to class, learn warm-ups in both styles.
Week 2	
Ideas	Start to work on some dance combinations we learned with a visiting South Asian dance group. We are going to work on an urban sequence, using some of the moves we learned from this group. This will be a bit Bollywood, but with lots of urban dance steps and moves in it. I will be dancing in a B-Boy group.
Classes	Go to regular class.
	Urban dance – Work on a short combination using some key South Asian moves. This will mean doing some music research.
Research	**Music research** – Ask music students for some ideas, plus look up my notes from the South Asian company workshop. Review the DVD we made of us in the workshop to remind ourselves of what we did.

 BTEC **Assessment activity 2**   **Unit C11** P2 M2 D2 **Unit C13** P1 M1 D1

Key features of dance

Throughout the course of this project, you will be assessed on how well you have learnt the key features of the urban style you are dancing.

The assessment will take place either in the studio or during actual performances. Your tutor will observe you as you work.

Grading tips

Unit C11

M2 To achieve merit, you should perform the key features of the style, not forgetting to use, for example, gestures and head moves. Make sure you practice to try and perfect your dances.

D2 This is all about flair. Your work must be confident, showing a close attention to detail and communicating the dance ideas to whomever is watching you, in class or rehearsal or in performance.

Case study: Leroy's work schedule 2

Week 3	
Activity	Notes
Classes	We are working on the two different styles now so that means taking class that covers technique for both of them.
Dance activity	**Contemporary** – Start working on the main motif with our tutor. We are going to put that together with some work we created during this unit where we choreographed our own dances. This dance will be a large group piece, with short partner pieces during the work. **Urban** – Using some music we have found, work on our Bollywood/urban dance.
Research	I am going to work out some solo and duet pieces, as the B-Boys. I will be working in the studio with my dance buddy on some difficult break-dancing moves. My partner and I will be providing the B-Boy moves. Urban Dance learning objective 1.

 Assessment activity 3
Unit C10
Unit C11

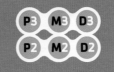

Urban dance and contemporary dance – Application of skills

To be successful you must demonstrate that you can apply physical and interpretive dance skills and show an awareness of stylistic qualities.

As you attend workshops, practices and rehearsals you must continue improving your work, adding to your own personal repertoire of steps and moves as you master different styles, and develop your movement vocabulary.

Evidence

Your logbook – Record all your sessions in your logbook. Note any problems or feedback and any improvements you or your tutor observes.

Tutor observations – These will also build up as part of your evidence for assessment.

Key term

Motif – a series of steps organised into a short sequence that can be developed into a longer and more complex dance.

Group rehearsals

Once the dances have been individually choreographed, rehearsed and developed it is time to put the pieces together and rehearse as a group with your tutor leading. Your tutor will decide and arrange the running order for the performance.

You will have spent a lot of time working on your dances, and this is your time to show how much you have learned and how much you have improved. It is essential that you arrive on time with all the kit you need.

Make sure you work hard in rehearsals to make your final performance as polished as possible.

Staging and blocking

If you are working on a major piece, you may need to use part of your rehearsal time to stage the dance. You will need to block out the moves to ensure that you can fit all of the steps into the space. You may need to modify your dance as a result of the staging, make sure you note any changes in your logbook.

Reviewing your progress so far

Your tutor or a member of your class may film the rehearsal to allow you to study your movements more closely and look for areas where you could improve. It is essential that you take this time to review your performance and watch the film with a critical eye. What comments would you make if the performer were a friend or a classmate rather than you? How would you help them to improve? As well as reviewing your own performance you must also be open to the suggestions of others in your class. Ensure that you record your review in your logbook. You may need to fill in an evaluation form detailing how you are planning to use the feedback you have gathered.

Further guidance on reviewing and evaluating dance routines can be found in Unit C13 Performing Dance.

Case study: Leroy's work schedule 3

Week 4	
Activity	Notes
Aims and objectives	Group will start to put ideas together.
	Tutor-led rehearsals begin, with all of us showing what we have learned.
	Tutor will tell us the running order.
First rehearsal	**Contemporary** – This is a major piece that needs to be staged. Block out the dance.
	Film the piece.
	Urban – Bring together the different sections. I am dancing in the main Bollywood/urban connecting dances, but also doing my duet work with the B-Boys crew.
	We show our B-Boys moves – they go down very well!
Evaluation & planning	Watch film of contemporary piece; assess response to B-Boy moves. Write up evaluations and plan my work for the next week

Individual dance workout

While you are rehearsing you can put together your own dance class to keep up your fitness levels, help your body strength and learn some new moves for yourself. This short class is simple and you should be able to do it every day. You can use it to warm-up before working on any steps and combinations you need for performance.

1. Find a space big enough to swing your legs and arms around, preferably with a mirror so you can see and correct faults.

2. Start with some roll downs. Standing straight, start the roll down from the top of your head and follow it all the way down through the spine until you have gone as far as you can. Relax your neck, shoulders and arms.

3. Stretch your arms, one by one, high into the air and to the side.

4. Sit on the floor with soles of feet together and bend your upper body forwards, over your legs and towards the floor. Hold for a count of five, release and repeat four times.

5. Do the same with legs stretched in front and wide apart.

6. Stretch legs in front, point and flex feet four times with feet parallel, then with feet turned out.

7. With legs wide apart, feet pointed and arms open to each side, reach one arm overhead and stretch up and then sideways over your head and down one leg, come back to centre, and repeat to the other side, four times each side.

8. In the same position, stretch forwards gently top of head towards the floor.

9. Repeat 7 and 8 with feet flexed.

10. Bring feet and legs together, arms by your sides, roll gradually back down so you are flat on the floor, then roll slowly up. Repeat four times, breathing out going down, breathing in when flat on the floor and out again when coming up. If this is too hard, bend knees with feet flat on the floor before you start. This helps you slowly build up enough strength in your centre until you can manage the full exercise.

11. Get up from the floor; do some bends of the legs, or pliés, with feet parallel and turned out, in first and second positions.

12. Stand up straight and do some leg and feet stretch and flex, tendus in ballet, to front side and back – arms wide, shoulders down.

13. Repeat the above, raising the legs higher.

14. First with feet parallel, jump with feet together, then feet apart. Then try the jumps with feet turned out. Remember to start and end with a bend, or plié, to prevent injury.

Always finish with a good stretch of all your muscles from head to toes. Once you have completed these work-out exercises, practise your steps and combinations.

Do this mini-class to music if it helps, and don't forget to ask your tutor for some help to design more work for your own class, such as exercises that fit in with what you are working on in class.

Remember

You may find it more motivating to rehearse with a dance buddy. You can encourage each other to find time for your individual dance workouts when you are feeling tired or would like to be doing something else!

Did you know?

Professional dancers take class every day.

Case study: Leroy's work schedule 4

Week 5	
Activity	Notes
Rehearsals	**Contemporary** – Whole group working on the main dance. This is long piece of dance choreographed and directed by our tutor. It is technically difficult and we have to keep trying our lifts and falls.
	Film the rehearsals so we can watch ourselves.
	Urban – Put the main motifs together with the B-Boy combinations.
Evaluation & planning	Watch films. Tutor to run feedback session so we can all evaluate each other and make some plans for the next rehearsals.
	Need to work on keeping up the energy levels in the urban piece as this is supposed to be very lively.
	Review logbook and rehearsal progress report.
	Group discussions about what costumes we will wear.

Assessment activity 4

| Unit C10 | P3 M3 D3 P4 M4 D4 |
| Unit C13 | P3 M3 D3 P5 M5 D5 |

From rehearsals to performances

You will be assessed as you move from rehearsals to performance. As your dancing improves, your tutor will give you opportunities for further assessments.

Evidence

Your logbook – Record all your sessions in your logbook. Note any problems or feedback and any improvements you or your tutor observes.

Tutor observations – These will also build up as part of your evidence for assessment.

Grading tips

Unit C13

M3 You must really try to develop a sense of the style you are dancing. For example, for hip-hop you will need to contrast your isolated moves with your smoother, more fluid steps.

D3 You must learn and reproduce all your dance combinations very accurately and with confidence. You should make sure you use the mirror objectively to watch yourself, at the same time as watching the tutor. Make sure you watch any DVDs made of your work, both in the studio and in rehearsal. This will allow you to see where you can further improve your performance.

M5 You must show commitment to your rehearsals, and consequently some improvement in your dancing.

D5 To achieve distinction, your improvements will be clear and obvious and have come from your genuine commitment to rehearsals throughout the project.

Case study: Leroy's work schedule 5

Week 6	
Activity	**Notes**
Dress and technical rehearsals	Rehearse dances onstage in costume. Final technical rehearsals with lighting and sound.
Performances	Whole company performances to our audience!

Remember

This whole assignment has involved work from three units, but there are opportunities here to undertake work that can be assessed for others as well. For instance, you could provide work for any of the other dance style units, such as Unit C12 Jazz Dance. Marks for this work can contribute to these units.

Think hard about how your performance could be improved.

PLTS

When evaluating your work you will show that you are a reflective learner.

Portfolio

As well as keeping your logbook you will have to work up a portfolio of written or recorded evidence. This will be combined for your assessment with observations made by your tutor or any visiting dance professionals. You will need to carry out a final evaluation of the performances after the festival. Find out what the audience thought of it if you can. You could record your evaluations on tape, on your centre's virtual learning environment, on your phone ready to download onto the centre VLE/workspace, or a blog if you find writing tricky. Make sure you keep a copy though. This could be the link to your centre's virtual learning environment, if there is one, or to the site where your work is stored.

Portfolios that achieve the highest marks are those where the learner has been thorough and totally objective about their progress. They will have noted down their ideas, thoughts and feelings throughout the course. They will have made realistic plans for the future.

BTEC Assessment activity 5
Unit C13   P4 M4 D4

Evaluating your work

It is important that throughout the course of your project you evaluate your work, looking at where you can make improvements. Your evaluations should be placed in your logbook.

Evidence

Your logbook – Record all your sessions in your logbook. Note any problems or feedback and any improvements you or your tutor observes.

Tutor observations – These will also build up as part of your evidence for assessment.

Grading tips

M4 You must review your work as you go along, showing why you think what you do and giving reasons for what you say. You should also be able to identify your strengths and weaknesses.

D4 Your review of your work must be detailed and specific, showing you understand how you might improve your dancing, perhaps through more practising of particular steps and moves. You should also set yourself realistic targets to improve your performances further.

Unit B8 Musical Theatre Performance

Unit C12 Jazz Dance

This project is all about showtime! It takes you through a major project preparing for a song and dance showcase. This project will give you opportunities to show off your strengths in dance and singing and will test you in the skills you already have.

Unit B8 Musical Theatre Performance asks you to work across all three disciplines of dance, drama and music performance but here you will be covering only the last two of these disciplines. You will have to develop work in acting to finish your assessments for Unit B8.

Unit C12 Jazz Dance asks you to develop skills in all the key features of the style, and to be able to demonstrate the relationship between many different kinds of music and jazz dance itself. It will not be possible to achieve all this in one show, but you will be able to work towards learning outcome 3, performing jazz dance.

Learning outcomes

After completing this project you should be able to achieve the following learning outcomes:

Unit B8 Musical Theatre Performance

2. Be able to use dance skills
3. Be able to use music performance skills

Unit 12 Jazz Dance

3. Be able to perform studies and combinations within the jazz style.

Assessment and grading criteria

This table shows you what you must to in order to achieve a pass, merit or distinction and where you can find activities in this book to help you.

To achieve a pass grade the evidence must show that you are able to:	To achieve a merit grade the evidence must show that, in addition to the pass criteria, you are able to:	To achieve a distinction grade the evidence must show that, in addition to the pass and merit criteria, you are able to:
Unit B8 Musical Theatre Performance		
P2 demonstrate dance skills with technical control **Assessment activity 1 page 230** **Assessment activity 3 page 232**	**M2** demonstrate dance skills in ways that show a good degree of technical control **Assessment activity 1 page 230** **Assessment activity 3 page 232**	**D2** demonstrate a strong technical command of dance skills **Assessment activity 1 page 230** **Assessment activity 3 page 232**
P3 demonstrate musical skills with technical control **Assessment activity 2 page 231** **Assessment activity 3 page 232**	**M3** demonstrate musical skills in ways that show a good degree of technical control **Assessment activity 2 page 231** **Assessment activity 3 page 232**	**D3** demonstrate a strong technical command of musical skills **Assessment activity 2 page 231** **Assessment activity 3 page 232**
P4 communicate a simple interpretation in performance through the application and combination of musical theatre skills **Assessment activity 3 page 232**	**M4** *(communicate intentions in performance with attention to detail and success in the consistent application of skills across the three disciplines)*	**D4** *(communicate intentions in performance clearly and effectively through the imaginative and consistent application of skills across the three disciplines)*
P5 review the main strengths and weaknesses of performance work. **Assessment activity 4 page 232**	**M5** review strengths and weaknesses of performance work with some reasoning. **Assessment activity 4 page 232**	**D5** review in detail the effectiveness of performance work with considered conclusions. **Assessment activity 4 page 232**
Unit C12 Jazz Dance		
P3 recall and reproduce learned dance combinations using jazz techniques in performance **Assessment activity 1 page 230** **Assessment activity 3 page 232**	**M3** recall and demonstrate a variety of jazz dance combinations, using dynamics, projection and focus in performance **Assessment activity 1 page 230** **Assessment activity 3 page 232**	**D3** accurately recall and demonstrate jazz dance combinations, to a high technical standard, using dynamics, projection and focus in performance **Assessment activity 1 page 230** **Assessment activity 3 page 232**

How you will be assessed

This project will be assessed by your tutor observing you in all classes and workshops. Some centres may invite other dance professionals to run workshops, and they feed back to your tutor on your progress during their workshop. You will also be assessed through your own logbook that you should keep going all through the course. You must record the work you do in all the styles you work on, making sure you objectively evaluate what you are doing and say how you plan to improve your dancing. You can refer to any evidence you have of your work recorded on DVD or video.

The work you produce for assessment could include:
- tutor observations
- peer observations
- witness statements from visiting professionals
- DVD recordings of classes, workshops and rehearsals
- DVD recordings of performances
- your logbook including reviews and evaluations of both rehearsals and performances.

Kiran, professional dancer

I started dancing when I was eight. I got into classes because my older sister used to take me to watch her when I was younger. I took classes in ballet, tap and modern jazz dancing and passed my grade exams.

When I was 16 I wanted to go to stage school, but instead I took BTEC Dance at my local college. I thought the course was great. We had regular classes every day in lots of different styles and I was in loads of shows. After college I took a short course at the Laban Centre in London and then began going to auditions. My first job was as a dancer in a music video – the record didn't sell and I'm not sure if anyone even saw me dancing! Since then I have had quite a few jobs like that and I'm now dancing in a show in London's West End – mainly jazz dancing. It's exhausting, but I love it.

Dance showcase

The scenario

For this project, the scenario is that you have been asked to prepare for a song and dance musical show produced by your centre. You will have half a term to prepare your numbers for the show, which will be made up of short pieces performed by the whole group, small groups or as solos. The audience will be your friends and parents as this will be a celebration of the achievements of the musical theatre department.

As Unit B8 Musical Theatre Performance asks you to work across all three disciplines of dance, drama and musical performance, you will not be able to gain all possible marks for this unit. Your acting skills will need to be assessed in a different project. Likewise, for Unit C12 Jazz Dance you will be unable to fulfil learning outcomes 1 and 2, as you will probably be dancing to a limited range of accompaniment. You will be able to demonstrate the relationship between different kinds of music and jazz dance itself, and develop skills in all the key features of the style in a different project.

Song and dance show timetable

There will be a strict timetable of classes and rehearsals so that everybody is ready to perform in time. Your department will work out the timetable, and this will follow the procedure of a professional company. In commercial theatre or variety shows, a professional producer or a production company will decide which members of their company they would like to see performing in which acts. The producers in this case will be the department at your centre. You will be asked to bring along your own ideas for your songs and dances based on what you have learned in workshops over the year. The timetable will be planned carefully to allow time to:

- select the songs and dances
- choreograph the dances (this could be done by your tutors, by you and your tutors or you and other learners on your own)
- teach the songs and dances
- rehearse the songs and dances
- review and evaluate the songs and dances, reworking them if necessary.

Did you know?

The timing of the jazz dance is very tricky and requires rhythmic accuracy. There are jazz walks, jumps and rolls, plus some opposing rhythms.

Key terms

Rhythmic accuracy – dancing closely to the required count, either of the music or just of the dance itself. Dancers usually count in phrases of 8 beats for music with a 4/4 time signature.

Opposing rhythms – dancing across the rhythm of the music, or another dancer.

Jazz walks – funky danced walks, usually led from the hips, with knees bent, sometimes with turns and jumps.

Rolls – danced rolls on the floor or in the air, incorporating a jump, e.g. a barrel roll where the torso is thrown over.

Choosing your pieces

Every learner must decide, with guidance from their tutor, what they want to perform in the showcase. What you choose must:

- be realistic

- show what you are capable of

- extend your own skills and understanding.

Practical evidence

The majority of the evidence for any showcase will be in the form of the performance itself. However, you will also be assessed by your tutor in class so it's important to be absolutely focused in all your studio sessions. You should also keep a record of the following in your logbook:

- plans for what you are going to do in class, names of assignments, details of performances

- reviews and evaluations of your own progress

- areas to work on at home or in your own time in the studio, so that your technique goes on improving throughout the project

- what you thought when you saw yourself on DVD – be objective

- what your peers thought if they saw your performance. Ask what they think, share ideas and record their responses in your logbook

- what the audience thought of your performance, if possible.

If you find writing difficult, you could record your evaluations on tape or DVD, in a blog or on your phone. Always ensure you keep a copy, though, this could be linked to your centre's virtual learning environment, to the website where your work is stored, or on your own computer or MP3 player.

Remember

If you have the chance to work with a visiting professional, make sure you ask questions and find out what it's really like out there in the professional world. Why not find out about their individual training route, how they got into the performing arts business in the first place and their career path to date?

Keep focused in all rehearsals and the performance.

Case study: Asta and Darshan's work schedule 1

Asta and Darshan are working towards a dance performance at their centre's end-of-term show. These Worked Example boxes follow their progress, and linked activities will take you through the same processes.

Week 1	**Dancing** – Usual Jazz Dance class. General warm-ups taught by students. Darshan leads a street jazz warm-up that includes loads of isolation exercises to help with the style.
	Singing – Asta leads the vocal warm-up in class with help from the tutor on the piano. Run through of one of the group numbers: 'Radio Gaga', by Queen.
	Discussion session – Try to decide what to perform.
	Asta chooses 'Memories' from the show *Cats* by Andrew Lloyd Webber as her solo number.
	Darshan will perform in a Stomp dance as well as sing in the finale.

Case study: Asta and Darshan's work schedule 2

Week 2	**Dancing** – Whole group starts to work on some dance combinations learned with a visiting dancer. He taught the group to work with loads of props for percussion, such as dustbin lids, drumsticks, wood, plastic bins, etc. Re-visit some of the steps and moves, work on short solos and put the pieces together. **Singing** – Go to regular class. Whole group works on a finale number with tutor. Soloists work on their number. Asta is keeping up her logbook, with details of the singing practice she is doing in her own time.
Week 3	**Dancing** – Darshan and the group working on Cats dance get together to rehearse this jazz piece. This is a prepared dance, choreographed by the tutor, performed to the show's intro music. Asta working on her own numbers.

Assessment activity 1 Unit B8 Unit C12

Learn two of the jazz dance combinations your tutor is using for the showcase, rehearse them and perform to the group.

Evidence

Your logbook – Include any reviews and evaluations on your performance in your logbook.

Grading Tips

Unit B8

M2 You should show technical control, being able to hold a balance, hold your extension up in your legs and arms and turn accurately. You must not make mistakes. Watch any DVDs made of your work, in both studio and rehearsal so you can check your work and plan how to improve.

D2 This is the level where your technical ability will be measured. To achieve distinction, this must be high. Practise very hard in the chosen style so that you are completely accurate. You must be totally confident with your material and in performance itself. You must know your cues and never be late for them. You will get there through dedicated practice and rehearsal.

Unit C12

M3 Just learning the dance and performing it will not be enough. You must demonstrate the jazz dance style, perform dynamically and project the dance to whoever is watching you. Don't look at the ground; use your focus to drive your dance towards your audience. Make sure you use the mirror in the studio to watch yourself and the rest of the dancers and performers to help you perfect your studies and combinations.

D3 To achieve distinction, every part of the dance must be accurate and focused in performance. Your technical ability is vital. You must show a high level of technical accuracy in your dancing, dance dynamically and project your work towards your audience. Ask your dance partners to watch you and give you notes to help you improve.

**Assessment activity 2
Unit B8**

Learn one of your songs and rehearse it ready for a mini-performance to the group. Record your thoughts on your performance.
Think about how much you have improved already and how you can continue to improve further and note it in your logbook.

Evidence

Your logbook – Any reviews and evaluations on your performance should be included in your logbook.

PLTS

By using your logbook to include reviews and evaluations of your performances in you will show your skills as a **reflective learner**.

Functional skills

You will use your **English** writing skills when including reviews and evaluations of your performance in your logbook.

Case study: Asta and Darshan's work schedule 3

Week 4	**Whole group reviews and evaluations** – Learners give a review of own work to tutor and rest of group. Each has a five-minute slot to deliver a short talk, presentation or evaluative talk about their work on the project so far. **Asta** – gives a short talk about her preparations for her solo number. She explains to the group about how her voice is coping with the demands of the song, illustrating with some sung phrases. Her presentation is filmed by Darshan. **Darshan** – takes the group through some of the work he has developed for the Stomp piece. He gets the group to join in, using anything they can lay their hands on. This review goes down very well. Asta films it.
Week 5	**Rehearsals** – Group do a run through to check timings. **Costume decisions:** Cats number will have black leotards and leggings. The Stomp dance group will wear baggy trousers, T-shirts and lace-up boots. 'Radio Gaga' will be performed in whatever the group have on for their final piece.
Week 6	**Rehearsals** – Whole group identifies own personal strengths and weaknesses. All groups rehearse on stage to block out entrances and exits. **Technical rehearsals** – Sound and lighting
Week 7	Final rehearsals for all captured on DVD so everyone can review their contributions. Group notes given by tutor and plans made for final polishing in own time. Performances. Final evaluations written up and handed in.

Remember

Rehearsals are a key part of developing as a performer through watching yourself, getting feedback, setting realistic targets and making plans. Ensure you make the most of them – use the objective criticism your tutor gives you to improve your performance.

PLTS

When you evaluate your work you use your skills as a **reflective learner**.

Remember

Skill and accuracy are very important for gaining a good grade. Unfortunately, if you cannot dance steps accurately and in time, or sing a tune, it will be hard to achieve high marks in either unit. BTEC is all about reaching a national standard of work that is set for the whole examination. This is exactly how the professional world works as well. It is tough being a professional singer or dancer.

BTEC
Assessment activity 3
Unit B8
Unit C12

Your final performance must genuinely communicate with the audience. You must consider how you are going to reach the audience through the way you deliver your songs and dances.

Evidence

A DVD recording of the performance.

Grading Tips

Unit B8

(M2) You must hit all your notes, be in time and on cue throughout the performance. Watch any DVDs made of your work, in both studio and rehearsal so you can check your work and plan how to improve.

(D2) Be absolutely in tune and sing the work showing you have mastered the technicalities of both the piece and the style. Your work must be almost faultless. Be totally confident with your material and in performance itself and make sure you know your cues.

BTEC
Assessment activity 4
Unit B8

Make evaluations of your performance after all rehearsals to help you understand the main strengths and weaknesses in your performance and how your work is improving as a result.

Evidence

Your logbook – Your evaluation could be written or recorded on tape, your phone or DVD. Refer to any feedback from your tutor or visiting professionals in your evaluation.

Grading Tips

(M5) Review your work and think about where your strengths and weaknesses lie, then say how you can do better.

(D5) Make sure your reviews are thorough and your conclusions about how you can improve are clear. You then need to demonstrate that your work has improved.

Project 4 Children's Show

Unit B6 Devising Plays

Unit B9 Developing Physical Theatre Performance

Unit D20 Mask Making

In this project you will devise and develop a show for younger children. You will develop physical theatre skills through your responses to a stimulus, create masks that you can use in your physical theatre performance and develop and perform a role through devised dance drama work that you communicate to the audience.

These units all require that you take part in more than one performance or task, so you will not gain all the marks you need for each of the learning outcomes, but this project will contribute to them.

Learning outcomes

After completing this project you should be able to achieve the following learning outcomes:

Unit B6 Devising Plays

3. Be able to communicate ideas, issues and/or feelings through presentation of devised work.

Unit B9 Developing Physical Theatre Performance

1. Be able to develop physical theatre skills
2. Be able to rehearse physical theatre for a performance
3. Be able to perform a physical theatre role.

Unit D20 Mask Making

3. Be able to make a mask for a performance or demonstration

Assessment and grading criteria

This table shows you what you must to in order to achieve a pass, merit or distinction and where you can find activities in this book to help you.

To achieve a pass grade the evidence must show that you are able to:	To achieve a merit grade the evidence must show that, in addition to the pass criteria, you are able to:	To achieve a distinction grade the evidence must show that, in addition to the pass and merit criteria, you are able to:
Unit B6 Devising Plays		
P4 perform a role with vocal and physical expression connecting with other performers most of the time **Assessment activity 4 page 242**	**M4** perform a role with vocal and physical accuracy connecting with other performers throughout **Assessment activity 4 page 242**	**D4** perform a role with vocal and physical imagination being responsive to other performers at all times **Assessment activity 4 page 242**
P5 communicate intentions to the audience with some success **Assessment activity 4 page 242**	**M5** communicate intentions to an audience effectively **Assessment activity 4 page 242**	**D5** communicate intentions to an audience with clarity **Assessment activity 4 page 242**
Unit B9 Developing Physical Theatre Performance		
P1 demonstrate physical theatre skills in workshops and performance **Assessment activity 1 page 238**	**M1** competently demonstrate physical theatre skills in workshops and performance **Assessment activity 1 page 238**	**D1** imaginatively demonstrate physical theatre skills in workshops and performance **Assessment activity 1 page 238**
P2 use physical theatre skills to develop a role for performance **Assessment activity 3 page 241**	**M2** use appropriate physical theatre skills to explore stimulus materials and develop a role for performance **Assessment activity 3 page 241**	**D2** use appropriate physical theatre skills to imaginatively explore stimulus materials and develop a role for performance **Assessment activity 3 page 241**
P3 perform a role using physical theatre skills **Assessment activity 4 page 242**	**M3** competently perform a role that explores the stimulus material or idea, using physical theatre skills **Assessment activity 4 page 242**	**D3** perform an imaginative and coherent role using physical theatre skills that fully exploits the stimulus material or idea **Assessment activity 4 page 242**
Unit D20 Mask Making		
P3 use techniques, materials and processes to design and make a mask for a performance or demonstration **Assessment activity 2 page 240**	**M3** use suitable techniques, materials and processes to design and make a creative mask that is suitable for use in a performance **Assessment activity 2 page 240**	**D3** show considered and skilled application of techniques, materials and processes to design and make an imaginative and effective mask for a performance **Assessment activity 2 page 240**

How you will be assessed

This project will be assessed by your tutor observing you in all classes and workshops, as well as through your performance. Some centres may invite other professionals to run workshops, and they could feed back to your tutor on your progress during their workshop.

There will also be your practical approaches to the design and making of your mask. Your work must be organised, safe and well carried out. You should also keep a logbook, recording all the decisions made and any evaluations carried out.

The work you produce for assessment could include:

- tutor observation statements
- peer observations
- witness statements from visiting professionals
- DVD recordings of classes, workshops and rehearsals
- DVD recordings of performances
- your logbook
- audience feedback.

Orla, 17, taking part in physical theatre workshops

I love physical theatre because there are no rules for how you can do things. I am a wheelchair-bound learner and it has been great to make physical theatre one of my units. I knew this would be hard but our tutor took us to see Candoco, a contemporary dance company of mixed able-bodied and disabled dancers. These performers gave me the confidence to realise that I had a lot to offer as well as a lot to learn. Also by taking BTEC Performing Arts I needn't be afraid of moving and taking risks, just like these amazing dancers.

I am going to be in the ensemble for this performance, which means I am part of the group who will play all the animals, create all the scenes and all the action.

Should be exciting!

Children's show

The scenario

This project provides you with the opportunity to create and perform a mask dance-drama in the physical theatre style to a young audience. The performance will form part of a children's show.

The project will be made up of a series of workshops where you will learn to explore the possibilities of physical theatre as a way of creating a dance drama. You will devise a role or roles for yourself and then develop them. This will result in a performance of a piece of narrative mask work, specially created to suit the young audience.

Your project might follow the schedule below:

1. Decide on a story to use as a basis for the show. This may be decided by your tutor, or you may be able to choose it for yourselves.

2. Learn and rehearse roles and scenes.

3. Design and make a mask.

4. Review and evaluate your dance-drama as you go on with rehearsals, and your work progresses towards performance.

5. Perform your dance-drama to an audience.

Practical evidence

Much of the work for this assignment will be produced in the workshop in the form of practical physical theatre and devising. To be successful it is vital that you stay focused in all your studio sessions. This is particularly important where you are working on physical theatre as it can involve moves, such as lifts and falls and carrying and taking weight, that can be dangerous if not carried out properly and safely.

In your logbook you could include the following:

- Plans for what you are going to do in class, names of assignments, details of performances.

- Ongoing reviews and evaluation of your own progress, including what you thought when you saw yourself on DVD – be objective.

- Any work you do at home. Remember that physical performers must stay active. See Project 2 Dance Festival for details of a mini workout you can do at home.

- Records of your design and progress on your mask.

- A final evaluation of the performance. If possible, this should include what the audience thought of it. You could record your evaluations if you find writing tricky; use your phone, tape recorder or DVD, but remember to keep a copy or a record of where you can find it.

Key terms

Physical theatre – uses movement as a way of expressing the story, the place or the characters; can have dialogue or not.

Mask drama – where all or some of the performers wear masks. This might be to create a particular character.

Narrative drama – tells a story.

Dance-drama – combines dance and drama together, such as a dance with speech, or a drama with movement.

Portfolios of evidence that achieve the highest marks are those where the learner has been thorough and totally objective about their progress. They will have noted down their ideas, designs, thoughts and feelings throughout the course. They will have made realistic plans for future improvements and often related what they have seen performed by others, on stage or in the studio, to their own work.

Case study: Orla's project 1

What's the story?

Orla's group is a mixed ensemble of able-bodied and disabled learners – two use a wheelchair. They have decided to use the story, 'How the Elephant got his Trunk', based on one of the *Just So Stories* by Rudyard Kipling, for their work.

The story can be broken down in the following way:

- Introduction – the elephant has no trunk.
- Elephant spreads rumours about his friends.
- Friends get angry at the elephant and set a trap.
- Elephant gets caught in the alligator trap and his friends have to free him.
- Result is a big stretched nose, called a trunk.
- Conclusion – from that day the on stretch marks are still visible.

Able-bodied and disabled learners can achieve in exactly the same way.

237

Activity: Choosing your story

Once you have chosen your story, read it carefully and break it down into its simplest plot elements, like Orla's group did with 'How the Elephant got his Trunk'.

Make a list of all the characters in the story and start thinking about how they might move and talk.

Keep copies of the story, your plot breakdown and character list in your logbook.

Functional skills

You will use your writing skills when listing the characters in your story.

Case study: Orla's project 2

Week 1	Whole group discussion about the show. Company warm-up. A mix of dance and drama activities including stretches, noises, animal shapes, still pictures.
Week 2	Whole company working on animal shapes, the way animals move. Mask workshop using college masks; visual impact on audience.

Assessment activity 1 Unit B9

Animating characters

When your story has been chosen, take part in classes to investigate how your characters move. Your tutor will assess you in this skill, so make sure you concentrate throughout the class.

Evidence

Your logbook – Record the sessions and any feedback from your tutor or other learners in your logbook. Include your plans to improve based on this feedback.

Grading Tips

M1 This unit does not ask for any written assignments, but you may have to provide written evaluations of how you are getting on. You can use drawings and sketches to help you show complicated moves and shapes. You must show off your physical theatre skills in both the workshop and in performance.

D1 To reach high marks you must be bold, take sensible risks, use your imagination and push yourself. The better you treat every opportunity to show off your physical skills, the higher your marks will be. To gain top marks, you must be imaginative.

Case study: Orla's workshop

Orla and Kasey taught a session on the shapes of animals. Working in pairs, they got the group to create some shapes for an elephant, then morph it into the crocodile. The pairs went on to create a dialogue between the two animals.

They then improvised a scene where the elephant is eavesdropping on the crocodile, who snaps down on his nose, trapping him.

The whole point was to make the movements really large and the sounds of the animals very loud and raucous.

The workshop gave the group some good ideas for the ensemble piece.

Remember

Health and safety points to note while making your mask.

- Be careful with the Vaseline, avoid your eyes.
- Lie down in a safe place.
- Take care with scissors when cutting the bandage.
- Wait until the PVA glue is dry before trying on your mask.

Activity: Creating a short scene

Working in pairs, use the story you are using for your project to create a short improvised scene. Make sure you use large movements – remember, if you wear a mask the audience will not be able to see your face, so what you do with your body is all the more important.

Ask your class for feedback and record in your logbook any changes you could make to improve your work.

Did you know?

Modroc masks work well with added ears and noses; you can also paint them in loud colours to blend in with the rest of the company.

Case study: Orla's project 3

| Week 3 | Group presentations and workshops. |
| | Start designing masks for the animal characters. |

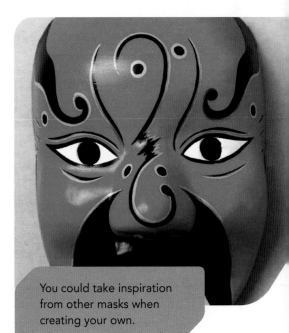

You could take inspiration from other masks when creating your own.

BTEC **Assessment activity 2** **Unit D20** P3 M3 D3

Making a mask

In class, design and make the mask for your performance. There are lots of ways of making masks: using folded card, papier mâché, decorating a bought plastic one. However, one way of doing this yourself is by using modroc, a very cheap modelling material consisting of bandage impregnated with plaster that can be easily moulded once dampened. This is a messy business but results can be amazing.

In pairs, get a partner to cover their face with Vaseline, lie down on the floor in a safe place and close their eyes. The second person then makes the mask using the following method.

1. Cut strips of Modroc bandage, 5cm by 2.5cm. Dampened them with warm water when they are ready to be used.

2. Build up layers over the face with the dampened strips until the mask is about 2–3 strips thick. Make sure breathing holes are made and leave the mask to dry on the face for a short while.

3. When it is dried sufficiently to become rigid, remove carefully and leave to dry thoroughly.

4. Once completely dry, start to build up features as required by the design you have made. You can build up features using tissue, cotton wool and more plaster; remember to make two holes at the sides so you can attach the mask around your head with elastic – this will be a personal mask made to fit the performer's own face.

5. Decorate or paint the mask as desired to suit the design.

6. Leave to dry, then paint over the whole mask, inside and out, with PVA glue to seal the surfaces and prevent damage or powdering of the plaster as it is worn.

7. Add two pieces of elastic to the holes on the sides to fit around the wearer's head.

8. Find a dark coloured balaclava or woollen beanie hat to wear while in the mask – this hides the hair and ears.

Grading tips

M3 You will have to keep records of your design ideas, how you make sure you are working safely, and how you ensure your mask works for the job in hand. When making your mask make sure it really fits you well and creates an idea of the character you are playing. The mask must be durable and able to withstand the rigours of performance.

D3 Use your imagination when creating your mask for your character or role. The mask must be fully up to the job of expressing your role or character in performance.

Case study: Orla's project 4

Week 4	The group works through each scene, trying to create movements and shapes for the whole of the story, while improvising lines from the story.
	The performance will feature different levels, and lifts and balances. Whole group workshop on lifts and balances, with particular attention to how to involve the wheelchair-bound learners in the balances.
	Voice and sound workshop.
	Role development, communication of character to audience.

Assessment activity 3

Unit B9

Developing your role

You are going to develop a role for your performance. You will be marked on how well you explore the material, the story, and create your work for performance. The more bold and imaginative you are with trying out and developing new ideas, the better will be your marks.

Grading tips

M2 As you explore your stimulus, in this case the story, you will learn and use particular skills.

D2 Use your imagination to make these skills work for you, for example, by trying your work out at different levels of tension, sometimes very tense, then very relaxed. See which works best. This way you will find the most effective way to play your role.

Case study: Orla's project 5

Week 5	Run-through.
Week 6	Masks ready.
	Start to develop final ideas for the characters in masks, such as ticks and individual expressions created through head movements.
	Group run-through.
Week 7	Rehearsals and visit venue.
Week 8	Performance.

Make the most of your mask during performances.

PLTS

You will need to be a **creative thinker** in order to develop you role fully.

Remember

When making performance works for young children always remember that they like to be involved. Try to think ways to engage them. Don't be afraid to make contact with your audience, directly if the script calls for it.

BTEC **Assessment activity 4**
Unit B6 P4 M4 D4 P5 M5 D5
Unit B9 P3 M3 D3

The final performance

While you may achieve some marks for small workshop performances, it will be the final performance that gives you your assessed mark. You should make sure that you show how much you have learned through the course of the project, and make sure that your performance shows imagination.

Functional skills

Your performance is very likely to need you to use your **English** speaking skills.

PLTS

The performance will require that you show that you are a **team worker** and an **effective participator**.

Remember

Note that for Unit B6, this is one of the two performances you will be taking part in.

Evidence

You are being assessed on how well you communicate your work through the performance. You may also be asked to make a record of how well you think it has gone; you could record this and keep a sound file on your college's VLE or on your computer, if you find writing difficult.

Tutor observations and audience feedback are other sources of evidence you can use.

Grading Tips

Unit B6

- **M4** You are not performing in the piece alone. You must connect with the other performers as well as your audience.

- **D4** Your work must be physically accurate – the more accurate it is, the better will be your marks.

- **M5** You must communicate all your intentions to the audience so this a focus of your final rehearsals.

- **D5** The audience must see and hear very clearly what you are trying to put across, so make sure you really understand what it is and try hard to make the meaning reach them.

Unit B9

- **M3** Your role must fit in with everything else that is happening on stage. For example, when you are in a chorus, make sure your work is positioned properly.

- **D3** Your assessor will be looking for performances that are coherent with the group, highly focused and absolutely in tune with the ensemble.

Project 5 Setting the Scene

Unit D17 Design for Performance

Unit D21 Set Construction

Everything that the audience can see and hear on stage has been selected or created by a designer. This involves the designer working to develop and agree the design ideas with the director, then relying on a team of skilled workers to create the set, costumes and props or to rig and operate the lighting and sound.

This project provides information and activities to guide you on what you can expect to do when you are assessed on your design skills in your research, design planning, design realisation and reviewing of your work.

Learning outcomes

After completing this project you should be able to achieve the following learning outcomes:

Unit D17 Design for Performance

1. Know the characteristics of performance environments
2. Be able to implement design production skills
3. Be able to realise design ideas
4. Understand own production work.

Unit D21 Set Construction

1. Know the use of set construction tools and materials
2. Know the set construction process
3. Be able to plan and construct a scenic element
4. Be able to demonstrate safe working practices throughout the set construction process.

Assessment and grading criteria

This table shows you what you must to in order to achieve a pass, merit or distinction and where you can find activities in this book to help you.

To achieve a pass grade the evidence must show that you are able to:	To achieve a merit grade the evidence must show that, in addition to the pass criteria, you are able to:	To achieve a distinction grade the evidence must show that, in addition to the pass and merit criteria, you are able to:
Unit D17 Design for Performance		
P1 describe characteristics of performance environments **Assessment activity 1 page 246**	**M1** discuss the key characteristics of performance environments **Assessment activity 1 page 246**	**D1** explain the main characteristics of performance environments **Assessment activity 1 page 246**
P2 demonstrate design production skills, materials and processes **Assessment activity 2 page 248**	**M2** demonstrate appropriate design production skills, materials and processes **Assessment activity 2 page 248**	**D2** demonstrate a high level of competence when using key design production skills, materials and processes **Assessment activity 2 page 248**
P3 use production skills, materials and processes to realise design ideas **Assessment activity 3 page 253**	**M3** realise the key design intentions through the selection and use of suitable production skills, materials and processes **Assessment activity 3 page 253**	**D3** effectively realise design ideas through the competent selection and use of appropriate production skills, materials and processes **Assessment activity 3 page 253**
P4 explain own design production work. **Assessment activity 2 page 248** **Assessment activity 3 page 253**	**M4** explain own design production work using some accurate terminology and showing some awareness of the designer's roles and responsibilities. **Assessment activity 2 page 248** **Assessment activity 3 page 253**	**D4** explain own design production work comprehensively and in detail, using accurate terminology. **Assessment activity 2 page 248** **Assessment activity 3 page 253**
Unit D21 Set Construction		
P1 identify set construction tools and their uses **Assessment activity 2 page 248**	**M1** describe set construction tools and their uses **Assessment activity 2 page 248**	**D1** explain the use of set construction tools and uses **Assessment activity 2 page 248**
P2 identify set construction materials and their uses **Assessment activity 2 page 248**	**M2** describe the main set construction materials and their uses **Assessment activity 2 page 248**	**D2** explain a wide range of set construction materials and uses **Assessment activity 2 page 248**

To achieve a pass grade the evidence must show that you are able to:	To achieve a merit grade the evidence must show that, in addition to the pass criteria, you are able to:	To achieve a distinction grade the evidence must show that, in addition to the pass and merit criteria, you are able to:
P3 carry out the set construction planning process competently, with support and guidance **Assessment activity 2 page 248** **Assessment activity 3 page 253**	**M3** carry out the set construction planning process successfully, with little support and guidance **Assessment activity 2 page 248** **Assessment activity 3 page 253**	**D3** carry out the set construction planning process effectively and independently **Assessment activity 2 page 248** **Assessment activity 3 page 253**
P4 demonstrate basic set construction skills in completing the scenic element **Assessment activity 2 page 248** **Assessment activity 3 page 253**	**M4** demonstrate a capable use of most of the set construction skills, making a competent scenic element **Assessment activity 2 page 248** **Assessment activity 3 page 253**	**D4** demonstrate a fully effective application of a wide range of set construction skills, making a well-made scenic element **Assessment activity 2 page 248** **Assessment activity 3 page 253**
P5 apply basic safe working practices throughout the set construction process. **Assessment activity 2 page 248** **Assessment activity 3 page 253**	**M5** apply safe working practices throughout the set construction process. **Assessment activity 2 page 248** **Assessment activity 3 page 253**	**D5** apply well-developed safe working practices throughout the set construction process consistently. **Assessment activity 2 page 248** **Assessment activity 3 page 253**

How you will be assessed

This project will be assessed by an internal assignment that will be designed and marked by the tutors at your centre. You will be assessed on your practical work, which will demonstrate your level of skill, as well as your descriptions, reflections and evaluations in your logbook.

The work you produce for assessment could include:

- tutor observation statements
- peer observations
- DVD recordings of classes, workshops and setting up for performances
- DVD recordings of performances
- your logbook of designs, notes, photographs, sketches and descriptions, etc.

Setting the scene

Set, prop, costume, lighting and sound design require specific skills. You will have the opportunity to learn and practise these skills in the classroom before you begin to apply them as you work towards a production. You may not be able to explore all design production skills; your tutor will guide you towards the skills that you need to complete Unit D17 Design for Performance. Set construction skills learned in Unit D21 are integral to the production of a scenic element.

Telling the whole story

Putting on a successful production requires creative and practical skills; everything that appears on stage helps to explain the production's intentions to the audience. The costume designer will think about what clues the actor's costumes will give the audience about their character and status. The set and props designers will help the audience to understand the location and context of the performance. The use of abstract colour and shape may be used to produce a more abstract design and gives clues about the themes of the performance. The set designer will also consider how the actors will use the set. The sound designer will choose music and sound effects. The lighting designer will work closely with the set and costume designers to choose appropriate colours, lanterns and lighting effects for the performance.

PLTS

Use your research findings to compile your response to this assignment shows that you are developing skills as an **independent enquirer**.

Successfully working together in groups or pairs shows you are a **team worker**.

Key terms

Performance venues – proscenium arch, traverse, in the round, promenade, thrust. Make sure that you use the correct terminology as described in Unit D16 Crewing for Stage Performance.

Performance genres – dance, physical theatre, plays, musicals, variety, gigs, talent shows, fashion shows.

 BTEC **Assessment activity 1** **Unit D17**

Developing understanding of design for perfomance

Investigate the characteristics of different performances spaces, Make sure you can identify the design requirements of different performance genres.

You may carry out your research in pairs or small groups. However, it is important that you produce your own individual response to the research. Most large repertory theatres have education officers who will be able to help you with your research. There is a wealth of valuable information online including theatre and museum websites. A visit to your local theatre will also be beneficial.

Evidence

Your logbook – You could include notes, diagrams of different performance space, annotated photographs and tables that describe the characteristices of different performance venues and research examples of design approaches for different performance genres.

Grading Tips

M1 Describe each performance venue in some detail, ensuring that you show you have a good understanding of the key design elements used to create a performance space.

D1 Each description of the performance venues should be fully detailed and your understanding of design elements should be accurately detailed.

The performance space

You need to recognise how each different performance space is equipped and organised. Consider how this affects:

- interaction between performers and audience

- design opportunities and limitations

- design of the space for different performance genres.

Activity: Choosing a venue

You have been given the job of choosing which venue would be most appropriate for a forthcoming production of the pantomime *Cinderella*.

1. From your knowledge of traditional pantomimes and any additional research, identify the design requirements for lighting, sound, props, set and costume for such a performance.

2. From your research select a venue in which you propose to stage the pantomime.

3. Explain the reasons for your choice, making sure that you use the correct terminology throughout.

   Make sure that your explanation includes:

   - an annotated picture and or diagram of the venue

   - a list of your research findings

   - an explanation of the design requirements for pantomime that includes a reference to the different performance genres included in the performance.

Did you know?

Design for performance began with Greek theatre. Theatre design has an interesting history that is worth investigating; some stage terminology is thousands of years old.

Design and production skills

Designers need to have both creative and practical skills. In their job they have to be able to come up with new and exciting, but appropriate design ideas and then have the practical and management skills to make it all happen. This process is 95 per cent hard work – that is the planning, researching and making – and five per cent magic: that is the moment when it all comes together on stage and your design vision is realised.

BTEC Assessment activity 2
Unit D17
Unit D21

Developing design production skills

In class, you will take part in a series of practical workshops to learn, develop and apply practical design construction materials and skills. Keep an account of the skills that you learn and all relevant health and safety considerations. Demonstrate an understanding of how these skills are used in the industry.

Evidence

Your logbook – Keep a record of all the materials and tools you have used, the skills and processes you have learned and the health and safety rules for the use of the materials, methods and processes.

Grading Tips

Unit D17

M2 Use relevant skills, techniques and materials to develop your design ideas. Realise the key design intentions through the selection and use of suitable production skills, materials and processes.

D2 Competently use production skills, materials and processes in your practical design work as you complete your design responsibilities. Effectively realise design ideas through the competent selection and use of appropriate production skills, materials and processes.

M4 Explain your own design production work using some accurate terminology. Your explanation will show that you understand the materials, processes and skills that you have used. It will show some awareness of the designer's roles and responsibilities and will make some comparison with professional designers' work.

D4 Explain your own design production work using mainly accurate terminology. Your explanation will be detailed and show an informed understanding of the materials, processes and skills that you have used. It will show that you have an informed understanding of the designer's roles and responsibilities. Your explanation will make a thoughtful and considered comparison with professional designers' work.

Unit D21

M1 In your logbook, describe the tools you have used and their functions. Diagrams would be useful.

D1 Explain in detail the use of the tools available.

M2 Describe the materials used, showing an understanding of their details and how to fix together using screws, nails and/or glue.

D2 Compare different ways of doing the same job and explain the application of set construction materials.

M3 Complete your research and planning with little support and guidance. Research the production demands and plan the construction process with some detail. Communicate your plans in simple but useable construction drawings and show an understanding of how much it will cost to realise your design ideas. Carry out the set construction and planning processes successfully, with little support and guidance.

Assessment activity 2 continued

D3 Complete the planning process with minimal support and guidance. Research the production demands and plan the construction process in careful detail. Communicate your plans in useable construction drawings and have a detailed understanding of how much it will cost to realise your design ideas. Carry out the set construction and planning processes effectively and independently.

M4 Select and use suitable set-construction skills to make your scenic element. Use the skills capably to create a scenic element that can be used in a performance with only a few minor adjustments and demonstrate a capable use of most of the set construction skills in making a competent scenic element.

D4 Select and use a variety of effective construction skills to make your scenic element. Demonstrate a fully effective application of a wide range of set-construction skills and use those skills confidently to create a well-made scenic element that is performance-ready.

M5 Show that you can work safely as you plan and make your scenic element, applying safe working practices throughout the set construction process. Support your practical work by reflecting on your application of health and safety in your account of the process.

D5 Show that you can consistently apply fully considered safe working practices as you plan and make your scenic element. Support your practical work by reflecting in full detail on your application of health and safety in your account of the process.

Design production

A designer needs to have an understanding of design production skills.
Your tutor may introduce you to some of the following skills.

Set Be able to:	• make a flat • make a simple scenic element • decorate a scenic element or set furniture.
Costume Be able to:	• make a simple costume • alter an existing costume • decorate a costume.
Props Be able to:	• source a prop • make a prop • decorate a prop.
Lighting Be able to:	• recognise the main lantern types • produce lighting plans and cue sheets • rig and focus lanterns for a performance.
Sound Be able to:	• set up and use sound recording equipment • set up and use sound playback equipment • compile sound cue sheets.

Key terms

Manual handling – lifting and carrying of heavy, large or awkward objects.

Ventilation – the adequate provision of air movement outlets when cutting timber or using paints or glues that emit noxious fumes.

Remember

It is important that you are aware of current professional design and production work. Look at:

- current theatre design magazines
- theatre journals and magazines
- theatre websites
- designers' websites
- British Society of Designers website

Find examples of professional work and analyse the processes and materials that they have used. Try to find a professional example for each new skill that you have learnt.

Annotate the picture of the professional example and add it to your logbook.

You should maintain a detailed account of each new skill, process or construction material that you learn about. Use photographs, DVDs or diagrams to record methods and processes. Try to get other people's opinions of how you have worked. For instance, after completing a lesson on making a flat your account might include:

- a diagram that explains how a flat is constructed
- a step-by-step guide that details every stage of making a flat
- a description of the materials that you have used
- a list of the tools and a description of how you have used them
- photographs that show how you constructed the flat
- an evaluation of the skills that you learned and applied
- a description of the health and safety rules for making a flat.

Health and safety

Your centre will have carried out a risk assessment for your workshop space. To work in the space you need to be aware of health and safety issues such as ventilation, how to correctly undertake manual handling and how to work safely at height. Your tutor will teach you the correct way to use the workshop so that you keep yourself and your fellow learners safe. Remember, health and safety is everybody's responsibility. It is integral to all aspects of your work so make sure that you apply the rules consistently. Don't be tempted to cut corners – it is not worth the risk.

In practical workshops you must make sure that you are appropriately dressed. You should:

- wear steel toe-capped boots or shoes
- tie back your hair
- not wear jewellery or belts that may become trapped or caught while using tools
- wear overalls for painting or glueing.

It may be useful to go to Unit D16 Crewing for Performance for terminology and health and safety definitions.

Problem solving

No matter how thorough your planning, sometimes things will still go wrong. Don't be thrown when this happens. In these situations you will have to be flexible and develop successful problem-solving skills – remember that the deadlines are not negotiable and that the production element will have to be ready on time. This might mean that you have to change or even let go of your best ideas, as sometimes you will have to compromise.

The design and production process

You may be given a design production task by your tutor so you can practice your skills. This is a chance to apply and develop the skills that you have learned to create a scenic element or prop.

These are the stages you should go through both for this activity and for Assessment activity 3.

Research	• The text to see how the set/prop is used. • The history/style/social context for your set/prop. • The work of other designers.
Design development	• Sketch your ideas. • Draw diagrams to explain your ideas. • Explore possible construction methods. • Explore possible construction materials. • Make models if you find it easier to work in 3D. • Come up with a few strong ideas. • Prepare provisional costs. • Select your final idea.
Finalising design	• Research materials. • Cost your prop. • Complete a production plan. • Prepare final drawings that explain exactly how you intend to make the prop.
Presenting design	• Present final plans to your tutor who will be acting as the director. • Explain and justify your ideas.
Resourcing materials/ tools	• Source materials, making sure that you get the best deal. • Keep to your budget. • Ensure that you have suitable tools, workshop and storage space. • Ensure that you know how to use the tools safely.
Making	• Work to your production plan. • Problem solve throughout the process. • Make the prop or scenic element. • Seek the opinion of others to check that you are on track.
Preparing for the get-in	• Finish the scenic element/prop so that it is performance-ready.

Take time in the planning and do your research thoroughly. Don't be impatient to get making until you have fully considered your methods, materials, tools, timing and costing. If you plan comprehensively and carefully, the making process should be quite straightforward.

Activity: Design and making task

Your tutor will set you a task to design and make a scenic element or a large prop. You will work in small teams to complete this task.

You will have to complete the task within a given, limited time-frame. This means that the designers and makers have to plan every aspect of the creative process in order to ensure they complete on time. This is a different process from making a piece of creative art, which may have no time limit and no pre-planned specific outcome. Deadlines are very important in the theatre production process. For example, a scenic element must be ready for the technical rehearsal.

Make sure you keep to schedule when designing and making your scenic element or prop.

Key terms

Interim assessment – an assessment of your progress part way through the project.

Formative assessment – assessment that helps you to recognise how you can improve what you are doing. You may set targets as a part of the process.

Interim assessment

When you have completed the design and making task you may take part in an interim assessment. Your tutor will invite you to present all of the evidence that you have generated for the task as you would for your final assessment. Your tutor will ask you to talk about your work and will use the grading criteria to assess your achievement so far.

As part of the assessment, either you or your tutor may make notes that could include formative assessment of:

- the skills that you have demonstrated
- the quality of the finish of the product
- your selection and use of materials
- your interaction with the others in your team and your management of the process.

After you have completed the first design project you will have an interim assessment. During the interim assessment you will agree and set targets for Assessment activity 3. This will be a chance to reflect on your skills and to plan how you may develop them further in your final project.

Assessment activity 3
Unit D17
Unit D21

Applying practical production skills

You will select and fulfil a production role; this role might require that you work individually or in pairs.

You will apply the skills that you have learned so far to design, plan and make a design contribution to a performance. This will be assessed in these stages:

- Agreement and research of design ideas in response to the stimulus, the venue and the production.
- Finalising of the design.
- Resourcing materials and tools.
- Realising the design element/contribution.
- Your management of the process.
- The final completed scenic element.

NB: If you complete a lighting, sound or costume project, then you will not produce any work for Unit D21.

Evidence

Your logbook – This could include:

- evidence of your planning
- a description of the materials that you have selected and a justification for their selection
- evaluations of how well you have applied the skills and processes that you have learned
- paperwork that you have generated or used (you can use photocopies)
- any feedback and action-planning from interim assessments
- other people's observations of your work, for both the final product and the process
- your assessment of the final product
- your reflection on how well you have applied health and safety rules for the use of the materials, methods and processes.

Grading Tips

Unit D17

M3 You should show that you have the ability to complete practical tasks. Your notes will include observations about how you have applied the skills you have learned and your final product will show that you have understood the design intentions.

D3 You will show, through your practical work, that you learned, understood and are capable of successfully applying production materials, techniques and processes. Your final product will be completely suitable for performance and you will fully consider how you have applied the skills you have learned in your evaluation.

Final assessment

This builds on the skills that you learned in the practice activity. You will repeat the design production process to make a significant production design element for a live performance. This will be the culmination of everything that you have learned.

Use the feedback from your interim formative assessment to plan how you work for this part of the project.

As a reminder, the process may include:

- production-needs analysis
- research
- design development
- finalising design ideas
- presenting design ideas
- resourcing materials and tools
- making
- get-in/rig focusing/plotting
- technical rehearsal/programming
- dress rehearsal
- the quality of your final product.

It is also important that you demonstrate good health and safety practice throughout the process and to ensure that you keep a full and detailed account explaining you understanding.

Remember that even a set that looks simple will need a lot of hard work and effort to get it looking just right.

Unit B4 Acting Skills and Techniques

Unit B6 Devising Plays

Theatre in Education (TiE) is much more than simply a form of drama performance. It is an experience through which the audience can develop knowledge and awareness and explore issues. Whether they are producing work for teenagers that raises awareness of issues such as drink and drugs or shows designed to help nursery children use their imaginations, TiE productions must be inspiring and thought-provoking.

During this project you will work as a TiE company to devise a piece of theatre designed to educate and entertain a specific audience. The project will not cover the whole of the two units, but will allow you to gain marks from assessments for some of the learning outcomes for both of them.

Learning outcomes

After completing this project you should be able to achieve the following learning outcomes:

Unit B4 Acting Skills and Techniques

3. Be able to interpret and develop characters

4. Be able to perform in an acting role.

Unit B6 Devising Plays

1. Be able to explore and develop material for a devised play

2. Be able to use a range of drama forms and techniques

3. Be able to communicate ideas, issues and/or feelings through presentation of devised work

4. Understand the effectiveness of devised work for performance.

255

Assessment and grading criteria

This table shows you what you must to in order to achieve a pass, merit or distinction and where you can find activities in this book to help you.

To achieve a pass grade the evidence must show that you are able to:	To achieve a merit grade the evidence must show that, in addition to the pass criteria, you are able to:	To achieve a distinction grade the evidence must show that, in addition to the pass and merit criteria, you are able to:
Unit B4 Acting Skills and Techniques		
P5 demonstrate ways of exploring, researching and creating a character/role **Assessment activity 5 page 266**	**M5** demonstrate responsive ways of exploring, researching and creating a character/role **Assessment activity 5 page 266**	**D5** demonstrate highly flexible and creative ways of exploring, researching and creating a character/role **Assessment activity 5 page 266**
P6 develop a character and make decisions about interpretation **Assessment activity 5 page 266**	**M6** develop a character and make considered decisions about interpretation **Assessment activity 5 page 266**	**D6** develop a character which shows use of imagination and/or insight in the choices and decisions made about interpretation **Assessment activity 5 page 266**
P8 communicate with an audience with occasional lapses in consistency. **Assessment activity 6 page 267**	**M8** communicate with an audience and remain focused and engaged in the drama. **Assessment activity 6 page 267**	**D8** communicate effectively with an audience and remain focused and engaged in the drama throughout. **Assessment activity 6 page 267**
Unit B6 Devising Plays		
P1 contribute some ideas an suggestions that are relevant to the work **Assessment activity 1 page 261** **Assessment activity 2 page 262** **Assessment activity 3 page 264** **Assessment activity 4 page 264**	**M1** develop ideas and suggestions which are clearly focused on the drama and attempt to shape the structure of the work **Assessment activity 1 page 261** **Assessment activity 2 page 262** **Assessment activity 3 page 264** **Assessment activity 4 page 264**	**D1** develop ideas and suggestions that make a positive contribution to the shape and form of the work with effective results **Assessment activity 1 page 261** **Assessment activity 2 page 262** **Assessment activity 3 page 264** **Assessment activity 4 page 264**
P2 select and use some drama forms and techniques as part of the development process **Assessment activity 3 page 264**	**M2** select and use a range of forms and techniques with some invention as part of the development process **Assessment activity 3 page 264**	**D2** experiment creatively with different forms and techniques as part of the developmental process **Assessment activity 3 page 264**

To achieve a pass grade the evidence must show that you are able to:	To achieve a merit grade the evidence must show that, in addition to the pass criteria, you are able to:	To achieve a distinction grade the evidence must show that, in addition to the pass and merit criteria, you are able to:
P3 develop a role and make some artistic decisions **Assessment activity 5 page 266**	**M3** develop a role and make considered artistic decisions **Assessment activity 5 page 266**	**D3** develop a role which shows use of imagination and/or insight in the choices and decisions made **Assessment activity 5 page 266**
P4 perform a role with vocal and physical expression connecting with other performers most of the time **Assessment activity 6 page 267**	**M4** perform a role with vocal and physical accuracy connecting with other performers throughout **Assessment activity 6 page 267**	**D4** perform a role with vocal and physical imagination being responsive to other performers at all times **Assessment activity 6 page 267**
P5 communicate intentions to the audience with some success **Assessment activity 6 page 267**	**M5** communicate intentions to an audience effectively **Assessment activity 6 page 267**	**D5** communicate intentions to an audience with clarity **Assessment activity 6 page 267**
P6 evaluate the main strengths and weaknesses of the final devised piece. **Assessment activity 7 page 268**	**M6** evaluate strengths and weaknesses of the final devised piece with reference to the preparation process and with some reasoning. **Assessment activity 7 page 268**	**D6** evaluate in detail the effectiveness of the final devised piece with reference to the preparation process and with considered conclusions. **Assessment activity 7 page 268**

How you will be assessed

This project will be assessed by an internal assignment that will be designed and marked by the tutors at your centre. You will be assessed on your ability to play an active part in the devising process and contribute to the performance of a Theatre in Education production.

The work you produce for assessment could include:
- tutor observation statements
- peer observations
- DVD recordings of classes, workshops, rehearsals and the performance
- an evaluation of the devised piece
- your logbook of the devising and rehearsal processes
- audience feedback.

Zak, drama student

The Theatre in Education project was the most difficult but the most rewarding and enjoyable project I undertook on my BTEC First in Performing Arts.

It was difficult because when devising a show for young children you need to take into account so many different things. We created a show to teach seven-to nine-year-olds about children who were evacuated during the Second World War. This meant we needed to research the topic to make sure the story we created was historically accurate and to highlight the main issues our audience needed to know about. We also had to make sure the play was interesting and enjoyable enough to hold the attention of a young audience. We included some songs and audience participation, which worked well.

The hard work paid off because the show went down really well in the four primary schools we visited. It was fun being 'on tour', just like being in a real theatre company. After the tour we received some lovely thank you letters from the children and we also got great feedback from their teachers who told us our play had really helped the children to understand the topic.

Theatre in Education show

The scenario

For this project, you will be required to work as a TiE company and create a piece of theatre that will educate, inform and entertain your given audience. You will need to decide on your theme or message, your audience and the form your piece will take. You will then devise, rehearse and perform your work. But first you need to find out a bit more about Theatre in Education.

Some TiE companies create work for very specific audiences e.g. pre-school children or young adults. Others produce work for a range of groups. The target audience for a TiE production will affect:

- the themes and issues addressed
- the style of the production e.g. use of interaction and audience participation.

Key term

Target audience – the audience that is being aimed at in any production e.g. teenagers, young adults or pre-school children.

Activity: TiE companies

Divide into groups and explore the work of one of the following TiE companies:

- APE Theatre Company

- Freedom Theatre UK

- Aesop's Touring Theatre

To access their websites, go to the Hotlinks section on p.2. You should gather details about:

- any particular themes and/or issues they tend to deal with

- details of the company's aims

- their target audience(s)

- the size and make up of the company

- how the company is funded (if they are subsidised, find out who they receive funding from)

- details of two of their recent productions (find out if they were original pieces or adaptations and what the themes were).

Share your findings with the rest of the class.

Activity: Forming a TiE company

Discuss in your group the things your company hopes to achieve. You need to address such issues as:

- who your target audience will be

- in what settings (e.g. schools, youth clubs, etc.) you will be performing.

With the help of your tutor, compile a short list of aims and objectives. For example, your company might wish to create work that helps children explore road safety issues.

You should also come up with an appropriate name for your company.

Finding a theme or subject

Work on a TiE production will often begin with a decision about the content of the production in terms of the issue or topic the piece will be based on.

Some TiE productions are created to raise awareness of social or other issues such as:

- binge drinking
- bullying
- road safety
- healthy eating
- homelessness.

Some companies produce work to support topics being taught in schools. TiE pieces could, for example, be used to support children's interest and understanding of the topics below.

The issue or topic chosen must, of course, be appropriate to the age and needs of the target audience.

Subject	Age group	Topic	Possible content
History	Years 1 & 2	What were seaside holidays like in the past?	Seaside holidays in the mid 20th century. Holidays today. What do souvenirs tell us about holidays?
RE	Years 1 & 2	Harvest festivals	What does harvest mean? What is thankfulness? How do Christians celebrate harvest? What is the Jewish festival of Sukkot?
Science	Year 3	Teeth and healthy eating	Different types of teeth. Losing your milk teeth. Keeping your teeth healthy. Eating to be healthy.
Geography	Year 7	Flood disasters – how do people cope?	What causes floods? How do communities and individuals respond to floods?
Science	Year 8	Sound and hearing	How are different sounds made? How do we hear sounds? Safety – can sound be dangerous?
History	Year 9	Black people of America – from slavery to equality	What is slavery/what is freedom? Where did black Americans originate? What was the Atlantic slave trade? What was segregation? How was freedom achieved? What did the civil rights movement do for black people?

Assessment activity 1

Unit B6 P1 M1 D1

Potential topics/issues

Divide into pairs or small groups and come up with ideas and suggestions for issues or topics that would be suitable for the target audience you will be creating your TiE piece for.

Produce a shortlist of two ideas to present to the class.

Take part in a discussion of all the ideas presented and, with the guidance of your tutor, make a decision about the topic or issue your TiE will be based on.

Evidence

Your logbook – Make notes on this activity in your logbook describing what has been discussed and the decisions made.

Grading Tips

M1 Your notes should discuss the topics and issues you put forward for discussion describing why they are appropriate to your target audience. In practical sessions you should help to develop ideas for a TiE piece in a clearly focused way contributing to the way the piece is shaped and how it is structured.

D1 Your notes should explain why the ideas generated by your research are appropriate to the topic/issue and how they will make a positive contribution to the piece. In practical sessions you will make a positive contribution to the work in progress using your ideas to effectively develop the piece.

Researching the issue or topic

Whatever the topic or issue you have chosen you must spend some time researching it to ensure you have a good understanding of the subject and its potential in terms of creating an interesting piece of drama. The case study on the following page shows research into teenagers and alcohol. Research like this will help you put together your final performance. Make sure you go into the same kind of detail, thinking of probing questions to look into.

Functional skills

Presenting your ideas and recording notes in your logbook will use your **English** speaking and writing skills.

PLTS

Thinking about what issue or topic would be suitable for your target audience will show that you are a **creative thinker**.

Working in groups for this task will show that you are a **team worker**.

Teenagers experimenting with alcohol often make the news. Try searching your favourite newspaper with 'teenager' and 'alcohol' as key words.

Case study: Initial research into teens and alcohol

Many teenagers experiment with alcohol. Studies show that the majority of young people under 16 have tried it at least once. While for most this will not lead to major issues, many youngsters are getting drunk on a regular basis. So-called binge drinking can lead to severe health and other problems.

Why teenagers drink

Many teenagers drink alcohol for the first time out of curiosity. Others feel pressured by their friends who drink. This is known as peer pressure.

Alcohol and health

In the short term, binge drinking can lead to a hangover the next day. This happens because heavy drinking causes dehydration and low blood sugar which can result in headaches and vomiting. Continued abuse of alcohol can lead to much more serious health problems, including urinary infections, fertility problems, liver, kidney and heart damage, alcoholism and mental health problems, and in extreme cases, even death.

Other issues

Many people do foolish and dangerous things when they are drunk. Some might start fights or take unnecessary risks. Accidents caused by falling or running into things are common among young people who have drunk too much. For young girls in particular the risk of sexual assault is increased when they are too drunk to make sensible decisions.

Potential starting points for drama

- A young person feeling pressured by friends to try alcohol.

- A group of friends looking back on a night out that ended badly.

PLTS

Your research into your chosen topic will require that you use your skills as an **independent enquirer**.

Functional skills

Making notes in your logbook will use your **English** writing skills.

Assessment activity 2
Unit B6

Research

Undertake an investigation into your chosen issue or topic.

Use the investigation to come up with ideas for potential starting points for the devising process.

Evidence

Your logbook – Make notes on your research and ideas in your logbook.

Devising and rehearsing

Effective scheduling

As with the creation of any performance piece, care has to be taken to use time effectively when developing your TiE drama. You will be working to a deadline, and it is easy to waste precious time because rehearsals have not been planned, or too much time is spent discussing or sitting around wondering what to do next.

Professional companies work to schedules. Here is an example of a typical schedule used on a daily basis by a small-scale theatre company when they are working on a new project:

1. Quick warm-up – games as well as a physical and vocal warm-up.

2. Plan of attack – go over the aims for the devising/rehearsal session.

3. Practical work on the material including:

- improvisation to explore and generate new material
- work on material suggested or scripted by group members
- develop and improvematerial already produced
- discuss and evaluate work done so far
- discuss the shape and structure of the show
- agree what needs doing, and set aims for the next session.

Audience interaction

During these sessions you will also need to consider ways you can make your TiE presentation interactive. There could be audience involvement built into the actual performance. Alternatively a workshop and discussion in response to the performance may be more effective.

Production style

Many TiE productions use very basic sets, costumes and props. This is because the majority of TiE companies tour a range of venues, many of which are not theatres, so the production must be flexible enough to fit into a variety of different spaces. Materials must also be portable and quick and easy to set up.

Support materials

Many TiE companies produce materials to support the content of their productions. These could be tutor/facilitator packs that include activities the audience might undertake in preparation for the performance or to extend learning and thinking about it afterwards.

BTEC **Assessment activity 3** **Unit B6**

Devising sessions

You need to develop your ideas into performance material. Your tutor will provide advice and guidance, but you will be expected to contribute to the development of your piece.

Be prepared to try out different drama forms and techniques. For example, you could use still pictures to explore the key moments of the story and hot seating to explore the individual characters in the piece. Also consider the use of props, levels, costume and music in your work.

You will also need to give regular work-in-progress showings, take part in discussions, respond to feedback from your tutor and your peers and amend work as needed.

Evidence

Your logbook – Make notes on your activities and progress in your logbook.

Observations – You tutor will observe your work during these sessions and will produce a report.

Recordings – Milestone sessions may be recorded to provide evidence of your contribution.

Grading Tips

M2 You should select performance styles and methods you think most appropriate to the mood and meaning of the piece and make meaningful contributions to the final style and form of the play.

D2 Your contribution to activities that experiment with drama forms and techniques will be positive and constructive. You will offer a suitable range of styles and forms with full understanding of their thematic purpose. The final devised play will have been successful in communicating the meaning of the content owing to the form and style used.

 BTEC **Assessment activity 4** **Unit B6**

Production requirements and support materials

Hold a production meeting to discuss set, costume and prop requirements as well as any requirements for support materials. During the meeting:

- decide on production roles and responsibilities
- consider whether any support materials will be required for your performance
- decide on the content and form of the materials and who will produce them.

Evidence

Your logbook – Make notes on your discussions. Detail what you will be taking responsibility for.

Grading Tips

M1 In your logbook, describe your ideas saying why they are appropriate to the piece.

D1 Fully explain your ideas in your logbook, discussing how they will positively impact the piece.

Developing your character

Preparing to play any role in a piece of drama involves individual preparation as well as participation in rehearsals. Once you have been allocated a role in the performance you will need to prepare to play the character.

Guidance and activities for developing a character can be found in Project 7 Page to Stage.

Role on the wall

A good way of collating information about the character you are playing is through a role on the wall diagram. This is essentially a diagram of a figure with information about the character written inside or around it.

Popular with the other girs in her year group (but many don't trust her).

Doesn't do well at school (can't see the point). Likes to mess about rather than working.

Aspires to be a celebrity. Likes nice clothes and tries to look older than she is.

Tends to bully anyone who gets in her way.

Outwardly confident but uses this to hide her insecurity.

Feels threatened by Ginny as she is also popular.

Likes Damian. Will do what she can to get his attention.

Figure 6.01: Role on the wall - Geri.

> ## Key term
>
> **Role on the wall** – putting an image of your character on a poster with all their character attributes to help you remember and develop the role.

Think about your character and keep focused during your performance.

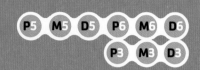

BTEC Assessment activity 5
Unit B4
Unit B6

P5 M5 D5 P6 M6 D6
P3 M3 D3

Developing your character

You will be responsible for developing your own role in the piece. You should work in class and individually to explore and research your character. This could be done by:

• creating a role on the wall character sketch

• writing a talking-head monologue for your character where they talk about something that happens to them during the play

• creating a mind map that illustrates your character's relationships with other characters in the play.

Evidence

Your logbook – Keep a record of your character-development activities and progress in your logbook.

Grading Tips

Unit B4

M5 You should use responsive ways to research and develop characters and carefully consider the choices you make in interpreting your role.

D5 Use imaginative and creative ways of exploring, researching and developing your character.

M6 When developing your character you should think about their background, motivations and relationships. Show that you understand the style of the piece you are performing in.

D6 You will use imagination and insight in the choices and decisions you make when developing your character.

Unit B6

M3 You should develop a character/role that has a specific identity and makes a positive contribution to the devised play. Your logbook will show some evidence of character research and use of explorative strategies to gain depth of understanding.

D3 You should use imaginative and creative ways of exploring and developing your character. You should undertake significant research into the character/role and fully master the techniques required to adapt to the chosen style of the piece.

The performance

The performance of any TiE piece is the culmination of much preparation. The company needs to arrive early at the venue – often a school or other community centre – to ensure items of set, props and other equipment are set up ahead of the start time and any unforeseen problems with the venue (such as awkward positioning of power sockets) can be identified and solutions found. Keeping to the agreed performance schedule is vital, particularly if the performance is in a school as the production will have to fit around the timetable.

When preparing for your own performance it is also vital to ensure you understand your responsibilities and are properly organised.

Young audiences can be challenging to perform to. If your show is for youngsters, a final dress rehearsal for an invited audience, for instance, younger brothers and sisters of company members, will help to iron out any problems.

Functional skills

You will use your **English** writing skills when developing your character.

Assessment activity 5
Unit B4
Unit B6

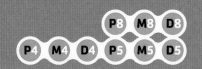

Performing

Take part in the performance of your TiE piece interacting with other performers and using physical and vocal skills to communicate your intentions to the audience.

Evidence

Recorded evidence – The performance will be recorded to provide evidence of your contribution and performance skills.

Grading tips

Unit B4

M3 During the performance you should remain focused and engaged. You should ensure your performance communicates the intentions of your character clearly.

D3 You should remain focused and engaged throughout the performance. You should ensure your performance communicates the intentions of your character effectively and imaginatively.

Unit B6

M4 You should perform a role that is clearly seen as part of the overall meaning of the piece. You will show variety in vocal and movement skills showing some variation of pace.

D4 You should demonstrate full clarity of character/role and perform with confidence and energy. Your vocal work will demonstrate a variety of pace, pause, pitch and tone. Movement skills will show pace and energy that is completely appropriate to the style you are performing in.

M5 Your performance should communicate the character you are playing in a clear and precise manner. The audience will generally be able to understand the purpose and intentions of your character's role in the piece.

D5 You should communicate your character with complete clarity. The audience should fully understand the intentions of the piece.

Evaluating the project

Evaluation of any theatre project is an important part of the work. In commercial theatre, evaluation evidence comes in many forms, including bookings, merchandise sales, reviews, etc. TiE companies often work on a smaller scale, but it is important to gauge the success of the work so that it can be improved. Lessons learned can help ensure the success of future projects.

Activity: Assessing the success

In your group, list as many methods you can think of to evaluate your project. A questionnaire is one method. How else can you obtain this information?

Decide on how you will gather responses about you show. Remember to consider the age of your audience when deciding how to gather responses.

BTEC Assessment activity 7   Unit B6

Evaluation

Take part in an evaluation discussion of the effectiveness of the show as well as the strengths and weaknesses of the devising process of the company.

Use any information gathered from your audience in your discussions.

After the discussion, complete an evaluation in your logbook.

Evidence

Recorded Evidence – The discussion will be recorded to provide evidence of your contribution.

Your logbook – Complete a written evaluation in your logbook.

Grading Tips

M6 Your evaluation should identify strengths and weaknesses in the performance and refer to the devising process. You should note the activities undertaken during the devising and rehearsal process that might have needed more attention to improve the final piece and those that worked well, contributing to the strengths.

D6 Your evaluation should identify significant strengths and weaknesses in the performance and explain in detail what actions during the creative process contributed to these. You should also provide detailed explanations as to what might have been done differently to avoid any weaknesses identified.

Project 7 Page to Stage

Unit B4 Acting Skills and Techniques

Unit B7 Performing Scripted Plays

These units will give you opportunities to develop and apply rehearsal, characterisation and performance skills and both require assessment of performances to an audience.

This project will allow you to achieve grading criteria from assessments for the learning outcomes for each of these units. You may be asked to rehearse and perform complete plays, substantial scenes and play extracts, showcases of acting scenes, or a combination of these.

Learning outcomes

After completing this project you should be able to achieve the following learning outcomes:

Unit B4 Acting Skills and Techniques

1. Be able to use vocal skills
2. Be able to use movement skills
3. Be able to interpret and develop characters
4. Be able to perform in an acting role.

Unit B7 Performing Scripted Plays

1. Be able to interpret a role taken from a play
2. Be able to develop a role for performance through rehearsal
3. Be able to take part in the performance of a play
4. Understand the effectiveness of the interpretation of a role.

Assessment and grading criteria

This table shows you what you must do in order to achieve a pass, merit or distinction, and where you can find activities in this book to help you.

To achieve a pass grade the evidence must show that you are able to:	To achieve a merit grade the evidence must show that, in addition to the pass criteria, you are able to:	To achieve a distinction grade the evidence must show that, in addition to the pass and merit criteria, you are able to:
Unit B4 Acting Skills and Techniques		
P2 use vocal skills in a way that is appropriate to the acting role with technical control **Assessment activity 4 page 284**	**M2** use vocal skills in ways that demonstrate a good degree of technical control in an acting role **Assessment activity 4 page 284**	**D2** demonstrate a strong technical command of vocal skills within an acting role **Assessment activity 4 page 284**
P4 use movement skills in a way that is appropriate to the acting role with technical control **Assessment activity 4 page 284**	**M4** use movement skills in ways that demonstrate a good degree of technical control in an acting role **Assessment activity 4 page 284**	**D4** demonstrate a strong technical command of movement skills within an acting role **Assessment activity 4 page 284**
P5 demonstrate ways of exploring, researching and creating a character/role **Assessment activity 1 page 274** **Assessment activity 2 page 279**	**M5** demonstrate responsive ways of exploring, researching and creating a character/role **Assessment activity 1 page 274** **Assessment activity 2 page 279**	**D5** demonstrate highly flexible and creative ways of exploring, researching and creating a character/role **Assessment activity 1 page 274** **Assessment activity 2 page 279**
P6 develop a character and make decisions about interpretation **Assessment activity 1 page 274** **Assessment activity 2 page 279**	**M6** develop a character and make considered decisions about interpretation **Assessment activity 1 page 274** **Assessment activity 2 page 279**	**D6** develop a character which shows use of imagination and/or insight in the choices and decisions made about interpretation **Assessment activity 1 page 274** **Assessment activity 2 page 279**
P7 perform a role showing a basic handling of the role with commitment **Assessment activity 4 page 284**	**M7** perform a role that is handled with commitment and some attention to detail **Assessment activity 4 page 284**	**D7** perform a role with focus, commitment, imagination and some sense of ease **Assessment activity 4 page 284**
P8 communicate with an audience with occasional lapses in consistency. **Assessment activity 4 page 284**	**M8** communicate with an audience and remain focused and engaged in the drama. **Assessment activity 4 page 284**	**D8** communicate effectively with an audience and remain focused and engaged in the drama throughout. **Assessment activity 4 page 284**

To achieve a pass grade the evidence must show that you are able to:	To achieve a merit grade the evidence must show that, in addition to the pass criteria, you are able to:	To achieve a distinction grade the evidence must show that, in addition to the pass and merit criteria, you are able to:
Unit B7 Performing Scripted Plays		
P1 develop a role and make decisions about interpretation **Assessment activity 1 page 274** **Assessment activity 2 page 279**	**M1** develop a role and make considered decisions about interpretation with some insight and imagination **Assessment activity 1 page 274** **Assessment activity 2 page 279**	**D1** develop a role which shows effective use of imagination and insight in the choices and decisions made about the interpretation **Assessment activity 1 page 274** **Assessment activity 2 page 279**
P2 attend rehearsals and performances demonstrating personal management and technical skills **Assessment activity 3 page 280**	**M2** attend rehearsals and performances and demonstrate engagement with the material with commitment and concentration **Assessment activity 3 page 280**	**D2** attend rehearsals and performances and demonstrate a purposeful sense of focus on the work throughout **Assessment activity 3 page 280**
P3 perform a role with vocal and physical expression connecting with other performers most of the time **Assessment activity 4 page 284**	**M3** perform a role with vocal and physical accuracy, connecting with other performers throughout **Assessment activity 4 page 284**	**D3** perform a role with imagination and vocal and physical accuracy, being responsive to other performers at all times **Assessment activity 4 page 284**
P4 communicate intentions to the audience **Assessment activity 4 page 284**	**M4** communicate intentions to an audience with success **Assessment activity 4 page 284**	**D4** communicate intentions to an audience with clarity and meaning **Assessment activity 4 page 284**
P5 review the main strengths and weaknesses of performance work. **Assessment activity 5 page 285**	**M5** review strengths and weaknesses of performance work with some reasoning. **Assessment activity 5 page 285**	**D5** review in detail the effectiveness of performance work with considered conclusions. **Assessment activity 5 page 285**

How you will be assessed

This project will be assessed by an internal assignment that will be designed and marked by the tutors at your centre. Each assignment will allow you to demonstrate understanding and apply skills and techniques you have learned in order to meet the grading criteria.

The work you produce for assessment could include:

- tutor observations
- peer observations
- witness statements from other staff
- DVD recordings of classes, workshops and rehearsals
- DVD recordings of performances
- your logbook including notes on characterisation (research, observations, ideas and inspirations, rehearsal notes, etc). Your log book can include written entries, audio/video diaries and blogs of reviews and evaluations of both rehearsals and performances.

Steve, professional actor

I first got into acting at age nine, when, having enjoyed doing school plays, I was sent to a youth theatre group in Birmingham. By age 15 or 16 I had decided that acting was where I wanted my future to lie. I had some great training at school and at youth theatre, so at the age of 18 I began to audition for professional jobs. I did a few tours and murder mystery jobs, but decided that I wouldn't get more high profile jobs without a good agent. I therefore auditioned and got into LAMDA's 3-year professional acting course. I trained for 3 years and found that the skills they had taught me would stand me in better stead than having an agent ever could. Signing with having an agent before graduating was a bonus though!

I've been touring for the last five months now, first with a Georgian play called *He's Much to Blame* and I've just finished a play about road safety for a TiE company. The best thing about acting is the variety of parts you can play – I'm looking forward to my next project!

Getting started

The scenario

There are no rules regarding which play(s) can be performed for the BTEC First in Performing Arts. Your tutor might choose plays for you that they feel will interest you and best develop your acting skills. Plays may be chosen because the theme or style will suit a planned performance event. It is also possible that you and your group can have some say in choosing plays you would like to perform.

Key Concept: From Page to Stage

The written play, often referred to as the 'script' or the 'text', is in many ways like a musical score or a set of instructions. It contains the information the director and actors need to put on a production of the play. Turning the written words of the playwright into a polished production requires interpretation. Interpretation is the careful analysis of what the playwright has written, both in the characters' dialogue and in the stage directions, to arrive at an appropriate way of performing the script so that the play's meaning will be successfully communicated to the audience.

Did you know?

The play script is a like a code. Approach the play and your character like a detective looking for clues in the text.

Interpreting the play

Themes and issues

Themes and issues in the play will be discussed between director and cast at the very start of rehearsals. These are the ideas and concerns communicated through the play's plot and characters. You need to understand these in order to interpret your character and tell the playwright's story successfully.

Activity: Themes and issues

For the play you are rehearsing, consider the following:
1. Why has the playwright focused on a particular theme?
2. How has the playwright treated the themes/issues through the style and content of the play?
3. What is the intended effect on the audience?

PLTS

The research you carry out into your play will show that you are an **independent enquirer.**

273

Characterisation
Interpreting your character

Once you have got to grips with the themes you will need to consider what impact they have on your character. Your director will guide you through this process during rehearsals. You will need to look at the information contained in the script and make decisions about how the play's meaning will be communicated to the audience.

 BTEC Assessment activity 1
Unit B4
Unit B7

(P5) (M5) (D5) (P6) (M6) (D6)
(P1) (M1) (D1)

Developing your character

Consider the role of your character within the play. How does your character's role show or develop the themes of the play? How can you develop your character to highlight these themes?

Evidence

Make sure you document the process of your character development and interpretation. This can be in the form of annotations to your script, a blog, a video diary, creative writing, role on the wall, etc.

Grading Tips

Unit B4

(M5) You must experiment with a variety of techniques associated with characterisation, either in response to direction from others, or independently.

(D5) You will need to explore and experiment imaginatively and creatively with a wide range of characterisation techniques and you must be prepared to try out different methods of creating a character.

(M6) Your character development must show carefully considered interpretive choices including background, motivations and relationships.

(D6) You must show that you have engaged enthusiastically with all aspects of character creation. You must show imagination and insight in making interpretive choices about the roles.

Unit B7

(M1) You will need to show evidence that you have given considerable thought to the imaginative life of the character (this is the understanding and detail that makes a three-dimensional character). Decisions you make about interpretation of the character will be made based on analysis of the piece and director's instruction as well as your research and exploration.

(D1) The results of your choices and decisions about interpretations will be effective, resulting in a valid and interesting characterisation. This will be due to good levels of imagination and understanding that you show in the characterisation process.

Writing styles

To help you to understand the material better you can analyse your chosen playwright's style of writing. This will help you interpret the material and come up with a successful characterisation.

The following questions help this analysis:

- What kind of language is used? Prose, rhyming verse or blank verse?
- Is the language realistic everyday speech, abstract or stylised?
- Do any characters speak directly to the audience?
- Do you understand the words easily, or do you need an explanation?
- What stage directions are provided?

You are most likely to encounter 'abstract' or 'stylised' language in Elizabethan, Medieval, Restoration or Classical plays where dramatists conventionally used verse and heightened speech. Stylised (unfamiliar) language in modern plays is used in experimental theatre. Epic theatre, for example, has characters speaking in verse or addressing the audience directly to emphasise issues of importance.

Stage directions

Modern plays usually provide specific stage directions, suggesting where there should be pauses, entrances, exits, lighting effects and so forth. Samuel Beckett wrote some plays that were only stage directions with no dialogue: *Quad*, for example, is only a series of complex instructions for movement with accompanying directions for lighting sound and costumes.

Directors can choose to ignore or change the stage directions in a play to suit their production concept. Very often the stage directions in a published play reflect the first production of that play in a particular theatre, so the directions might not be practical in other theatres.

Stage directions are also useful to actors for giving clues about the characters they are playing. How a character enters, exits and moves, for instance, can say a lot about who they are.

Finding clues to character

When you have your play, go through it carefully, picking out as many clues as you can about your character. What you find out will lead to many decisions about your character and how they react and respond to other characters.

Key terms

Annotations – notes you add to a book, text or picture giving explanations or comments. A play script might be annotated, for instance, to show moves, stage positions, notes on delivery and actions, etc

Characterisation – the features and qualities of a character, as developed by the actor under the guidance of the director.

Prose – a way of describing language written in its ordinary continuous form, reflecting typical everyday expression rather than language written in rhythmic line structure or rhyme.

Rhyming verse – a number of lines of text/dialogue grouped together where the last word of a line rhymes with the last word of the previous line or the line before.

Blank verse – lines structured like rhyming verse, but unrhymed.

Did you know?

Classical plays did not normally include stage directions: actions were described in the characters' dialogue.

Activity: Exploring your character

Having looked at the overall style of the writing for your play, now examine in detail the dialogue and stage directions for your character.

When reading your own lines, you need to decide why the character says and does what they do: what motivates them throughout the play.

Ask yourself the following questions:

1. What does the character say about themselves (about their past, their lifestyle, their goals, fears and ambitions)?

2. Does your character always say what they are is really feeling or thinking or are they hiding something (a sub-text)?

3. What do others say about your character?

4. How do others treat your character?

Also look for clues in the style of writing and the stage directions to help you develop and interpret the character. These could include:

- a particular accent, a way of speaking or vocal mannerism

- physical mannerisms, gestures or habits

- instructions to perform special actions such as dancing, fighting or complex physical actions.

Note your observations, thoughts and conclusions in your logbook (or blog, video diary, etc.). You might also annotate your script with notes on character, delivery of speech, movement, etc.

Did you know?

The director usually reads the whole play at least ten times before starting rehearsals. As an actor, you need to read the whole play a number of times as well to really understand it.

Activity: Character relationships

In discussion with your director and the rest of the cast, decide on the relationships between the characters. This is important in understanding the structure of the play. Knowing the relationships will help you decide on how your character should respond to other characters, and why.

The best and easiest way to show and understand the characters' relationships is by creating a diagram. This can be done individually or as a group. Keep a copy of the diagram and a record of your discussions in your logbook to help you with character development.

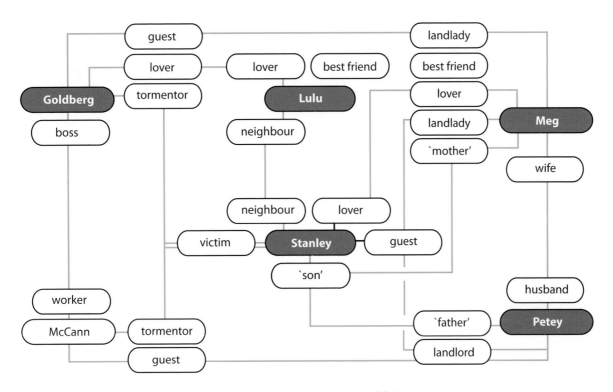

Figure 7.1: The character relationships in *The Birthday Party* by Harold Pinter.

Researching and developing character

A good actor will look beyond the script to flesh out their characters. Here are some typical research topics an actor should carry out to find out more about their character and the world they inhabit.

Topic	Character development
Time or period when the play is set	Does this information affect your interpretation of character, such as their gestures, the way they speak, posture, dress, use space, etc?
Where the play is set	The play's location can affect many decisions on character interpretation – accent, culture, climate, political situation, historical situation.
Lifestyle of the character	This might include their place in society, job, financial situation, living conditions, religion, tastes in food or entertainment.
Staging and style of performance	The play might be performed exactly as written, or your director may suggest a staging. You need to be aware of the type of stage, e.g. thrust or in-the-round, and the style of the production, e.g. naturalistic, melodrama or experimental.

BTEC Assessment activity 2
Unit B4
Unit B7

P5 M5 D5 P6 M6 D6
P1 M1 D1

Good sources of research.

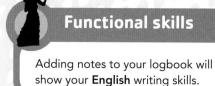

Functional skills

Adding notes to your logbook will show your **English** writing skills.

Research

When developing a character, an actor has to know and understand the world the playwright has created and in which the character lives. You will need to research the background of the character and their world, as well as the background of the play itself. Use a variety of sources in your research, such as:

- printed sources – books, newspapers and magazines, including reviews of other performances of the play
- pictures – artwork, photographs
- sculptures – very useful if the play is set in the past
- performances – of the same play, or plays by the same writer or in the same genre
- films – of the play or from the same period or location as the play, or covering similar content or themes
- documentaries – on fashion, behaviour, history, lifestyle, etc.
- internet – information on the playwright, theatre company websites, study notes, reviews, etc.

Evidence

Your logbook – Keep any materials you find to help your research (photocopies, drawings, materials, etc) with your logbook to refer back to when developing the character. But it is not enough to simply place these items in your logbook. You should add notes and annotations, either commenting on how the information helped you make decisions when developing the character, or referencing the information to a section in the play where it is relevant to your interpretation.

Applying your research

The research you have completed should have given you lots of information that will help you flesh out your character and bring them to life. You will need to decide which aspects of what you have learned will help your character development, and how to use them in the play.

The following pages shows how Luke – a learner on the BTEC First Performing Arts course, playing one of the prisoners in *Our Country's Good* by Timberlake Wertenbaker – applied research to his interpretation, as shown in this extract of notes from his logbook.

Worked example: Luke's logbook – characterisaton

After reading the play and discussing it, I also read the book *The Playmaker* by Thomas Keneally and watched a TV documentary on crime and punishment in the 1700s.

Character: Robert Sideway

Date of Birth: January 14th 1758

Address: East London (transported to New South Wales 1788)

Features: Head shaved, skinny, tall, covered in sores and bites, rotting teeth.

Research result: Prisoners were shaved to prevent lice. Colony very hot, nasty insects. Disease called scurvy affected gums and made teeth fall out.

Voice: Puts on affected 'dandy' voice, which sometimes slips into common London accent.

Why: Robert is a conman and pickpocket pretending to be a noble.

Movement and appearance: Nimble and supple, but puts on over the top graceful gestures. Costume was elegant but now torn and sweat stained.

Why: He stole his fine clothes just before he was arrested and has worn them ever since.

Props: Handkerchief waved around for effect, also to mask rotten teeth, wipe sweat, swat insects and hide smell of other convicts.

Research result: Wealthy types often showed off by waving around expensive handkerchiefs.

Rehearsals

 BTEC | ## Assessment activity 3 | Unit B7

Technical work in rehearsal

You will be assessed throughout the rehearsal period on rehearsal skills including personal management, exercises, improvisations and development activities. These skills contribute not only to the success of your character/role development, but the overall success of the production as a team effort.

Evidence

Your logbook – Tutor observation of your contribution and progress during rehearsals, warm-ups and workshops; notes in your logbook detailing the rehearsal process.

Grading Tips

M2 You will need to attend rehearsals regularly and demonstrate, through your participation and contribution, your understanding of how the rehearsal process allows you to explore and develop character.

D2 You will rehearse with absolute concentration and energy, showing purpose and commitment to the work.

Case study: Extract from rehersal schedule

Company: The Tractorshed Theatre Company
Production: *The Best Little Whorehouse in Texas*
Rehearsal schedule – Week commencing 14th February

Day/Time	Cast	Act/Scene	Notes
Mon 14.00–16.30	Mona, Ed, Girls	Act 2 Scene 4 & 5	MD to run 'Hard Candy Xmas' and 'Bus to Amarillo'
Tue 09.30–12.00	Mona, Girls	Act 1 Scene 2, 3	Choreo for: 'Pissant Country Place' & 'Girl You're a Woman'
Wed 11.45–12.45	Doatsey, Edsel, Rufus, CJ, Ed	Act 1 Scene 8	
Thu 11.45–12.45	Ed Earl, Doatsey, Edsel, Rufus, CJ	Act 2 Scene 3	MD to run 'Good Ol' Girl'
Fri 14.00–17.00	Whole Company	Act I	Off-book deadline Act I

Rehearsal schedule

Your director will prepare a rehearsal schedule. This will ensure everything happens on time and the show develops at the right pace.

Key elements in the schedule will include a read-through, explorations, blocking, deadline for learning your lines (known as 'off script' or 'off book'), props rehearsals, technical and dress rehearsals.

When you get your schedule, note all the key dates and save a copy of your schedule in your logbook. You will be assessed on your ability to meet deadlines (such as learning lines, songs and choreography) as well as your regular attendance and punctuality.

Learning lines

You cannot give a proper performance with the script in your hand, and your director will tell you at what point you need to be off script or off book in rehearsals.

When?

It is best to learn your lines once you have read the play through a number of times and have rehearsed enough to know what the lines mean and why the character is saying them – also when you know the shape and feel of each scene.

How?

Actors use many different methods to learn their lines. Some methods are described in Unit B4 Acting Skills and Techniques on page 64.

Character development through rehearsal

Early rehearsals should include explorations and off-text exercises. Your director will usually decide on the best exercises to suit the play. The following activities feature some well-known methods to help you explore and develop character. They can be used as evidence activities for your portfolio.

PLTS

Your research into characters will require you to use your skills as an **independent enquirer** and a **self-manager**.

Activity: Observation

Look for character ideas and inspiration by studying other people – friends, relatives, people in the street or on TV. Keep notes and sketches in your logbook and experiment with applying movements, habits, ways of speaking and actions to your character.

Activity: Hot-seating

Functional skills

The hot-seating and improvisation activities will ask you to use both your **English** speaking and listening skills. Keeping notes of the activities and what you find out whilst doing them will use your **English** writing skills.

This exercise is like an interview, but requires you to answer a series of questions not as yourself, but as your character. Once you have read the play and rehearsed all the scenes, split into pairs, and think of some questions to ask your partner's character. Then interview each other and record the hot-seat on video or audio, or make notes on your responses in your logbook. Look back at your answers and see how much more you now know about your character.

You will find some questions easy to answer, but may be asked about things beyond what the script suggests (such as what your favourite colour is). It is important to answer as you think the character would.

Activity: Improvisations

Improvisation can be used in rehearsal to explore characters by placing them in situations not contained in the play. These can include improvising what could have happened to the character before the story starts, and what might happen after the story of the play finishes. You could also explore an event mentioned in the play but not seen, or try placing characters in different situations to see how they would behave.

Improvisation will help you develop your understanding and depth of character. Keep notes in your logbook, and say what you have learned about your character.

Blocking

Blocking is the process the director goes through to set the action. It takes place over a number of rehearsals and involves deciding on entrances, exits, stage positions, key movements, groupings of actors, etc. Blocking helps communicate the play's meaning and presents a clear stage picture, ensuring nothing important is masked or obscured through clumsy positioning.

As your director blocks your scenes, you must note when and where you enter and exit, where you will be on stage and your key moves. Draw a diagram of the stage, showing any items of set or furniture, with arrows to show your moves and positions as well as the positions of other characters in the scene.

Blocking may get changed as the play develops in rehearsal, so make notes in pencil.

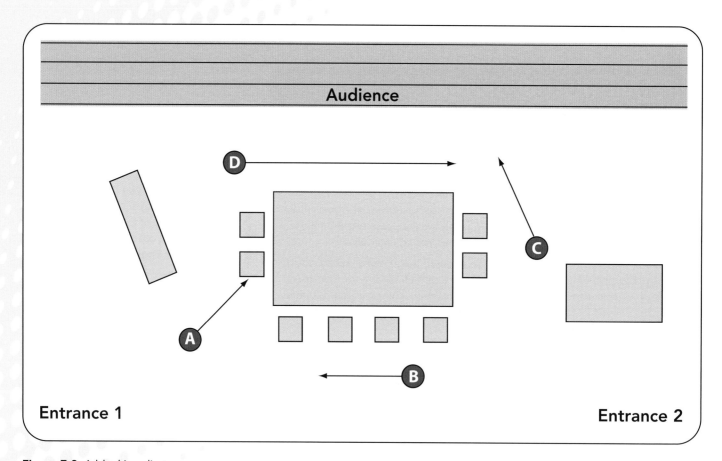

Figure 7.2: A blocking diagram

Assessment activity 4
Unit B4
Unit B7

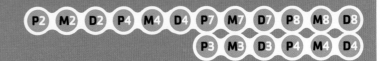

The play's the thing

The culmination of all the hard work you and your fellow actors put into rehearsal is the final performance itself. You will be assessed on:

- technical skills, control and command of vocal and movement acting skills
- vocal and physical expression
- connection with and response to other performers/characters
- your ability to communicate with the audience and stay committed and engaged in the drama.

Evidence

Your performance – Your tutors will record the performance(s) on DVD/video and they will usually write tutor observation notes. Sometimes they will ask other staff to provide witness observations, and it is often a good idea for the audience to provide feedback, although for assessment, the tutor's judgement is normally used to decide on actual achievement.

Grading tips

Unit B4

M2 You will need to apply vocal skills and techniques successfully and appropriately to your acting role. They will need to be controlled, consistent and in keeping with the nature of your character and the demands of the scenes and actions in the play.

D2 Your vocal performance will be skilful enough for you to 'inhabit' your role, meaning you will have such a strong technical command of your vocal techniques, that your vocal performance will seamlessly communicate the character, scene and situation to the audience.

M4 You must use and apply movement skills and techniques successfully and appropriately to your acting role. You will be expected to demonstrate control of movement as well as the application of movement, mannerism and gesture appropriate to your interpretation of character, scene and action.

D4 Your physical performance of character will show a technical command of movement skills and techniques, allowing for a performance where you fully 'inhabit' your role.

M7 You must perform your character/role showing commitment. Your performance will show attention to detail, as shown in detailed use of your voice, movement, reactions and inter-actions with other characters.

D7 Your performance will be focused (combining of energy, concentration and being absorbed in the character and the play), as well as showing imagination and some sense of ease. The performance will be fluent and seamless, so you really appear to inhabit the character.

M8 You will need to sustain your characterisation without losing concentration focus, and be engaged with the action, meaning you will have a sense of involvement and belief in the play when performing.

D8 You will need to maintain full focus and engagement with the character/play throughout the performance, thus allowing you to communicate effectively with the audience. You will remain in control of every aspect of your performance.

BTEC Assessment activity 4 continued

Grading Tips

M3 Your performance will be accurate vocally and physically. Accuracy means a clear, appropriate and consistent performance of the character/role, paying attention so that relationships, reactions and interactions (with other characters and the world of the play and its actions) make sense within the context of the play.

D3 You will give an imaginative performance, as shown in the depth of detail, insight and experiment (there may be elements of the interesting, unusual or 'risk-taking' in your performance). You will also be responsive to other performers, meaning your reactions and relationships occur convincingly in response to the actions of others (there may also be instances when your character reacts spontaneously to events as they occur).

M4 Your performance will successfully communicate the intentions of the play to the audience, through consistent and credible characterisation, understanding and commitment.

D4 Your performance will communicate the intentions of the play with a good degree of clarity, and the meaning of the play (theme, mood, concept, as well as the nature and motivations of your character) will be put across to the audience.

BTEC Assessment activity 5　Unit B8

Reflections

You will watch a recording of the show as a group and consider audience feedback. You will then review the main strengths and weakness of your work during rehearsal and performance.

Evidence

This can include:

- a video-recorded discussion and analysis in an interview with your tutor or in small groups
- a written review of your own performance and character development
- a video box review. This is a bit like the diary room in *Big Brother* – you will be asked to provide your reflections on the performance, usually alone, recording your thoughts on video.

Grading Tips

M5 You should clearly describe your strengths and weaknesses and say how you would improve in terms of rehearsal, preparation and performance.

D5 Provide a full account analysing your strengths and weaknesses in rehearsal and performance. Analysing means saying why your strengths allowed you to rehearse/perform effectively and why your weaknesses may have prevented successful performance. You should be able to say how you would rectify weaknesses in your performance through rehearsal and preparation, as well as how the rehearsal contributed to your strengths.

Unit E26 Exploring Music Composition

Unit E28 Developing Music Theory

Music and drama have always been linked. From opera and musical theatre to film and TV drama, music plays an integral part in the communication of the plot of a piece of drama, as well as helping to provide a setting or adding to the emotion of a scene.

This project will require you to compose a short piece of incidental musical to represent a character in a piece of drama. You will need to generate a number of original musical ideas in response to a brief and develop one of them into a completed composition.

Learning outcomes

After completing this project you should be able to achieve the following learning outcomes:

Unit E26 Exploring Musical Composition

1. Be able to generate original musical ideas from starting points

2. Know how to extend, develop and manipulate musical material

3. Be able to form musical material into completed compositions

Unit E28 Developing Music Theory

1. Be able to harmonise melodies using chords.

Assessment and grading criteria

This table shows you what you must to in order to achieve a pass, merit or distinction and where you can find activities in this book to help you.

To achieve a pass grade the evidence must show that you are able to:	To achieve a merit grade the evidence must show that, in addition to the pass criteria, you are able to:	To achieve a distinction grade the evidence must show that, in addition to the pass and merit criteria, you are able to:
Unit E26 Exploring Musical Composition		
P1 create five original musical ideas that could form a basis for a composition **Assessment activity 1 page 290**	**M1** create five original musical ideas that could form a basis for a composition, demonstrating a range of distinctive characteristics **Assessment activity 1 page 290**	**D1** create five original musical ideas that could form a basis for a composition, demonstrating a wide range of distinctive characteristics and showing imagination **Assessment activity 1 page 290**
P2 identify the techniques used to extend, develop and manipulate three original musical ideas (partial coverage) **Assessment activity 2 page 295**	**M2** describe the range of techniques used to extend, develop and manipulate three musical ideas (partial coverage) **Assessment activity 2 page 295**	**D2** explain the range of techniques used to extend, develop and manipulate three musical ideas (partial coverage) **Assessment activity 2 page 295**
P3 create a fully-formed musical composition, demonstrating the ability to handle musical elements appropriately **Assessment activity 4 page 304**	**M3** create a fully-formed musical composition, demonstrating the ability to handle a range of contrasting musical elements appropriately and in a structured way **Assessment activity 4 page 304**	**D3** create a fully-formed musical composition, demonstrating the ability to handle a wide range of contrasting musical elements appropriately, in a structured way and demonstrating imagination **Assessment activity 4 page 304**
Unit E28 Developing Music Theory		
P3 apply identified primary chords, in root position, in the harmonisation of diatonic melodies **Assessment activity 3 page 301**	**M3** apply identified primary and secondary chords, in root position, in the harmonisation of diatonic melodies. **Assessment activity 3 page 301**	**D3** apply identified primary and secondary chords, in root position and first inversions, in the harmonisation of diatonic melodies. **Assessment activity 3 page 301**

How you will be assessed

This project will be assessed by an internal assignment that will be designed and marked by the tutors at your centre. You will be assessed on your ability to create at least two original musical ideas from a given brief developing and extending one of them into a fully formed musical composition.

The work you produce for assessment could include:
- tutor observation statements
- peer observations
- your logbook that includes ideas and work in progress
- a presentation or written log that explains techniques used to extend, develop and manipulate musical ideas
- DVD recordings of classes, workshops and rehearsals
- a final composition presented as a score or recording.

Sacha, 16, first steps to composition

I was a bit apprehensive when I was told about this project. I have played the guitar for a couple of years and enjoyed music in Key Stage 3, but the idea of composing a complete music track was scary.

When we began to work on the project I realised, however, that big musical pieces can actually begin with small ideas. I was amazed at how a short theme of only a few notes could be extended and developed to create a full melody, and I really enjoyed experimenting with the different techniques we were taught. I also got completely absorbed by the idea of composing a piece that would represent a character in a play or film. I used some of the same skills we have been taught in acting classes to develop my understanding of my chosen character and used this to come up with ideas for my music. I am now really proud of what I achieved in this project and can't wait to do some more composition.

Music and drama

The scenario

In this project you are required to compose a dramatic piece of music to be used as a theme for a character from a play, film or video game. The piece should be based around a short leitmotif. You may choose a character from an existing play, film or video or create a new character. But before you start, you need to understand a bit more about incidental music and how it is created.

Incidental music

The great white shark makes its way menacingly through the ocean towards an unsuspecting swimmer. (*Jaws* – 1975 directed by Steven Spielberg, music by John Williams.)

The superhero effortlessly swings through the city in pursuit of the Green Goblin. (*Spider-Man* – 2002 directed by Sam Raimi, music by Danny Elfman.)

Imagine these scenes played without the incidental music composed to heighten the drama of the moment. Incidental music can provide atmosphere to a scene, warn of impending danger or provide a character with a recognisable melody. The use of incidental music in drama dates back as far as theatre itself to the ancient Greeks. In more recent times it has become an important element of film, TV and radio drama.

Key term

leitmotif – a recurring musical theme that is associated with a character or place.

The *Jaws* music, before the shark attacks, is instantly recognisable.

Activity: Incidental music

Watch some extracts from films or TV dramas that include the use of incidental music.

Discuss the relationship between the music and what you see on screen. How does the music add to the drama of the scene?

Leitmotif

A leitmotif is usually a short melody, but it can also be a rhythmic phrase or chord progression. Leitmotif was widely used by composers during the 19th and early 20th century. Sergei Prokofiev used the technique in his composition *Peter and the Wolf*, a narrated orchestral piece in which each character – Peter, his grandfather, the cat, the wolf, etc – has its own musical theme.

In the 20th and 21st centuries, many composers of music for film, TV and even video games have used leitmotif to represent specific characters. John Williams is a composer who has worked a lot with the director Steven Spielberg. He often uses leitmotif in his work. Williams' score for the 1975 film *Jaws* includes an ominous motif to represent the shark, which is constructed around only two notes. His work on the *Star Wars* films also makes much use of leitmotif, including themes for characters Luke Skywalker, Princess Leia and Darth Vader.

Activity: Examples of leitmotifs

Begin by listening to *Peter and the Wolf* by Sergei Prokofiev. Note how specific instruments and themes represent the different characters.

Find a range of more modern examples to listen to; e.g. watch an extract from *Star Wars – The Empire Strikes Back* and listen for the motifs used for Darth Vader, Yoda, Luke Skywalker and Princess Leia.

Discuss how each leitmotif suits the character it represents, e.g. how do the following character types tend to be represented by the music?

- the villain
- the hero
- the heroine – love interest
- the comedy character.

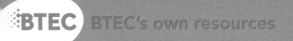
Developing your leitmotif

When generating leitmotif ideas, a composer needs to begin by considering the character type the motif will represent.

BTEC | ## Assessment activity 1 | Unit E26 P1 M1 D1

Ideas for your leitmotif

Come up with five different ideas for a leitmotif to represent five different types of character from a play, film or video game. The leitmotifs should each be based on a short melody (4–8 bars in length) that represents the type of character you are aiming to portray through the music.

During this activity you should show that you can generate ideas and explore possibilities for development.

Evidence

Your logbook – Record all your motif ideas in your logbook. Make notes describing how and why you generated the ideas, why you think each motif suits the character, and which ones you feel are most successful and why.

Grading Tips

(M1) You should include a variety of distinctive characteristics, for example, well-constructed melodic content, chord progressions and catchy hooks.

(D1) Try to be imaginative when you are creating your motifs, creating themes that are distinctive, embody the character they represent and will grab the listeners' attention.

PLTS

Generating ideas for a leitmotif will allow you to develop personal learning and thinking skills as a **creative thinker**.

Functional skills

Recording your motif ideas will allow you to show your **English** writing skills.

Developing a melody: extending

Once you have come up with a short melody for use as a leitmotif for your chosen character you will need to extend and develop it into a longer piece. There is a range of methods that can be used to extend a short melody into a longer passage of music.

Take this two-bar musical idea:

which we will represent with this graphic:

Repetition and imitation

One of the simplest ways of extending the idea is through repetition. This is where the melody is repeated on one or more occasions, as in the following graphic:

original melodic idea   original melodic idea

If the melody is repeated on a different instrument this is known as imitation, that is the second instrument imitates the melody played on the original instrument. This creates contrast.

flute   clarinet

Sequence

A device commonly used by composers to extend a melodic idea is a rising or falling sequence. This is where the original melodic idea is repeated at a slightly higher or lower pitch. For example, if your original idea begins on the note 'C' a rising sequence can be created by repeating the melody starting on a 'D' (i.e. with all the notes played one tone higher) then an 'E' and so on.

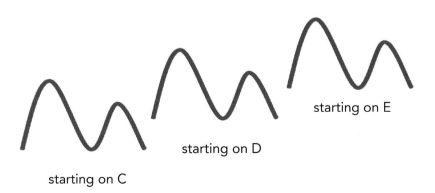

starting on E

starting on D

starting on C

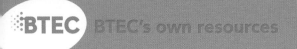

Activity: Using repetition, imitation and sequence

Explore ways to extend and develop the leitmotifs created in the previous assessment activity using:

- repetition
- imitation
- rising sequence
- falling sequence.

Developing a melody: manipulating

Another way of developing a melody is by manipulating the quality of the pitches of the notes and its rhythmic features.

Decoration

Adding more twists and turns to a melody is known as decoration and can add interest and contrast while still maintaining some of the features of the original idea.

original idea   idea with decoration

Here is how this might look notated:

original idea

original idea with decoration

Can you identify which notes in the decorated version have been added or changed?

Augmentation and diminution

Making a melody longer or shorter is another way of manipulating a musical idea.

Augmentation means making each of the note values in your melody longer so that quavers become crotchets, crotchets become minims, and so on. This means the rhythmic qualities of notes in the melody are still the same in relation to each other, but the melody itself will take twice as long to be played.

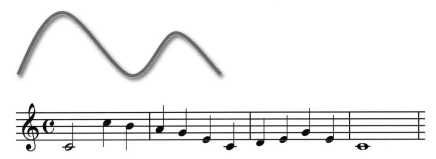

original idea augmented

You can, of course, do the opposite and shorten the note values of the melody, so that quavers become semi quavers, crotchets become quavers, and so on. This is known as diminution.

Retrograde

Another way of developing a melodic idea is to manipulate the pitches of the notes and the intervals (distances) between them.

Retrograde essentially involves playing the melodic idea backwards starting with the last note and ending with the first.

original idea in retrograde (backwards)

Activity: Using decoration, augmentation, diminution and retrograde

Explore ways to extend and develop the leitmotifs created in the previous assessment activity using:

- decoration
- augmentation
- diminution
- retrograde.

Activity: Creating a longer motif

Create a longer version (8–16 bars in length) of one of your leitmotifs using some of the extending and manipulating techniques you have explored. The following shows a worked example of an 8-bar motif.

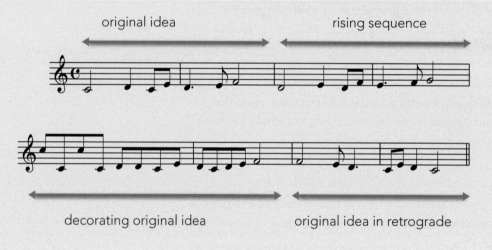

Contrasting material

When composing a musical theme, as well as extending and manipulating your original idea you should produce some new musical ideas to complement and contrast with your motif. A good way of doing this is by creating what is known as an answering phrase. This is a phrase that retains some of the rhythmic and/or melodic elements of the original idea while including some new material.

If your original idea looks like this, for example:

You might create an answering phrase such as this:

Same rhythm as first 2 bars of original idea

last 2 bars head back to the key note (the starting note)

Notice how the answering phrase balances with the original idea. That is, it is the same length and it uses similar rhythmic features.

Activity: Adding an answering phrase

Experiment with answering phrases for your original leitmotif.

Create answering phrases that could be used to extend and develop your leitmotif.

BTEC Assessment activity 2 — Unit E26

Extending, developing and manipulating musical ideas

For this activity you should choose and work on three of your five original ideas.

For each of the three leitmotifs you should explore and experiment with ways of extending, developing and manipulating your original materials and use the techniques shown to create three extended melodies of at least 16 bars. During this activity you should review and reflect on your compositional ideas and act on the outcomes to modify and improve your work.

Evidence

Your logbook – Include your extended pieces in your logbook along with the descriptions of the techniques you have used.

Grading Tips

M2 In your logbook, explain why you chose to use the particular techniques you did when extending your pieces. Ensure you describe how the techniques have been used.

D2 Ensure you explain the results of employing the specific techniques.

Harmonise melodies using chords

Once a melody has been written, the next step on the road to a fully formed composition is often the addition of some kind of accompaniment. In order to do this it is important to understand how to harmonise a melody using chords.

Triads

The simplest type of chord is a triad, which, as its name suggests, is made up of three notes.

The major triad includes a major 3rd and a perfect 5th over the root (bottom) note.

For example:

Perfect 5th	G	C	D	A
Major 3rd	E	A	B	F#
Root	C	F	G	D

The minor triad is made up of a minor 3rd and a perfect 5th over the root note.

For example:

Perfect 5th	G	C	D	A
Major 3rd	Eb	Ab	Bb	F
Root	C	F	G	D

This is what a triad looks like when notated:

Activity: Playing and writing major and minor triads

On a keyboard, try playing a range of major and minor triads beginning on different notes.

Notice the difference in sound between the major and minor triads.

Primary triads

When harmonising (adding chords to) a melody, the most useful chords are the three primary triads for the key of the melody.

The primary triads are built on the 1st, 4th and 5th notes of the scale of the key.

In the key of C major, the primary triads would be built on C, F and G.

The triads are named using the root note of the triad, as below, or roman numerals I, IV and V.

C	D	E	F	G	A	B	C
1	2	3	4	5	6	7	8

I   IV V

Activity: Triads

What notes would be in the three primary triads in each of the following keys?

- G Major
- F Major
- D Major
- A Minor

Write the names of the notes and notate the triads on the stave.

Adding primary chords to a melody

The reason why the three primary triads are so useful is that, together, they contain every note of the scale in the key you are working in. For example, the scale of C major contains the following notes:

C D E F G A B

The three primary triads are made up of the following notes:

I = CEG, IV = FAC, V = GBD.

So, as you can see from the following chart, there is a triad that fits with every note of the scale and, in the case of the notes C and G, there are two possible triads that could be used.

Melody note	C	D	E	F	G	A	B
Possible triads	I or IV	V	I	IV	I or V	IV	V

When adding chords to a short melody, there are a few simple rules that will help make the results sound good:

Rule 1 – Don't change chords too often

You may find that the same chord can be used to harmonise a full phrase within a melody.

For example; here a I chord can be used to harmonise all of the notes in the following musical phrase:

Melody note	C	E	G	E
Chord	I			

Rule 2 – Some notes can be ignored

If most of the notes in a musical phrase can be harmonised by the same chord you can probably ignore the few that don't fit with the chord.

For example, the D does not fit with the notes in the I chord but, as it doesn't appear for long and the other notes in the phrase do fit, this will sound fine.

Melody note	C	D	E	G
Chord	I			

Rule 3 – Take care at the beginning and end of your melody

Always try to begin and end with a I chord as this is the strongest of the three.

At the end of your melody, try one of the following chord patterns:

V followed by I

or

IV followed by I

This is called a cadence and will create a solid ending for your melody. Think of it as being like a full stop at the end of a sentence.

The following worked example shows the way you can harmonise a simple melody:

I.............. IV...... V.... IV..... I........ V.... I....

Secondary triads

Once you have mastered the use of primary triads you should move on to the use of secondary triads.

Secondary triads are built on the 2nd and 6th notes of the scale and are minor triads.

In the key of C major, the triads are as follows:

II = Dm*, IV = Am.

*the 'm' stands for minor.

These triads will add interest to a piece, but should be used more sparingly than the primary triads. They should not be used to harmonise the first or last note of the melody.

Melody note	C	D	E	F	G	A	B
Possible primary triads	I or IV	V	I	IV	I or V	IV	V
Possible primary triads	IV	II	VI	II		VI	

Activity: Secondary triads

What notes would make up the two secondary triads in each of the following keys?

- G Major
- F Major
- D Major
- A Minor

Write the names of the notes and notate the triads on the stave.

Activity: Experimenting with secondary triads/chords

Revisit the melodies you harmonised with primary triads. Try substituting some of the primary triads with secondary triads. The following worked example shows the addition of secondary triads.

I............. IV...... V.... IV..... VI........ II.. V.. I....

Root position and 1st inversions

The notes within a triad do not always have to be used in what is known as root position.

By placing the root note of the triad (i.e. the lowest note when the triad is in root position) at the top you can create a 1st Inversion of the triad.

C	C
C	C
C	C
C	
Root Position	Inversion

Activity: Playing triads in 1st inversion

On a keyboard, try playing a range of triads in root position and then in 1st inversion.

Notice the difference in sound between the root position and 1st inversion triads.

Changing chords

First inversions can often be used to provide a smooth transition from one chord to the next.

For example, here is a C triad in root position followed by a G triad also in root position i.e. GBD.

Now look at the same chord progression but with the second chord played an octave lower as a 1st inversion i.e. BDG.

Play or listen to each progression being played.

Which sounds the best?

If you thought the second example sounded better that is because there was a smaller amount of movement between the notes of the two chords in the second example. This makes for a smoother transition.

Functional skills

Any notated melodies you produce will show your **English** writing skills.

BTEC Assessment activity 3 **Unit E28** P3 M3 D3

Harmonising two melodies

You should now use the skills you have learned to harmonise three melodies of at least 16 bars in length using primary and secondary triads.

These melodies could be given to you by your tutor, but at least one should be chosen from those you developed when working on your leitmotifs earlier in this project.

Remember the rules for using primary and secondary triads and use some triads in 1st inversion.

Evidence

Your logbook – Include your harmonised pieces in your logbook. You may present your harmonised melodies as notated pieces or as recordings created using a sequencing package. You should clearly identify the triads you have used.

Grading Tips

M3 Ensure you add secondary chords in root position (chords II and VI but not chord VII).

D3 Ensure you use primary and secondary chords in root position and 1st inversion.

Forming musical material into completed compositions

You should now be ready to create your final composition based on a chosen leitmotif. When putting together a complete composition it is a good ides to begin with a plan or structure.

Repetition and contrast

Most pieces of music have a structure that is based on some amount of repetition, for instance, of the main theme along with some contrast. Musical forms, such as binary, ternary and rondo, include some repetition of a main A section as well as contrasting sections (B, C, etc.)

Further guidance and activities related to musical structure are included in Unit E31 The Development of Music.

Your composition will require that you really concentrate to get a good end product.

Activity: The stucture of your piece

Come up with an initial plan for the structure of your composition that includes both repetition and contrast. How many sections will the piece have? How long will each section last?

See the following worked example of a plan:

Section	Number of bars	Description
A	16	Main section – leitmotif played on the glockenspiel with string synth accompaniment
B	16	Contrasting section in minor key – same instruments
A	8	Main section – first 8 bars only
C	16	Contrasting section in major key. Clarinet plays a new melody with string synth accompaniment
A	16	Main section – all 16 bars

Getting the A section right

Much of the work on your A section is already done. You have an extended melody that includes the leitmotif for the character and you have already added some chords to harmonise the piece. You will now need to make decisions about instrumentation. Will your piece, for example, be played by live musicians (e.g. a clarinet player accompanied by a pianist) or would you prefer to use a computer sequencing package to create the final piece?

The other sections

There are many ways of creating contrast in a composition. For example, you could:

- move to a new key e.g. from major to minor

- move the melody or accompaniment to different instruments

- change the register of the melody e.g. moving it up or down an octave

- change the tempo or the time signature

- change the dynamics e.g. loud to soft

- create a new melody that has different qualities from the main section, e.g. if your main melody uses long sustained notes create a contrasting melody that includes fast moving running passages.

Creating a balance between the different sections of your piece is an important element in the success of your composition. The other sections should be different enough to provide the required contrast but have enough in common with the A section to make them sound like they are part of the same piece of music.

Assessment activity 4
Unit E26

Your final composition

You should now use the work you have produced so far in this project to create a fully formed composition in the style of a piece of incidental music that represents a character from a play, film or video game.

Your composition should show that you can create a composition around a leitmotif and use different musical elements to extend and develop the idea. Your completed composition should also have a clear structure.

To succeed, your piece should be imaginative using the elements you have selected in a creative manner.

Evidence

Your completed composition – This may be presented as a score, a recording of a live performance or a sequenced performance of the piece using a computer software program.

Grading Tips

M3 You will need to show that you can handle a variety of contrasting musical elements correctly and in a structured way (for example AABA).

D3 You will need to show that you can handle a wide range of contrasting musical elements correctly and in a structured way.

Project 9 Music Night

Unit A3 Performing Arts Production Process

Unit E30 Solo Musical Performance

Planning and taking part in performances is central to a professional musician's working life. This project will give you an insight into what it could be like to be a professional musician. The project requires you to plan a 'Music Night', a music event to showcase the individual talents of the instrumentalists and singers in your group.

As well as contributing to the planning of the event you will need to prepare two contrasting solo pieces for your own performance

Learning outcomes

After completing this project you should be able to achieve the following learning outcomes:

Unit A3 Performing Arts Production Process

1. Know how to carry out planning requirements for a performing arts product.

Unit E30 Solo Musical Performance

1. Know how to choose appropriate pieces of music for performance

2. Know how to prepare for a solo performance

3. Be able to perform music to an audience.

Assessment and grading criteria

This table shows you what you must to in order to achieve a pass, merit or distinction and where you can find activities in this book to help you.

To achieve a pass grade the evidence must show that you are able to:	To achieve a merit grade the evidence must show that, in addition to the pass criteria, you are able to:	To achieve a distinction grade the evidence must show that, in addition to the pass and merit criteria, you are able to:
Unit A3 Performing Arts Production Process		
P1 identify the necessary planning requirements for a performing arts product **Assessment activity 1 page 309**	**M1** describe the necessary planning requirements for a performing arts product **Assessment activity 1 page 309**	**D1** explain the necessary planning requirements for a performing arts product with insight, foresight and confidence **Assessment activity 1 page 309**
Unit E30 Solo Musical Performance		
P1 identify music for a concert programme that is generally appropriate to their performance standard **Assessment activity 2 page 311**	**M1** provide a description of the music selected for a concert programme that is appropriate to their standard of performance **Assessment activity 2 page 311**	**D1** justify the choices of music for a concert programme that are appropriate to their standard of performance **Assessment activity 2 page 311**
P2 identify examples of musical practice techniques that are used to improve performance on their instrument **Assessment activity 3 page 313**	**M2** describe the music practice techniques that they have used to improve performance on their instrument **Assessment activity 3 page 313**	**D2** evaluate the music practice techniques that they have used to improve performance on their instrument **Assessment activity 3 page 313**
P3 present a recorded portfolio of at least four contrasting pieces of music that are performed accurately to an audience, showing some sense of musical style. (Partial coverage*) **Assessment activity 4 page 314**	**M3** present a recorded portfolio of at least four contrasting pieces of music that are performed accurately, showing a sense of style and musical communication with the audience. (Partial coverage*) **Assessment activity 4 page 314**	**D3** present a recorded portfolio of at least four contrasting pieces of music that are performed accurately, showing expression, a clear sense of style and demonstrating musical communication with the audience. (Partial coverage*) **Assessment activity 4 page 314**

* Two of the four contrasting pieces required for this criterion are covered by this project.

How you will be assessed

This project will be assessed by an internal assignment that will be designed and marked by the tutor at your centre. You will be assessed on your contribution to the planning of a Music Night as well as your individual preparations and performance as a soloist.

The work you produce for assessment could include:
- tutor observation statements
- peer observations
- DVD recordings of classes, workshops and rehearsals
- DVD recordings of performances
- your process logbook that includes details of decisions made and notes from planning meetings
- your personal practice logbook
- audience feedback.

Etta, 16, trumpet player

I have been playing the trumpet since primary school. I play in the school wind band and we practise every week and usually do a concert at the end of each term. I don't usually play on my own as a soloist, so I was really looking forward to this project. The most difficult part was choosing the two pieces I would play in the concert. I wanted to show that I can play classical pieces as well as more popular stuff. My trumpet teacher helped me find some very good pieces and I finally decided on a traditional piece by the 17th-century English composer Henry Purcell along with an arrangement of a piece from *The Lion King*.

The final concert was amazing as there was such a range of instruments played as well as lots of people singing. The show went down really well with the audience. What was really good was the way in which we all supported and encouraged each other.

Have you thought about whether the people who will accompany you are as capable as you?

Choosing pieces for performance

The purpose of this project is to allow you to demonstrate your skills on your instrument or as a vocalist. It is therefore important that you choose pieces that will best showcase your skills. When choosing pieces to perform in a recital or other event, there are a number of considerations that you should take into account.

The difficulty of the piece

Many musicians make the mistake of choosing pieces that are too difficult. The desire to stretch yourself in terms of your technical abilities is not to be discouraged, but this should be done over an extended period of time while working towards long-term targets. For a performance that is just round the corner, pieces that are suitable to your current ability level are more appropriate.

The length of piece

Another consideration when selecting pieces for the event is their length. You may need to limit the length of the pieces you choose to fit in with the overall programme. Remember, everyone else has two pieces to perform, and you need to ensure that the whole programme is balanced.

The preparation time needed

The pieces you play or sing will need to be fully practised and polished in good time for the event. You will need to assess how long this is likely to take. Do you have time to bring them both up to performance standard?

Availability of accompaniment

Is an accompaniment required for the pieces you are considering? Most songs and solo instrumental pieces need a piano accompaniment. You must ensure you have someone willing and able to accompany you and that there is sufficient time for you to rehearse with them. If you are thinking of performing to a backing track, make sure you choose an appropriate track and that there is adequate amplification equipment available at the performance venue.

Suitability for target audience

Finally you should consider your intended audience. Your choice of pieces should be suitable for the audience and provide them with an interesting and entertaining experience.

Assessment activity 2 Unit E30 (P1) (M1) (D1)

Your programme

Come up with a shortlist of between four and six solo pieces for performance at your showcase event.

Describe each piece in terms of its appropriateness, taking into consideration your ability as a singer or instrumentalist, your intended audience and any constraints posed by the event such as the length of the piece, time need for preparation and availability of accompaniment.

Come up with a final list of two pieces to be performed at the Music Night event giving reasons for your choices.

Evidence

Your logbook – Include a full discussion of the choices made.

Grading Tips

M1 You should describe the pieces you are performing, including information about when and where the pieces were composed and the nature of the pieces.

D1 You should fully justify the choices made:
- Why did you select the final two pieces and reject the others?
- What factors influenced your choices?

Preparing for a solo performance

On the day of the event, the musician must be ready to perform to the best of their ability. Like an athlete training for a race, this involves a great deal of personal preparation.

Technical preparations

If you are a dedicated musician you should already have a regular practice regime that involves a warm-up and technical exercises. Depending on the instrument you play this might include:

- scales and arpeggios – these are useful exercises for any instrument and the voice

- breathing exercises – these are useful for woodwind and brass players as well as singers and might involve playing or singing long notes to improve stamina

- rudiments –such as flams and paradiddles for drummers

- lip-slurs – for brass players to strengthen the embouchure.

Key terms

Flam – a pattern that consists of a quiet grace note played with one hand followed by a louder primary stroke with the other hand.

Paradiddle – a four-stroke pattern in the form of RLRR or LRLL.

Embouchure – the shape made by the lips and muscles surrounding the mouth when playing a wind instrument.

Activity: Technical exercises

Make a list of appropriate technical exercises for the voice or the instrument you play. For each exercise, describe how it is performed and how it is used to improve technique.

As well as undertaking a series of appropriate technical exercises you should also spend time rehearsing the pieces you are planning to perform. It is important that you adopt the correct practice techniques that will improve your ability to play or sing the pieces. This will usually include breaking the piece down into short phrases and practising it a phrase at a time.

Unit E32 Working as a Musical Ensemble includes guidance and activities to help you understand how to practise effectively.

Accuracy

It is important that you perform the pieces you have prepared accurately in terms of pitch and rhythm. During rehearsals, make notes of any feedback given to you by your tutor and work to correct any mistakes.

Other preparations

As well as individual practice, there will be other preparations that need to be made. Having a rehearsal or dry run at the venue is a good idea, if feasible, as this will allow you to get a feeling for the space and what the acoustics will be like (although this will change when the venue has an audience in it). You may also need to get used to the equipment you will be working with. Having a sound check is vital if any amplification equipment is to be used and a full technical run-through is essential if lighting or other effects are to be used.

Rehearsals with your accompanist and/or any recorded tracks you are using are also very important. For a musician or singer who has been practising a piece alone, the introduction of an accompaniment can be difficult and it may take time for the performer to get used to it.

It is a good idea to rehearse entrances and exits. An event will look unprofessional if the performers look disorganised. Topping and tailing is a good way of practising these changes. It involves the performers entering, playing only the first and last few bars of each piece they perform, then exiting, so it can be done in a short space of time. If you are planning to introduce the pieces you are playing, practise what you are going to say so that it looks and sounds relaxed and professional.

Have you done enough rehearsal for your performance?

Assessment activity 3 Unit E30

Preparation techniques

Keep a practice logbook to record the technical and other preparations you undertake and discuss how the various music practice techniques you use contribute to your improvement.

Evidence

Your logbook – Record your preparations, rehearsals and assessments of your improvements.

Grading Tips

(M2) You will need to demonstate the practise techniques you have used. You could do this by videoing practise sessions or performance and keeping a copy for your logbook.

(D2) You should include an evaluation of the music practice techniques in your logbook that explains how any specific techniques used, such as warm-ups, technical exercises or practice methods, have improved your performance.

If you have carefully carried out the necessary preparations both individually and as a group, your event should be a success. But even so, things can still go wrong. Following these rules and tips should help you in your final preparations and performance.

Intonation

Intonation (or tuning) is a vital ingredient of a successful performance. If you are an instrumentalist, take great care when tuning up for a performance. If you are singing, during the sound check make sure that you can hear yourself through any monitoring being used.

Nerves!

One of the greatest enemies of performers is nerves. You might have played a piece correctly a hundred times at home but as soon as you walk out in front of the audience your hands shake, your mouth feels dry and you panic that you can't remember the first line! It is perfectly normal to feel nervous before a performance and many performers feel that some degree of nerves is a good thing. If you do tend to get nervous before a performance, try these techniques:

- Practise really thoroughly beforehand so that when the nerves kick in you can play the piece almost as if on automatic pilot.

- Stay calm and quiet. Keep backstage chat to a minimum. When you are waiting to perform, take deep breaths and relax. Try closing your eyes and imagining you are in a really calm place.

- Have some still water to hand to sip if your mouth gets dry. This is particularly important for singers and brass and woodwind players.

Key terms

Articulation – how phrases are played, e.g. smoothly.

Dynamics – the volume of an individual phrase.

Tempo – the speed of an individual phrase.

Tone – the sound quality of individual notes or phrases, e.g. harsh, mellow.

Communication, expression and style

All the right notes in the right places will result in an accurate performance. However, more is needed for a truly musical performance. Expression is what lifts a performance from something rather mechanical to something very special. It is how the musician communicates the style and mood of the piece to the audience. In songs, this is about communicating the meaning of the lyrics; in an instrumental piece, about conveying its mood and character.

Expression includes the use of tempo, dynamics, tone and articulation.

Activity: Expression marks

Many musical scores include expression marks that tell the performer how the piece should be played. These include a number of Italian terms.

Find out what the following instructions mean and record the definitions in your logbook.

- rallentando
- tenuto
- pianissimo
- legato

- con moto
- accelerando
- staccato
- presto

- crescendo
- lento
- diminuendo
- dolce

- forte
- con brio
- fortissimo
- andante.

Remember

Only two of the four contrasting pieces required for P3, M3 and D3 are covered by this assessment activity.

Assessment activity 4
Unit E30

P3 **M3** **D3**

Performance techniques

Perform the two pieces you have prepared at the Music Night event.

Evidence

Your performance – A recording of your performance plus any tutor or audience feedback.

Grading Tips

M3 You should perform accurately and demonstrate a musical connection with the audience.

D3 You should perform accurately, showing expression and a clear sense of style and demonstrating musical communication with the audience.

Glossary

Annotations – notes you add to a book, text or picture giving explanations or comments. An annotated play script may show moves, stage positions, notes on delivery and actions.

Arena – where the stage is surrounded on three or four sides by the auditorium, which is raised and tiered higher than the stage.

Articulation – how musical phrases are played e.g. smoothly or with notes separated.

Artistic policy – the type of work a company produces and the reasons why they produce it.

Arts Council – an organisation that distributes government funding (money) for the arts.

Avant-garde – new and unusual or experimental ideas in the arts.

Blank verse – lines structured on the like rhyming verse, but unrhymed.

Blocking – the physical arrangement of the actors on stage.

Budget – the amount of money allocated to a production.

Canon – a sequence of steps danced by different dancers or groups of dancers but each dancing a different part of it at any one time.

Capacity – the size of audience that a venue can hold.

Characterisation – the features and qualities of a character as developed by the actor, under the guidance of the director.

Choreographic theory – the rules that govern the way dances are made.

Choreography – the way dance is created, how steps and moves are put together.

Chorus – in ancient Greek drama, a group of actors who sang and danced, often commenting on the content of the play. Nowadays the term describes performers who sing and dance as an ensemble in musical theatre.

Combination – a similar idea to enchainment, but usually used in more modern dance styles, such as jazz dance, or street jazz.

Comedy – a funny and light-hearted play full of amusing events, often making fun of people's faults and misfortunes.

Contrast – juxtaposition of different passages (in terms of melody, instruments or voices used, key, tempo or dynamics) for musical effect.

Cool-down – a gentle series of exercises to cool down muscles and help them to disperse the waste products, (such as lactic acid), that build up when muscles are working hard.

Cue – a signal for something to happen, for example a lighting or sound effect.

Cue sheet – a grid that records the details of each lighting and sound cue.

Dance drama – combines dance and drama together, such a dance with speech, or a drama with movement.

Director's notes – notes taken by the director during the technical and dress rehearsals. At the end of the day the director shares the notes with the whole company. It is important to have a notepad and pen so that you can record what you have been asked to do.

Dress rehearsal – the final rehearsal before the opening night where the show is run in full costume.

Dynamics – speed of the moves and steps in a dance, or changes in volume of a musical piece.

Embouchure – the shape made by the lips and muscles surrounding the mouth when playing a wind instrument.

Enchainement – exercises and steps linked together into a short sequence, usually used in classical ballet classes.

Epic – developed by German playwright/director Bertolt Brecht, epics often feature many scenes depicting drama over long periods of time, and use techniques to 'distance' audiences from the story to allow them to concentrate on the themes and issues.

Farce – a form of comedy, fast-paced and featuring a series of bizarre misunderstandings and ridiculous events.

Fit-up – the process of setting up scenery, lighting and other equipment for a show.

Flam – a pattern that consists of a quiet 'grace note' played with one hand followed by a louder primary stroke with the other hand.

Flats – any flat elements of the set. These can often be large and unwieldy.

Flies – space above the stage where lines and equipment are used to move pieces of scenery.

Flutter tonguing – where the performer flutters their tongue while blowing into the instrument to create a 'frrrr' sound.

Get-in – the process of moving scenery, lighting and other equipment into the venue.

Ground row – a flat that is placed horizontally on the floor upstage. It often has a profile of hills, trees, etc.

Inflection – changes in how high and how low the voice is when the actor is speaking.

In-the-round – the acting space is in the centre of the audience.

Intonation – the rise and fall of the voice when speaking.

Jazz walks – funky danced walks, usually led from the hips, with knees bent, sometimes with turns and jumps.

Key – a list of all the symbols used on a plan and what they represent.

Key box – an accepted way of communicating key information on a plan.

Leitmotif – a recurring musical theme that is associated with a character or place.

Libretto – the dialogue sections of a musical.

LX tape – one-inch wide PVC tape used for marking out the set. Different colours are used for each scene.

Marking out – marking the position of the set onto the rehearsal room floor using LX tape. This is so that the actors can familiarise themselves with the positioning of the set.

Mask drama – where all or some of the performers wear masks. This might be to create a particular character.

Masking – standing in front of other actors, blocking the audience's view.

Melodrama – used to describe a popular form of entertainment in the 1800s, full of exciting action but nowadays seen as too exaggerated to be classed as 'realistic' drama.

Mode – a series of pitches used to create a piece of music.

Motif – a series of steps organised into a short sequence that can be developed into a longer and more complex dance.

Multimedia – multimedia theatre mixes live performance, recorded sound, film and computer graphics as well as acting, dance and acrobatics. It is sometimes associated with experimental works, but many major shows make use of effects to provide a spectacle.

Musical – drama usually combining an acted storyline with singing and choreography.

Narrative drama – tells a story.

Off book – when actors know their lines and no longer use their script.

Opposing rhythms – dancing across the rhythm of the music, or another dancer.

Paradiddle – a four-stroke pattern in the form of RLRR or LRLL.

Performance genres – dance, physical theatre, plays, musicals, variety, gigs, talent shows, fashion shows.

Performance venues – proscenium arch, traverse, in the round, promenade, thrust.

Physical theatre – uses movement as a way of expressing the story, the place or the characters; can have dialogue, or not.

Pitch – the correct level and sound of the voice as required for the character and role at any particular moment of a vocal performance.

Pitch bending – sliding from one note to another.

Plot – the events of the play and sequence in which they occur.

Political propaganda – information designed to promote particular ways of thinking.

Production manager – works with the creative and production teams. They ensure that all aspects of the production process are kept on target and within budget.

Programmatic – music that tells a story or represents moods, emotions or physical places.

Programming – selection of lanterns and levels for a particular lighting effect. When selected the lanterns and levels are programmed into the lighting desk and given a cue number.

Prompt copy/prompt script – an annotated script showing information about all aspects of lighting, sound, cues, blocking a well as where props and scenery will be used

Props table – usually situated at the side of the stage and managed by the stage management team. Props are taken from here for use onstage and then returned to the table after they have been used in performance.

Proscenium arch – the stage is framed by a wall, typically with an arch or rectangular opening separating the front of the stage from the auditorium.

Prose – a way of describing language written in its 'ordinary' continuous form, reflecting typical 'everyday' expression rather than language written in rhythmic line structure or rhyme.

Repertoire – the range of musical works or dances performed by a person or group.

Repetition – where passages are repeated for a particular musical effect.

Revue – theatre show incorporating acting scenes, songs, dances, stand-up comedy, etc.

Rhyming verse – a number of lines of text/dialogue grouped together typically where the last word of a line rhymes with the last word of the previous line, or the line before.

Rhythmic accuracy – dancing closely to the required count, either of the music or just of the dance itself. Dancers usually count in phrases of 8 beats for music with a 4/4 time signature.

Risk – the level of the danger that exists in the work space.

Role on the wall – putting an image of your character on a poster with all their character attributes to help you remember and develop the role.

Rolls – danced rolls on the floor or in the air, incorporating a jump, e.g. a barrel roll where the torso is thrown over.

Rostra – plural of rostrum, meaning a raised area.

Scale drawing – line drawing giving a birds-eye view of the performance space. The plan will show the area of the stage and the position of the set on the stage. It is used by the stage manager to position the set onstage and by the lighting designer to plan the lighting.

Scenic elements – all pieces of the set e.g. flats, backdrops, set furniture, drapes, ground row, treads, rostra, staging systems.

Season – a period in the company's calendar e.g. September–January. Many production companies produce two 'seasons' of work per year.

Setting back – setting up the stage for the next performance.

SMART – targets that are: Specific, Measurable, Attainable and Time-based.

Spill – when light falls where it is not wanted, e.g. on the audience, on the proscenium arch.

Stagger through – first run through rehearsal of a production at when all the separate dance, music and drama elements are put together.

Standby cue – a 'get-ready' signal to alert the operator that the next cue is only a few lines away.

Symphonic poem – an extended piece for orchestra that is programmatic. Also known as a tone poem.

Talk back/cans – a headsets system that enables the backstage crew to communicate and run the show from their separated backstage positions. Usually the DSM will call the show over the cans system.

Target audience – the audience that is being aimed at in any production e.g. teenagers, young adults or pre-school children.

Technical rehearsal – a run-through of the show to allow the technical members of the production team to practise their cues and identify any problems.

Technique – the set of things you can do that relate to a particular dance style. For example, if you are taking ballet class, your technique will include how much you can turn out your legs and feet,to get into second position or master a grand plié, how well your body is aligned as you move, jump and turn. For street jazz your technique will include how well you can isolate parts of you body and move them around the beat of the music.

Tempo – the speed at which the piece is played.

Thrust – a stage that projects out into the auditorium with the audience surrounding it on three sides.

Timbre – the character of the sound.

Tragedy – serious drama, usually with a sad ending, where one or more main characters die.

Traverse – where the audience sit either side of the stage.

Unison – a group of dancers dancing the same series of steps together – i.e. at the same time.

Unsigned – bands not signed up to a particular record label to produce, promote and distribute their work.

Upstaging – standing towards the rear of the stage from the actor who is speaking to you, making it difficult for them to deliver the line as they have to face away from the audience.

Ventilation – the adequate provision of air movement outlets when cutting timber or using paints or glues that emit noxious fumes.

Vibrato – a pulsating effect.

Visual cue – a cue based on an actor's action rather than a line of speech.

Warm-up – a series of exercises carried out at the beginning of class or before a performance. The purpose is to carefully mobilise the body by stretching, bending and twisting muscles so they become more flexible and less susceptible to injury.

Index